mother/child father/child Relationships

edited by
Joseph H. Stevens, Jr.
and
Marilyn Mathews
Georgia State University

The National Association for the
Education of Young Children

Photographs by

Barbara Young, *p. 2*
Pat Taylor, *p. 84*
Paul J. Cryan, *p. 146*
Robert Maust, *p. 222*

Copyright © 1978. All rights reserved.
National Association for the Education of Young Children
1834 Connecticut Avenue, N.W.
Washington, DC 20009

Library of Congress Catalog Card Number: 77-95173
ISBN Catalog Number: 0-912674-58-X

Printed in the United States of America.

Table of Contents

Preface 1

I. Mother/Child: Who Influences Whom? 3

Chapter 1 Parent to Infant Attachment 5
Marshall H. Klaus and John H. Kennell

Chapter 2 The Role of the Attachment Bond in Effective Parenting 31
Patricia Teague Ashton

Chapter 3 Maternal Attitudes and the Development of Mothers and Children 51
Michael L. Hanes and Sandra Kanu Dunn

Chapter 4 Socialization by Parents and Peers and Experiential Learning of Prosocial Behavior 69
Ervin Staub

II. How Does the Father Influence Development? 85

Chapter 5 The Father's Role in the Infant's Social World 87
Michael E. Lamb

Chapter 6 Fatherhood: The Myth of the Second-Class Parent 109
Marsha Weinraub

Chapter 7 Paternal Behavior: Implications for Child-rearing Practice 135
James C. Young and Muriel E. Hamilton

III. The Influence of Family Characteristics and Structure 147

Chapter 8 The Aftermath of Divorce 149
E. Mavis Hetherington, Martha Cox, and Roger Cox

Chapter 9 Minority Families 177
Harriette Pipes McAdoo

Chapter 10 Alternative Family Styles: Effects on Young Children 197
Bernice T. Eiduson and Thomas S. Weisner

IV. Methodological Issues and the Problem of Application 223

Chapter 11 The Care of Young Children: Some Problems with Research Assumptions, Methods, and Findings 225
Jean V. Carew

Contributors 244

Author Index 246

Subject Index 252

Preface

It would be presumptuous to attempt to define parent-child relationships in one volume. But the importance of these relationships and the paucity of publications integrating important research in this area have demanded this first effort. We were encouraged by the interest and willingness of excellent researchers and students of parent-child relationships to contribute. Our purpose has been to select research that appears to have the greatest bearing on the work of practitioners who counsel with parents. A major frustration was the omission of other significant, vital work that contributes to a more comprehensive view of the parent-child relationship. While in no way definitive, this book will, we hope, add substantively to the existing literature and stimulate others to close more of the gaps in what is known about parent-child relationships and what is disseminated to practitioners.

Three types of chapters are included in this book: (1) reports of significant research studies, (2) reviews of research, and (3) position papers outlining critical issues in relation to research and practice. The research reports are of seminal, ground-breaking work done in important areas; these provide new perspectives and new knowledge. The chapters by Klaus and Kennell; Hetherington, Cox, and Cox; and Eiduson and Weisner are of this nature. Reviews of research were prepared to integrate, critique, and summarize areas in which there are substantial data and which were of critical importance to our understanding of parent-child relationships. Chapters by Ashton, Hanes and Dunn, Staub, Lamb, Weinraub, and McAdoo reflect this orientation. In addition, two chapters outlining issues surrounding our study of the parent and child and applications of this knowledge are included—one by Young and Hamilton, and the second by Carew.

The authors of each chapter labored without remuneration to prepare substantive, pertinent discussions of research. This reflects a commitment to improving the quality of life for children and families in this country, a mission shared with members of the National Association for the Education of Young Children.

Joseph H. Stevens, Jr.
Marilyn Mathews
February 1978

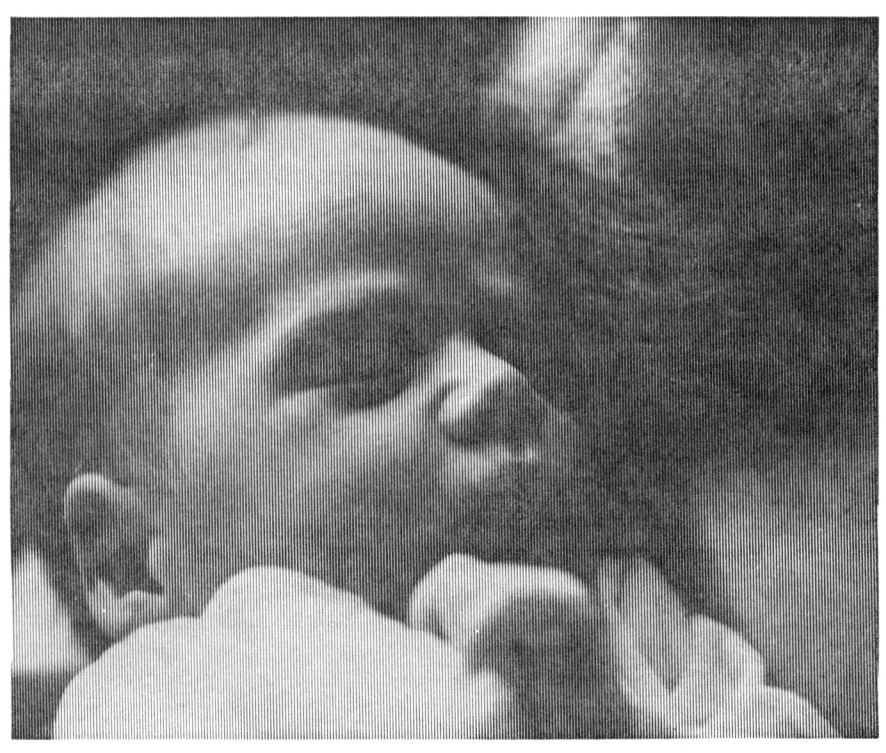

I

Mother/Child: Who Influences Whom?

Until recently mother-child relationships have been studied from a unidirectional framework. It was assumed that within the mother-child relationship only the mother's behavior was of consequence for the child's development. Now it is recognized that the infant contributes significantly in helping to maintain this interaction within mutually pleasurable and beneficial ranges. Until recently neonates were viewed as little more than blobs totally at the mercy of their environment. Their development was wholly dependent upon their caregivers—the adults around them. Now research evidence has considerably modified this view. Infants are recognized as proactive, competent organisms who exhibit decided preferences for particular types of auditory and visual stimuli. Infants select to attend to human faces and human voices, and they appear to move in response to the rhythm of the human voice. They avoid and attempt to draw back from aversive, annoying stimuli. In addition to exhibiting preferences, infants manifest characteristics and behaviors that appear to influence their caregivers. Characteristics such as adaptability and consolability seem to contribute significantly to maternal feelings of competence. Infants' readability (the degree to which their behavior is differentiated and predictable) may be another characteristic which influences the quality of mother-child interaction. It now appears that when the infant's behavior is clearer, more precise, and more predictable, the establishment of pleasurable and developmentally sound mother-child interactions is more probable. We know now that infants and young children make a significant contribution to the quality and quantity of the interaction between themselves and their mothers. The nature of this interaction (as well as the nature of the interaction with the father, grandparents, and other members of the family's social network) has major consequences for the child's development and probably for the mother's development. As children mature, their relative contribution to this interaction will increase.

Both the mother and child contribute significantly to the establishment of an optimal interaction. What parents do in interaction with their children has significant impact on the children's development. More important is the timing of this behavior: what the parent does *in response* to the behavior of the child. For example, it is not the number of times the mother smiles or praises but the pairing of these smiles and praises with developmentally significant behaviors that is most critical. Probably to maximize optimal child development and optimal parent development, the establishment and maintenance of reciprocal responsiveness is critical. Little fine-grained research has been done to examine how the parent changes or develops during childrearing.

The developmental significance that such patterning of parent and child behavior has is illustrated in the research discussed throughout this book, especially in the first chapter by Klaus and Kennell. They found that such reciprocity begins immediately after birth. The mother (and the father) may be particularly sensitive to certain stimuli neonates typically exhibit. These neonatal behaviors release patterns of parental exploratory behavior, the whole of which facilitate the early bonding of parent to child. This research also makes us patently aware that parents are probably profoundly influenced by the childrearing process; adult development, not just child development, is affected. Ashton's discussion of attachment of the young child to the parent reinforces the importance of the qualitative aspects of parent-child interaction, particularly parental responsiveness to infant signals, for optimal social development.

Hanes and Dunn describe the difficulties in defining and operationalizing maternal attitudes. Likewise, the relationship between observed behavior and reported attitudes appears not to be a clear one. However, there seem to be significant relationships between women's views of their roles as mothers and other aspects of their female roles. Some consistency in attitudes from pregnancy to the postpartum period has been found. Hanes and Dunn reiterate the importance of a general orientation of responsivity to, sensitivity to, and emotional involvement with the child.

Staub outlines how the development of prosocial behaviors in children is influenced by specific aspects of parental behavior: parental nurturance, warmth, use of control, and use of positive induction and reasoning. Reciprocal peer interaction in later developmental periods also appears to support the development of prosocial behavior.

Marshall H. Klaus and John H. Kennell

1 Parent-to-Infant Attachment

Over the past forty years, investigators from a wide variety of disciplines have painstakingly elaborated the process by which the human infant becomes attached to his* mother (Bowlby 1958; Spitz 1965). They have described the disastrous effects on the infant of long-term maternal separation in terms of his motor, mental, and affective development. This chapter describes the development of attachment in the opposite direction, from parent to infant—how it grows, develops and matures, and what distorts, disturbs or enhances it. This attachment is crucial to the survival and development of the infant. Its power is so great that it enables the mother or father to make unusual sacrifices necessary for the care of their infant, day after day, night after night, responding to his cry and protecting him from danger. Throughout his lifetime, the strength and character of this attachment will probably influence the quality of all future bonds and links to other individuals.

An "attachment" can be defined as a unique relationship between two people which is specific and endures through time. Although it is difficult to define this lasting relationship operationally, we have taken as indicators of this attachment, behaviors such as fondling, kissing, cuddling, and prolonged gazing, behaviors which serve both to maintain contact and exhibit affection to the particular individual. While this definition is useful in experimental observations, it is important to distinguish between attachment and attachment behaviors. Close attachment can persist during long separations of time and distance even though there may at times be no visible sign of its existence. A call for help even after 40 years may bring a mother to her child and evoke attachment behaviors equal in strength to those of the first year.

The impetus to intensively study the mother-to-infant bond occurred 10 to 15 years ago when staffs of intensive care nurseries observed that sometimes, after all extraordinary efforts had been taken to save small

---

*The pronouns "he," "him," "his" are used in their generic sense in this chapter to refer to both male and female infants.

Reprinted by permission from *Recent Advances in Pediatrics No. 5* edited by D. Hull (1976). Churchill Livingstone, Edinburgh, London, New York.

premature infants, they would return to emergency rooms battered and partially destroyed by their parents even though they had been sent home intact and thriving. More careful studies of this phenomenon have consistently shown that battering and failure-to-thrive without organic cause appear in a disproportionate number of infants who were premature or hospitalized for other reasons during the newborn period. (Failure-to-thrive without organic disease is a syndrome in which the infant does not grow, gain or develop normally at home during the early months of life, and yet shows leaps in development and weight gain with routine hospital care.) Table 1 presents observations on the incidence of infant battering and failure-to-thrive without organic disease and its relationship to separation in the early days of life. Re-analysis of a number of these studies has shown an association between early separation and these disastrous conditions. The occurrence of these and other mothering disorders has provided a continuing stimulus to unravel the process of parental attachment.

Table 1. Effect of Separation on Battering and Failure to Thrive Without Organic Cause

	Authors	Number in study	Number affected	Percentage separated
Failure to thrive	Ambuel and Harris, 1963	100	27 prematures	27
	Shaheen, Alexander, Truskowsky, and Barbero, 1968	44	16 prematures	36
	Evans, Reinhart, and Succop, 1972	40	9 prematures	22.5
Battering	Elmer and Gregg, 1967	20	6 prematures	30
	Skinner and Castle, 1969	78	10 prematures	13
	Klein and Stern, 1971	51	12 low birth weight infants	23.5
	Oliver, Cox, Taylor, and Baldwin, 1974	38	8 prematures	21

Had we read closely the first text on neonatology by Budin (1907), we could have foreseen these tragic consequences of early separation. In this book, *The Nursling* published in 1907, he wrote, "Unfortunately, . . . a certain number of mothers abandon the babies whose needs they had not had to meet and in whom they had lost all interest. The life of the little one has been saved it is true but at the cost of the mother." He recommended that mothers be encouraged to breast feed their premature babies and advised them to nurse full terms as well, to increase their milk production. He designed and promoted glass incubators which allowed a mother to look at her infant easily and permitted mothers to visit and care for their infants since they seemed to be so much more attentive to the infant's needs than were the hospital staff. Sadly, his original recommendations were not heeded.

Over the last six years, however, more and more mothers have been allowed to enter premature nurseries in the United States. None the less, in a recent survey of 1400 nurseries in the U.S. done in 1970 by Barnett and Grobstein (1974), only 30 percent of mothers were permitted to enter nurseries and of these, only 40 percent allowed the mother to touch her baby in the first days of life. It is apparent from the data and definition of deprivation (Barnett et al. 1970) that most normal deliveries in the U.S. are followed by several days of deprivation for the mother (Tables 2 and 3). A woman who delivers a premature infant suffers complete deprivation from the first day if she can only see her infant through a glass window for eight weeks. Only mothers who deliver at home and room in with their infants from the moment of birth experience no deprivation.

This report describes recent studies of the process by which a parent becomes attached to the infant and suggests applications of these findings to the care of the parents of a normal infant, a premature infant, and a malformed infant.

Table 2. Levels of Intractional Deprivation and Component Variables*

Levels of deprivation	Duration of interaction	Sensory modalities of interaction	Caretaking nature of interaction
I. No deprivation	Full time	All senses	Complete
II. Partial deprivation	Part time	All senses	Partial
III. Moderate deprivation	Part time	All senses	None
IV. Severe deprivation	Part time	Visual only	None
V. Complete deprivation	None	None	None

*From Barnett, C. R., Leiderman, P. H., Grobstein, R., and Klaus, M. H.: Neonatal separation: the maternal side of interactional deprivation, Pediatrics **45**:197-205, 1970.

Basic Considerations

It has been difficult to assess the factors which determine the parenting behavior of an adult human who has lived for 20 to 30 years. A mother and father's actions and responses towards their infant are derived from a complex combination of their own genetic endowment, the way the baby responds to them, a long history of interpersonal relations with their own families and with each other, past experiences with this or previous pregnancies, the absorption of the practices and values of their cultures, and probably most importantly how each was raised by his own mother and father. The mothering or fathering behavior of each woman and man, his or her ability to tolerate stresses,

Table 3. Deprivation Levels Over Time, Related to Birth Situations*

Birth situation	Deprivation levels, days and weeks postpartum							
	Day 0	Day 1	Day 3	Day 7	Week 8	Week 9
Home, full term	I, no deprivation	I, no deprivation	I, no deprivation	I, no deprivation	I, no deprivation	I, no deprivation
Hospital, full term, rooming-in	III, moderate deprivation	I, no deprivation	I, no deprivation	I, no deprivation	I, no deprivation	I, no deprivation
Hospital, full term, regular care	III, moderate deprivation	II, partial deprivation	II, partial deprivation	I, no deprivation	I, no deprivation	I, no deprivation
Premature, mother allowed into nursery	V, complete deprivation	IV, severe deprivation	III, moderate deprivation	II, partial deprivation	II, partial deprivation (discharge nursery)	I, no deprivation (home)
Premature, regular care (separated)	V, complete deprivation	IV, severe deprivation	IV, severe deprivation	IV, severe deprivation	II, partial deprivation (discharge nursery)	I, no deprivation (home)
Unwed mother, refuses contact	V, complete deprivation	V, complete deprivation	V, complete deprivation	V, complete deprivation	V, complete deprivation	V, complete deprivation

*From Barnett C. R., Leiderman, P. H., Grobstein, R., and Klaus, M. H.: Neonatal separation: the maternal side of interactional deprivation, Pediatrics **45:**197-205, 1970.

and his or her need for special attention differ greatly and depend upon a mixture of these factors. Figure 1 is a schematic diagram of the major influences on paternal and maternal behavior and the resulting disturbances which we hypothesize may arise from them. At the time the infant is born, some of these determinants (framed with a solid line) are ingrained and unchangeable. Other determinants (framed with a dotted line) can be altered, such as the attitudes, statements and practices of the doctor in the hospital, whether or not there is separation from the infant in the first days of life, the nature of the infant himself, his temperament, as well as whether he is healthy, sick or malformed.

Shown also on the schematic diagram (Fig. 1) are a series of mothering disorders ranging from mild anxiety (such as persistent concerns about a baby following a minor problem which has been completely resolved in the nursery) to the most severe manifestation—the battered child syndrome. It is our hypothesis that this entire range of problems may result, in part, from separation and other unusual circumstances that occur in the early newborn period as a consequence of present hospital care policies. The most easily manipulated variables in this scheme are the separation of the infant from his mother and the practices in the hospital during the first hours and days of life. It is here, during this period, that recent studies have in part clarified some of the steps in mother-infant attachment. The development of mother-to-infant rather than father-to-infant attachment will be the central focus of this chapter since more data from both clinical observations and controlled studies is available for mothers. Information relating to the father-infant bond will be presented parenthetically.

During the first stage of pregnancy, a woman must come to terms with the knowledge that she will be a mother. The second stage involves a growing awareness of the baby in the uterus as a separate individual, usually starting with the sensation of fetal movement (quickening), a remarkably powerful event. During this period, the woman must begin to change her concept of the fetus from a part of herself to a living baby who will soon be a separate individual.

After quickening, a woman will usually begin to have fantasies about what the baby will be like, attributing some human personality characteristics to him and developing a feeling of attachment. Unplanned, unwanted infants may now seem more acceptable. Objectively, there will usually be some outward evidence of the mother's preparation in such actions as the purchase of clothes or a crib, the selection of a name, and the rearrangement of space to accommodate the baby (nest building). Mothers who remain relaxed during labor and who cooperate and have good rapport with those caring for them are more apt to be pleased with their infants at the first sight (Newton and Newton 1962). Unconsciousness during delivery does not cause the mother to reject her infant in an obvious manner as has been observed in some animals.

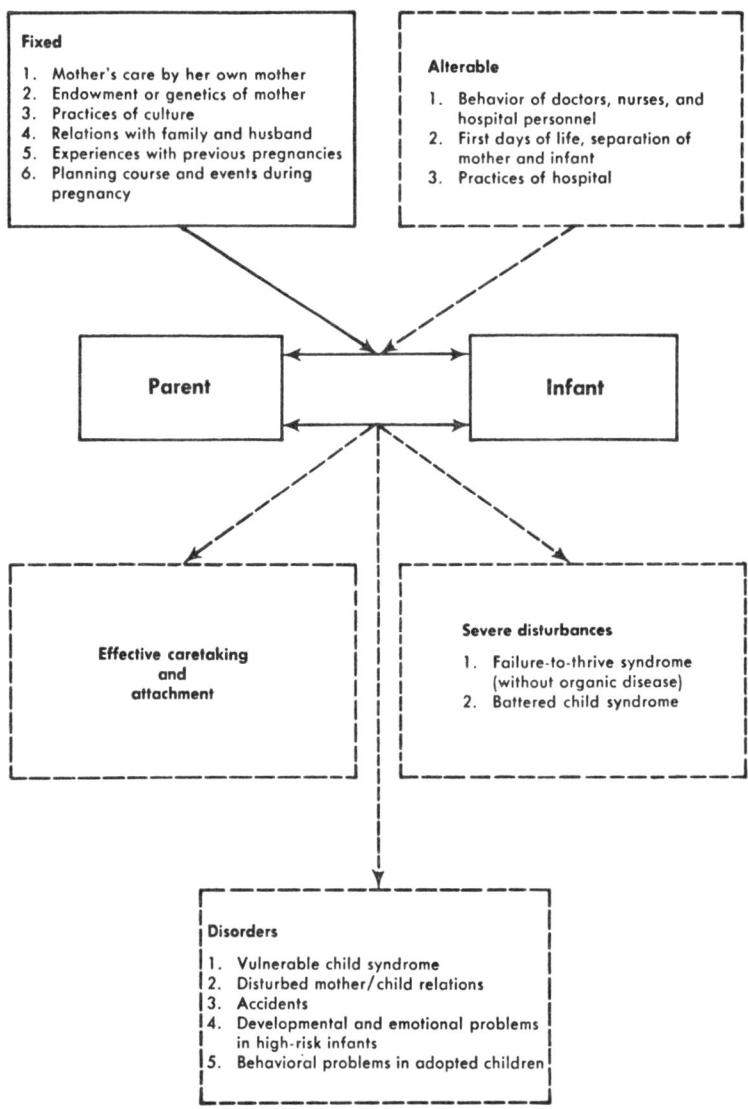

Figure 1. Hypothesized diagram of the major influences on maternal behavior and the resulting disturbances. Solid lines represent unchangeable determinants; dotted lines represent alterable determinants.

However, early unconfirmed reports suggest that there may be a tenfold increase in child abuse after delivery by Caesarean section when compared with vaginal deliveries.

Species-Specific Behavior

Detailed observations of many species have shown that adaptive species-specific patterns of behavior, including nesting, exploring, grooming and retrieving, before, during and after parturition have evolved to meet the needs of the young.

For example, the domestic cat, whether in the United States or England, behaves in a characteristic way at the time of delivery. Towards the end of her pregnancy, she finds a warm dark place, preferably with a soft surface, in which to give birth. Throughout labor and delivery, she spends increasingly more time licking her genital region. After delivery, she continues licking, but with the newborn kitten as her object. The placenta is usually promptly eaten. After the birth of the last kitten, the mother lies down encircling her kittens, and rests with them for about 12 hours (Schneirla, Rosenblatt and Tobach 1963). Each mammalian species studied has its own characteristic behavioral sequence around the time of delivery and following the birth (Hersher, Richmond and Moore 1963).

We have searched for similar specific behavior in the human mother in the hope that close observations of very early interaction between mother and infant might provide clues or principles that may not be evident at other times. If humans exhibit such specific patterns of behavior, knowledge of the sequence might be clinically applicable in situations where mothers and infants are at present separated early, such as prematurity or sickness during the neonatal period. In addition, it is our hypothesis that there is an immediate interlocking, and a reciprocal set of behaviors for attachment which must quickly operate because of the infant's precarious state after delivery.

Filmed observations made after delivery in a hospital show that a mother presented with her nude, full-term infant begins with fingertip touching of the infant's extremities and within a few minutes proceeds to massaging, encompassing palm contact of the trunk (Klaus et al. 1970). Mothers of premature infants in incubators also follow a small portion of this sequence but proceed at a much slower rate. According to Rubin (1964), when mothers are given their infants fully clothed, it takes several days for them to move to palmar stroking of the trunk. We have observed that fathers go through some of the same routines.

In sharp contrast to the woman who gives birth in the hospital, a woman delivering at home with a midwife appears to be in control. She chooses both the room in the house and the location within the room where she would like the birth to take place as well as the close friends who will be present to share this experience with her. She is an active participant rather than a passive patient during her labor and delivery. Immediately after delivery, she appears to be in a remarkable state of ecstasy. In fact many mothers have reported they had sensations similar to orgasm at the time of delivery (Lang 1974). The exuberance is contagious and the observers share the festive mood of unreserved elation after the delivery. Striking in films is the observers' intense interest in the infant, especially in the first 15 to 20 minutes of life. Although controlled studies have not yet been done to test the effects of this experience on the mother-infant relationship, it seems clear that the conditions surrounding delivery greatly affect the mother's initial mood and interaction with her infant.

In the observed home deliveries, the mother cradles her infant in her arms immediately after his birth and begins touching his face with her fingertips. Thus, we have fragmentary evidence that human mothers engage in a species-specific sequence of touching behaviors when first meeting their infants even though the speed and pattern of this sequence may be modified by environmental conditions.

In early contacts, a strong interest in eye-to-eye contact has been expressed by mothers of both full-term and premature infants. When the words of mothers who had been presented with their infants in privacy were taped, 70 percent of the statements referred to the eyes. The mothers said, "Let me see your eyes," and "Open your eyes and I'll know you love me." Robson (1967) has suggested that eye-to-eye contact appears to elicit maternal caregiving responses. Mothers seem to try hard to look "en face" at their infants, that is, to keep their faces aligned so that their eyes are in the same vertical plane of rotation as their babies'. Complementing the mother's interest in the infant's eyes is the early functional development of his visual pathways. The infant is alert, active, and able to follow during the first hour of life (Brazelton, Scholl and Robey 1966) if maternal sedation has been limited and the administration of silver nitrate delayed.

This area has been greatly augmented by the recent explosion of information in a closely related field. Detailed studies of the amazing behavioral capacities of the normal neonate have shown that the infant sees, hears and moves in rhythm to his mother's voice in the first minutes and hours of life and that there may be a beautiful linking and synchronized dance between the mother and infant.

Recent exciting observations by Condon and Sander (1974) reveal that newborns move with the structure of adult speech. " . . . When the infant is already in movement, points of change in the configuration of his moving body parts become coordinated with points of change in sound patterns characterizing speech . . . " In other words, as the speaker pauses for breath or accents a syllable, the infant almost imperceptibly raises an eyebrow or lowers a foot. The investigators demonstrated that live speech is particularly effective in entraining infant movement by showing that neonate movement did not show correspondence with either tapping noises or disconnected vowel sounds

Parent-to-Infant Attachment

as is noted with natural, rhythmic speech. Interestingly, synchronous movements were found at 16 hours of age with both of the two natural languages tested, English and Chinese. As the authors note,

> This study reveals a complex interaction system in which the organization of the neonate's motor behavior is entrained by and synchronized with the organized speech behavior of adults in his environment. If the infant, from the beginning, moves in precise, shared rhythm with the organization of the speech structure of his culture, then he participates developmentally through complex, sociobiological entrainment he later uses in speaking and communicating.

Thus it appears that the normal neonate is equipped in the first hours of life to follow his mother with his eyes and to move in time with her words. The appearance of the infant and its broad array of sensory and motor abilities evoke responses from the mother and provide several channels of communication which are essential in the process of attachment and the initiation of a series of reciprocal interactions. Lang (1974) noted that immediately after a home delivery, most mothers suckle their infants. The infants she observed did not suck but licked the area around the nipple.

MacFarlane (1975) has shown that six days after birth the infant will have the ability with significant reliability to identify by scent his own mother's breast pad from the breast pads of other women. The mother has an intense interest in looking at her newborn baby's open eyes. In the first 45 minutes of life, the infant is awake and alert and will follow his mother for 180 degrees with his own eyes. The licking of the nipple will induce a marked increase in prolactin secretion in the mother and at the same time oxytocin to contract the uterus and decrease bleeding. With the mother's strong desire to touch and see her child, nature has provided for the immediate and essential union of the two. The alert newborn rewards his mother for her efforts by following her with his eyes, thus maintaining their interaction, and kindling the tired mother's fascination with her baby.

Lind and his associates in Stockholm have shown that a surprising increase in blood flow to the breast occurs when a mother hears the cries of her own infant (Lind, Vuorenkoski and Wasz-Hoeckert 1972). These intricate interactions have focused our attention on the cascade of interlocking sensory patterns that quickly develop between mother and infant in the first hours of life.

There is suggestive evidence that many of these early interactions also take place between the father and his newborn child. Parke (1974) in particular has demonstrated that when fathers are given the opportunity to be alone with their newborns, they spend almost exactly the same amount of time as mothers holding, touching, and looking at them.

In his work with a mother and her three month old twins, Stern (1971) observed that the pattern of interaction between a mother and her child has a characteristic rhythm. Intricate interchanges occur within a period of a few seconds. And when these interactions are repeatedly out of phase, for example, if one partner looks away just as the other looks at him, many aspects of the relationship between the two individuals are disturbed. Our observations suggest that this dance of mother and infant, which may or may not be in rhythm, is first initiated in the immediate postpartum period. As Brazelton and his colleagues have stated, "This interdependency of rhythms seems to be at the root of their 'attachment' as well as communication" (Brazelton, Koslowski and Main 1974). Thus, it seems important that the family have privacy in the first hours of life, in which the new and older members may become attuned to each other.

On the basis of our observations and the reports of parents, we believe that every parent has a task to perform during the postpartum period. She must look and "take in" her real live baby and reconcile the fantasy of the infant she imagined with the one she actually delivered. Many cultures recognize this need by providing the mother with a *doula,* or "aunt" who mothers her and relieves her of other responsibilities so that she can devote herself completely to this task (Raphael 1973).

A Sensitive Period

It has been found that in a large number of animal species, separation of mother and baby immediately after birth can severely distort mothering behavior. For example, if the goat is separated for 1 hour from her kid immediately after delivery, she is likely to butt it away when it is returned. However, if a separation of similar duration begins 10 minutes after delivery, the dam will re-accept her kid upon reunion and allow it to nurse (Klopfer 1971). Thus, there appears to be a sensitive period in the first minutes of life in which any alteration in the normal pattern of interaction can result in aberrant subsequent mothering behavior.

In monkeys, a separation immediately after birth for 1 hour does not seem to affect the female's interest in being near her neonate. However, if the separation begins at birth and is for as long as 24 hours, the mother's preference for neonates seems to have disappeared. Lab-reared females separated at birth for a couple of hours will not re-accept their infants, whereas feral females will do so within two days. The fact that feral females will not immediately accept their infants suggests that separation at birth is a stressful experience. Even after living with their infants for several months before being separated, some monkey mothers show markedly altered behavior at the time of reunion (Meier 1965; Sackett and Ruppenthal 1974).

There is evidence that when human mothers are separated from their babies during the first hours and days after delivery, they may have difficulty forming an attachment. Studies of mothers of premature infants who spent their first weeks of life in neonatal intensive care nurseries highlight this problem. In those nurseries where the mothers are not allowed to visit, doctors find that mothers temporarily forget they have babies and find reasons to put off taking them home.

A small number of studies have focused on the possibility of an early sensitive period in the human mother. Observations at Stanford and in our own unit have been made with mothers of prematures, half of whom were permitted into the nursery in the first hours and half of whom could not come in until the twentieth day. At Case Western Reserve University, mothers who had early contact with their infants looked at them significantly more than late contact mothers during a filmed feeding at the time of discharge. Furthermore, preliminary data on the IQs of these two groups of children at 42 months indicate that children in the early contact group scored significantly higher (mean=99) than did children in the late contact group (mean=85). Strikingly, a significant correlation was found between IQ at 42 months and the amount of time women looked at their babies during the one month filmed feeding ($r=0.71$). This is consistent with our hypothesis that early contact affects aspects of maternal behavior which may have significance for the child's later development. At Stanford, when mothers separated from their premature babies from 3 to 12 weeks were compared with those of prematures permitted early contact, there were more divorces (five compared to one) and more infants relinquished (two compared to none) in the group of mothers with prolonged separation (Leifer et al. 1972). It should be noted that these were all middle-class families, and they all had initially planned on keeping their infant.

During the past five years, six studies of the sensitive period of mothers and their full-term infants have either been completed or are underway.

In a tightly controlled study of 28 primiparous mothers and their full-term infants, half the mothers were given 1 hour in the first 3 hours and 15 more hours of contact with their infants in the first three days of life than were the controls. The mothers who had early and extended contact were more likely to stand near their infants and watch during the physical examination, showed significantly more soothing behavior, engaged in more eye-to-eye contact and fondling during feeding, and were more reluctant to leave their infants with someone else at one month than were mothers not given the extended contact experience (Klaus et al. 1972). At one year the two groups of mothers were still significantly different. Extended contact mothers spent more time near the table assisting the physician and soothing their infant while he was being examined, and reported themselves to be more preoccupied with the baby when they went out (Kennell et al. 1974). At two years, when the linguistic behaviors of the two groups of mothers while speaking to their children were compared, extended contact mothers asked twice as many questions, and used more words per proposition, fewer content words, more adjectives and fewer commands than did the controls (Ringler et al. 1975). It is impressive evidence for a sensitive maternal period that just 16 extra hours of contact in the first three days of life had such far-reaching effects.

In a small but carefully controlled study, Winters (1973) gave six mothers in one group their babies to suckle shortly after birth and compared these with six mothers who did not have contact with their babies until approximately 16 hours later. All had originally intended to breast feed and none stopped because of physical problems. When checked two months later, all six mothers who had suckled their babies on the delivery table were still breast feeding, whereas only one of the other six was still nursing.

Recently, Drs. Kennell, Klaus, Mata, Sosa, and Urrutia started a long-term study in two hospitals in Guatemala. In the Social Security Hospital, one group of 19 mothers was given their babies on the delivery table during the episiotomy repair period, then allowed to stay with them in privacy for 45 minutes. Each mother-infant pair was nude under a heat panel. The other group of mothers was separated from their babies shortly after delivery, in the routine for both hospitals. Except for this difference in initial contact, the care of the two groups was identical. The infants were discharged with free milk at two days, as is the practice of the hospital.

When the babies were checked at 35 and 90 days after birth, the mean weight of those in the early contact group was significantly greater than that of the control group. The socio-economic, marital, housing, and income status of the mothers in the two groups were not significantly different.

In Roosevelt Hospital, a similar study was carried out and at 35 days there were no significant differences in weight gain. Other data are not yet available to help account for these discrepant findings.

In Pelotis, Brazil, Sousa et al. (1974) recently compared the success of breast feeding during the first two months of life in two groups of 100 women who delivered normal full-term babies in a 20-bed maternity ward. In the study group, the newborn baby was put to breast immediately after birth and continuous contact between the mother and baby was maintained during the lying-in period. The baby lay in a cot beside his mother's bed. The control group had the traditional contact with their infants—a glimpse shortly after birth and then visits for approximately 30 minutes every 3 hours, starting 12 to 14 hours after birth. The babies were kept in a separate nursery. Successful breast feeding was defined as the mother's not using complementary feedings other than tea, water, or small amounts of fruit juice until two months after birth. At two months of age, 77 percent of the early contact mothers were successfully breast feeding in contrast to only 27 percent of the controls. A weakness in this design which limits the strength of the findings is that during the experimental period there was a special nurse working in the unit to stimulate and encourage breast feeding. Although not definitive in itself, this study adds weight to our hypothesis.

In a third study in 1974 at Roosevelt Hospital in Guatemala, a different group of nine mothers was given their babies nude under a heat panel after they had left the delivery room. A second group of 10 was separated according to the usual routine. The babies in both groups were sent to the newborn nursery for the next 12 hours, after which they went to the mother in a seven-bed room for the first breast feeding. At 12 hours, each mother's interactions with her infant were noted by an observer who did not know to which group they belonged. Observations of the mother's fondling, kissing, looking "en face," gazing at, and holding her baby close were made for 15 seconds of every minute for 15 minutes (Fig. 2). The group with early contact showed significantly increased attachment behaviors.

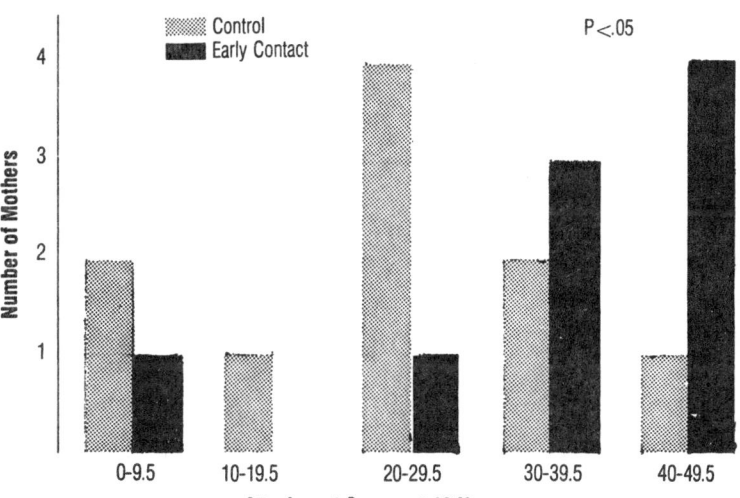

Figure 2. Attachment behavior (fondling, kissing, looking "en face," holding baby close) at 12 hours postpartum in two groups of mothers. Experimental mothers received their infants for 45 minutes after delivery; control mothers did not have this additional contact.

Studies of the effects of rooming-in have also confirmed the importance of the early postnatal period. At Duke University a number of years ago, an increase in breast feeding and a reduction in anxious phone calls was noted when rooming-in was instituted (McBryde 1951). In Sweden, mothers randomly assigned to rooming-in arrangements were more confident and felt more competent in caregiving. They also appeared to be more sensitive to the crying of their own infants than were mothers who did not have the rooming-in experience (Greenberg, Rosenberg and Lind 1973). In an interesting and significant observation of fathers, Lind (1973) noted that paternal caregiving was markedly increased in the first three months of life when the father was asked to undress the infant twice and establish eye-to-eye contact with him for 1 hour during the first three days of life.

It is our own belief that other principles also govern the attachment process. Though solid evidence is scanty, the following additional rules appear to be important.

1. The process of attachment is structured so that the father and mother will become attached optimally to only one infant at a time. In 1958, Bowlby stated this principle for the attachment process in the other direction (infant to mother) and termed it "monotropy" (Bowlby 1958).

2. During the early process of the mother's attachment to her infant, it is necessary that the infant respond to the mother by some signal such as body or eye movements.

3. People who witness the birth process become strongly attached to the infant.

4. It is difficult and possibly mutually incompatible for some people to both become attached and detached at the same time as in simultaneously attempting to go through the processes of attachment to one person while mourning the loss or threatened loss of the same or another person.

5. Early events have long-lasting effects. Anxieties in the first day about the well-being of a baby with a temporary disorder may result in long-lasting concerns that may adversely shape the development of the child (Kennell and Rolnick 1960).

Practical Considerations

Up until 100 years ago, events surrounding the delivery had changed little over the centuries. Elaborate customs of the society helped parents through this time. In the last century, however, increasing emphasis has been placed on the medical and scientific aspects of delivery, but less attention has been paid to the equally valid psychological considerations. A question may be raised: has the enormous improvement in medical management, which has lessened the physical dangers, contributed to a waning concern about the many other problems a mother faces during pregnancy? In 1959, Bibring wrote, "What was once a crisis with carefully worked-out traditional customs of giving support to the woman passing through this crisis-period has become at this time a crisis with no mechanisms within the society for helping the woman involved in this profound change of conflict-solutions and adjustive tasks." This deficiency accounts for the development of the many support systems in our society. The wide assortment of childbirth classes which attempt to continue previous customs are good examples. These groups help the mother through the delivery period as well as aiding her in later infant and child care. They also lessen the tensions, fears, and fantasies that occur during normal pregnancies. By joining a group of mothers, with whom she can chat and share her feelings, a woman can alleviate the many emotional upsets that occur during normal pregnancy. We therefore believe that these courses, particularly those in which mothers participate actively, have a valuable supportive role during pregnancy.

To minimize the number of unknowns for a mother while she is in the hospital, she and her husband should visit the maternity unit to see where labor and delivery will take place. She should also learn about the anesthetic (if she is to receive one), delivery routines and all the procedures and medication she will receive before, during, and after delivery. By reducing the possibility of surprise, such advance preparation will increase confidence during labor and delivery. For an adult, just as for a child entering the hospital for surgery, the more meticulously every step and event is detailed in advance, the less the subsequent anxiety. The less anxiety the mother experiences while delivering and becoming attached to her baby, the better will be her immediate relationship with him.

The mother must have continuing support and reassurance during her labor and delivery, whether from her husband, a midwife, or a nurse. She also must be satisfied with the arrangements that have been made to maintain her home during her hospitalization. In Holland, when the mothers deliver at home, mother-helpers come into the home at the time of delivery and take over the care of the family. The mother-helper helps the midwife to deliver the infant. This gives the mother the freedom to concentrate on the needs of the baby and to enjoy her family in the process, and it relieves pressure on the father, reserving his energies for the family.

In an effort to reduce the amount of tension on the mother, she should labor and deliver in the same room, preventing the necessity of rushing to a delivery room in the last minutes of labor. Once the delivery is completed and the mother has had a quick glance at the infant, it is important for her to have a few seconds to regain her composure and, in a sense, catch her breath before she proceeds to the next task—taking on the infant. This breath-catching usually occurs during the period when the placenta is being delivered, while the mother is being cleansed and is having any necessary suturing. It has been our experience that it is best not to give a mother her baby until she indicates that she is ready to take it on. It should be her decision.

In many hospitals it is customary to put the baby on the mother's chest for 1 or 2 minutes shortly after delivery. This is helpful, but coupled with the lack of privacy, the narrow table and the short time period does not allow sufficient opportunity for the mother to touch and explore her baby. Although it is a reasonable procedure, it is not sufficient to optimize maternal attachment.

After delivery, it is extremely valuable for the father, mother, and baby to have a period alone in either the delivery room or an adjacent room (i.e., a recovery room). Obviously, this is only possible if the infant is normal and the mother is well. The mother should have the infant with her on the bed so she can hold him. The infant should not be off in a bassinet where she can only see his face. She should be given the baby nude and allowed to examine him completely. We have found it valuable to encourage the mother to move over in her regular hospital bed, so that she only takes up about half of it, leaving the other half for her partially dressed or nude infant. A heat panel easily maintains or, if need be, increases the body temperature of the infant. Several mothers have told us of the unforgettable experience of holding their nude baby against their own bare chest, so we recommend skin-to-skin contact. The father sits or stands at the side of the bed by the infant. This allows the parents and infant to become acquainted. Because the eyes are so important for both the parents and baby, we withhold the application of silver nitrate ($AgNO_3$) to the eyes until after this rendezvous.

We have found it valuable for the mother, father, and infant to be together for about 30 minutes. After 10 to 15 minutes, the mother and baby often fall into a deep sleep. In Guatemalan hospitals, where drugs and anesthesia are used more sparingly, most mothers were usually awake after 45 minutes of privacy with their infants. The mother and father never forget this significant and stimulating shared experience. It helps to firmly bond the actual, real infant to both parents. We must emphasize that this should be a private session.

Affectional bonds are further consolidated in the succeeding four to five days through continued close association of baby and mother, particularly when she cares for him. Close contact with her husband and other children is also obviously important.

Immature or Sick Neonates

We recommend the following procedures:

1. We have found it useful and safe when a premature weighing 1.5 to 2.5 kilograms is delivered, and appears to be doing well without grunting and retractions, for the mother to have the baby placed in her bed in the first hour of life with a heat panel above them. We do not recommend this unless the physician feels relaxed about the health of the infant.

2. A mother and her infant should be kept near each other in the same hospital, ideally on the same floor. When the long-term significance of early mother-infant contact is kept in mind a modification of restrictions and territorial traditions can usually be arranged.

3. We have found it helpful if the baby does not have to be moved to a hospital with an intensive care unit, to give the mother a chance to see and touch her infant, even if he has respiratory distress and is in an oxygen hood. The house officer or the attending physician stops in the mother's room with the transport incubator and encourages her to touch her baby and look at him at close hand. A comment about the baby's strength and healthy features may be long remembered and appreciated.

4. We encourage the father to follow the transport team to our hospital so he can see what is happening with his baby. He uses his own transportation so that he can stay in the premature unit for 3 to 4 hours. This extra time allows him to get to know the nurses and physicians in the unit, to find out how the infant is being treated, and to talk with the physicians in a relaxed fashion about what we expect will happen with the baby and his treatment in the succeeding days. We allow him to come into the nursery and explain in detail everything that is going on with the infant, often offering him a cup of coffee. We ask him to help act as a link between us and his family by carrying information back to his wife, and request that he come to our unit before he visits his wife so that he can let her know how the baby is doing. We suggest that he take a Polaroid picture, even if the infant is on a respirator, so that he can describe to his wife in detail how the baby is being cared for. The mothers often tell us how valuable the picture is in keeping some contact with their infant, even while physically separated.

5. A mother should be permitted to enter the premature nursery as soon as she is able to maneuver easily. When she makes her first visit it is important to anticipate that she may become faint or dizzy when she looks at her infant. We always have a stool nearby so that she can sit down, and a nurse stays at her side during most of the visit describing in

detail the procedures being carried out, such as the monitoring of respiration and heart rate, the umbilical catheter, the feeding through the various infusion lines, and the functioning of the incubator.

6. We also encourage grandparents, brothers, sisters and other relatives to view the infant through the glass window of the nursery so that they will begin to feel attached to the infant.

7. It is necessary to find out what the mother believes is going to happen or what she has read about the problem. We try to move at her pace during any discussion to ensure that she understands.

8. In discussing the infant's condition by telephone with the mother who is still in the referring hospital, we ask the father to stand nearby so that we can talk to them both at the same time and they can hear the same message. This group communication reduces misunderstandings and usually is helpful in assuring the mother that we are telling her the whole story.

9. If there is any chance that the infant will survive, we are optimistic in our talks with the parents from the beginning. There is no evidence that if a favorable prediction proves to be incorrect and the baby expires, the parents will be harmed by the early optimism. There is almost always time to prepare them before the baby actually dies. If the infant lives and the physician has been pessimistic, it is almost impossible for parents to become closely attached after they have figuratively dug a few shovelfuls of earth. We recognize that this recommendation goes contrary to many old customs and places a heavy burden on the physician. It is our belief that if the infant does expire, we must still work with the mother and help her with the mourning period.

10. Once the possibility that a baby has brain damage has been mentioned, the parents will not forget it. Therefore, unless we are 100 percent sure that the baby is damaged, we do not mention the possibility of any brain damage or retardation to the parents. On many occasions we have had neonates who have appeared to be brain damaged but who later were obviously perfectly normal.

11. It is important to emphasize that if we have a clear objective finding, such as a cardiac abnormality or a specific congenital malformation, we see no reason to hide this from the parents. We would never lie to a parent.

12. As soon as possible we describe to both the father and the mother the value of touching the infant in helping them get to know him, in reducing the number of apnoeic episodes (if this is a problem), in increasing weight gain, and in hastening his discharge from the unit.

13. It is important to remember that feelings of love for the baby are

often elicited through eye-to-eye contact. Therefore if an infant is under bilirubin lights, we turn them off and remove the eye patches so that the mother and her infant can really see each other.

14. From our previous observations, we have found that keeping a book in which to record parental phone calls and visits is useful in determining which mothers are likely to require additional help from a social worker or extra discussions about the health of their infant. If a mother visits less than three times in two weeks, in the nursery, the chance of her developing some sort of mothering disorder such as failure-to-thrive, battering, or giving up the baby, increases. Therefore, if the visiting pattern of the mother is less than most mothers, the mother is given extra help in adapting to the hospitalization (Fanaroff et al. 1972).

Congenital Malformations

The birth of an infant with a congenital malformation presents complex challenges to the physician who will care for the affected child and his family (Johns 1971; National Association for Mental Health 1971). Despite the relatively large number of infants with congenital anomalies, our understanding of how parents develop an attachment to a malformed child remains incomplete. Although previous investigators agree that the child's birth often precipitates major family stress (Johns 1971; National Association for Mental Health 1971; Roskies 1972), relatively few have described the process of family adaptation (Hare et al. 1966; Johns 1971; Roskies 1972) during the infant's first year of life. A major advance was Solnit and Stark's conceptualization of parental reactions (Solnit and Stark 1961). They emphasized that a significant aspect of adaptation is the necessity for parents to mourn the loss of the normal child they had expected. Other observers (Waterman 1948; Zuk 1959; Michaels and Shucman 1962) have noted the pathological aspects of family reactions including the chronic sorrow which envelops the family of a defective child (Olshansky 1962). Less attention has been given to the more adaptive aspects of parental attachment to children with malformations.

Parental reactions to the birth of a child with a congenital malformation appear to follow a predictable course. For most parents, initial shock, disbelief, and a period of intense emotional upset (including sadness, anger, and anxiety) are followed by a period of gradual adaptation, which is marked by a lessening of intense anxiety and emotional reaction (Fig. 3). This adaptation is characterized by an increased satisfaction with and ability to care for the baby. These stages in parental reactions are similar to those reported in other crisis situations, such as terminally ill children (Friedman et al. 1963). The shock, disbelief, and denial reported by many parents seem to be an understandable attempt to escape the traumatic news of the baby's malformation, so discrepant with usual parental expectations for a newborn that it is impossible to register except gradually (Geleerd 1965).

The intense emotional turmoil described by parents who have given birth to a child with a congenital malformation corresponds to a period of crisis, defined as "upset in a state of equilibrium caused by a hazardous event which creates a threat, a loss, or a challenge for the individual" (Bloom 1963; Rappoport 1965). A crisis includes a period of impact, a rise in tension associated with stress, and finally a return to equilibrium. During such crisis periods a person is at least temporarily unable to respond with his usual problem-solving activities to solve the crisis. Roskies (1972) noted a similar "birth crisis" in her observations of mothers who had given birth to children with birth defects caused by thalidomide.

Solnit and Stark (1961) have likened the crisis of the birth of a child with a malformation to the emotional crisis following the death of a child, in that the mother must mourn the loss of her expected, normal infant. In addition she must become attached to her actual living, damaged child. However, the sequence of parental reactions to the birth of a baby with a malformation differs from that following the death of a child in yet another respect (Fig. 3). The mourning or grief work appears not to take place in the usual manner because of the complex issues raised by continuation of the child's life and the demands of his physical care. The parents' sadness, which is important initially in their relationship with their child, diminishes in most instances once their parents take over the physical care. Most parents reach a point at which they are able to care adequately for their children and cope effectively with disrupting feelings of sadness and anger. The mother's initiation of the relationship with her child is a major step in the reduction of anxiety and emotional upset associated with the trauma of the birth. As with normal children, the parents' initial experience with their infant seems to release positive feelings which aid the mother-child relationship following the stresses associated with the news of the child's anomaly and in many instances, the separation of mother and child in the hospital (Zuk 1959).

Practical Suggestions for Parents of Malformed Infants

1. We have come to believe that it is far better to leave the infant with the mother for the first two to three days, if medically feasible. If the child is rushed to the hospital where special surgery will eventually be done, the mother will not have enough opportunity to become attached to him. Even if the surgery is required immediately, as for bowel

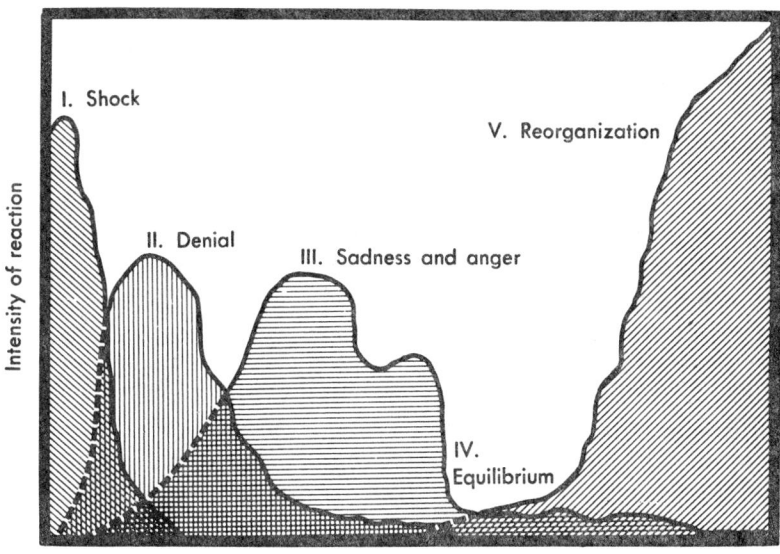

Figure 3. Hypothetical model of the sequence of normal parental reactions to the birth of a child with congenital malformations. (From Drotar, D., Baskiewicz, A., Irvin, N., Kennell, J. H., and Klaus, M. H.: *Pediatrics* 56:710-717, 1975.)

obstruction, it is best to bring the baby to the mother first, allowing her to touch and handle him, and point out to her how normal he is in all other respects.

2. It is our impression that the parents' mental picture of the anomaly is often far more alarming than the actual problem. Any delay during which the parents suspect that there may be a problem greatly heightens their anxiety and causes their imaginations to run wild. Therefore, we suggest that it is helpful to bring the baby to both parents when they are together as soon after delivery as possible.

3. We believe that parents should not be given tranquilizers. This tends to blunt their responses and slows their adaptation to the problem. However, a small dose of Seconal at night is often helpful.

4. It has been our clinical experience that parents who are adapting reasonably well initially often ask many questions and at times appear to be almost over involved in clinical care. In our unit we are pleased by this and more concerned about parents who ask few questions and who appear stunned and overwhelmed by the problem. Parents who become involved in trying to find out what the best procedures are, who ask many questions about care—why this, why that—are sometimes very bothersome but often make the best adaptation in the end.

5. Many anomalies are very frustrating not only to the parents but to the physicians and nurses as well. There is a temptation for the physician to withdraw from the parents and their infant. The many questions asked by the parent who is trying to understand the problem are often very frustrating for the physician. The parent often appears to forget and asks the same questions over and over again.

6. We have found it best to move at the parents' pace. If we move too quickly, we run the risk of losing the parents along the way. It is beneficial to ask the parents how they view their infant. "Maybe you could tell me how you see the infant?"

7. Each parent may move through the process of shock, denial, anger, guilt and adaptation at a different pace so the two parents may not be synchronized with one another. If they are unable to talk with each other about the baby, there may be a marked disruption in their own relationship. Therefore, we use the process of early crisis intervention, meeting several times with the parents. During these discussions, we ask the mother how she's doing, how she feels her husband is doing, and how he feels about the infant. We then reverse the questions and ask the father how he's doing and how he thinks his wife is progressing. The hope is that they will think not only about their own reactions, but will begin to consider each other's as well.

Summary

The hospital now determines the events surrounding birth and death. These two most important events in the life of an individual have been stripped of all the long-established traditions and support systems which were established over centuries to help families through these transitions that have such long-lasting effects on everyone involved.

Since the newborn baby is utterly dependent upon his parents for his survival and optimal development, it is essential to understand the process of attachment as it develops from the first moments after the child is born. Although we have only a beginning understanding of this complex phenomenon, those responsible for the care of mothers and infants would be wise to re-evaluate hospital procedures that interfere with early, sustained mother-infant contact, to consider measures which promote a mother's contact with her nude infant and to help her appreciate the wide range of sensory and motor responses of her neonate.

References

Ambuel, J., and Harris, B. "Failure to Thrive: A Study of Failure to Grow in Height or Weight." *Ohio Medical Journal* 59 (1963): 997.
Barnett, C. R.; Leiderman, P. H.; Grobstein, R.; and Klaus, M. "Neonatal Separation: The Maternal Side of Interactional Deprivation." *Pediatrics* 45 (1970): 197-205.
Barnett, C. R., and Grobstein, R. 1974: personal communication.
Bibring, G. "Some Considerations of the Psychological Processes in Pregnancy." *Psychoanalytic Study of the Child* 14 (1959): 113.
Bloom, B. "Definitional Concepts of the Crisis Concept." *Journal of Consulting Psychology* 27 (1963): 42.
Bowlby, J. "Nature of a Child's Tie to His Mother." *International Journal of Psychoanalysis* 39 (1958): 350-373.
Brazelton, T. B.; Koslowski, B.; and Main, M. "The Origins of Reciprocity—The Early Infant Interaction." In *The Effect of the Infant on Its Caregiver*, edited by M. Lewis and L. A. Rosenblum. New York: John Wiley & Sons, 1974.
Brazelton, T. B.; Scholl, M.; and Robey, J. "Visual Responses in the Newborn." *Pediatrics* 37 (1966): 284-290.
Budin, P. *The Nursling*. London: Caxton, 1907.
Condon, W. S., and Sander, L. W. "Neonate Movement Is Synchronized with Adult Speech: Interactional Participation and Language Acquisition." *Science* 183 (1974): 99-101.
Elmer, E., and Gregg, D. "Developmental Characteristics of Abused Children." *Pediatrics* 40 (1967): 596.
Evans, S.; Reinhart, J.; and Succop, R. "A Study of 45 Children and Their Families." *Journal of the American Academy of Child Psychiatry* 11 (1972): 440-454.
Fanaroff, A. A.; Kennell, J. H.; and Klaus, M. H. "Follow-Up of Low Birth-Weight Infants: The Predictive Value of Maternal Visiting Patterns." *Pediatrics* 49 (1972): 288-290.
Friedman, S. B.; Chodoff, P.; Mason, J. W.; and Hamburg, D. A. "Behavioral Observations on Parents Anticipating the Death of a Child." *Pediatrics* 32 (1963): 610.
Geleerd, E. R. "Two Kinds of Denial. Neurotic Denial and Denial in the Service of the Need to Survive." In *Drives, Affects and Behavior*, vol. 2, edited by M. Schur. New York: International Universities Press, 1965.
Greenberg, M.; Rosenberg, I.; and Lind, J. "First Mothers Rooming-In with Their Newborns: Its Impact upon the Mother." *American Journal of Orthopsychiatry* 43 (1973): 783-788.
Hare, E. H.; Lawrence, K. M.; Paynes, H.; and Rawnsley, K. "Spina Bifida Cystica and Family Stress." *British Medical Journal* 2 (1966): 757.
Hersher, L.; Richmond, J.; and Moore, A. "Maternal Behavior in Sheep and Goats." In *Maternal Behavior in Mammals*, edited by H. Rheingold. New York: John Wiley & Sons, 1963.
Johns, N. "Family Reactions to the Birth of a Child with a Congenital Abnormality." *Medical Journal of Australia* 7 (1971): 277.
Kennell, J. H.; Jerauld, R.; Wolfe, H.; Chesler, D.; Kreger, N.; McAlpine, W.; Steffa, M.; and Klaus, M. H. "Maternal Behavior One Year after Early and Extended Post-Partum Contact." *Developmental Medicine and Child Neurology* 16 (1974): 172-179.
Kennell, J. H., and Rolnick, A. "Discussing Problems in Newborn Babies with Their Parents." *Pediatrics* 26 (1960): 832-838.
Klaus, M. H., and Fanaroff, A. *Care of the High-Risk Neonate*. Philadelphia: W. B. Sanders, 1973.

Klaus, M. H.; Jerauld, R.; Kreger, N.; McAlpine, W.; Steffa, M.; and Kennell, J. H. "Maternal Attachment—Importance of the First Post-Partum Days." *New England Journal of Medicine* 286 (1972): 460-463.

Klaus, M. H.; Kennell, J. H.; Plumb, N.; and Zuehlke, S. "Human Maternal Behavior at the First Contact with Her Young." *Pediatrics* 46 (1970): 187-192.

Klein, M., and Stern, L. "Low Birth-Weight and the Battered Child Syndrome." *American Journal of Diseases of Children* 122 (1971): 15.

Klopfer, P. "Mother Love! What Turns It On?" *American Scientist* 49 (1971): 404-407.

Lang, R. *Birth Book*. Ben Lomond: Genesis Press, 1972.

Lang, R. 1974: personal communication.

Leifer, A.; Leiderman, P.; Barnett, C.; and Williams, J. "Effects of Mother-Infant Separation on Maternal Attachment Behavior." *Child Development* 43 (1972): 1203-1218.

Lind, J. 1973: personal communication.

Lind, J.; Vuorenkoski, V.; and Wasz-Hoeckert, O. "The Effect of Cry Stimulus on the Temperature of the Lactating Breast Primipara: A Thermagraphic Study." In *Psychosomatic Medicine in Obstetrics and Gynaecology*, edited by N. Morris. Basel, Switzerland: S. Karger, 1973.

MacFarlane, J. A. "Olfaction in the Development of Social Preferences in the Human Neonate." In *The Parent-Infant Relationship*, Ciba Foundation. Amsterdam: Elsevier, 1975.

McBryde, A. "Compulsory Rooming-In in the Ward and Private Newborn Service a Duke Hospital." *Journal of the American Medical Association* 45 (1951): 625.

Meier, G. W. "Maternal Behavior of Feral- and Laboratory-Reared Monkeys Following the Surgical Delivery of Their Infants." *Nature* 206 (1965): 492-493.

Michaels, J., and Shucman, H. "Observations on the Psychodynamics of Parents of Retarded Children." *American Journal of Mental Deficiency* 66 (1962): 568.

National Association for Mental Health Working Party. "The Birth of an Abnormal Child: Telling the Parents." *Lancet* 2 (1971): 1075.

Newton, N., and Newton, M. "Mothers' Reactions to Their Newborn Babies." *Journal of the American Medical Association* 181 (1962): 206-211.

Oliver, J. E.; Cox, J.; Taylor, A.; and Baldwin, J. "Severely Ill-Treated Young Children in North-East Wiltshire." Research Report No. 4. Oxford University Unit of Clinical Epidemiology, 1974.

Olshansky, S. "Chronic Sorrow: A Response to Having a Mentally Defective Child." *Social Casework* 43 (1962): 190.

Parke, R. "Family Interactions in the Newborn Period: Some Findings, Some Observations and Some Unresolved Issues." In *Proceedings of the International Society for Study of Behavior Development*, edited by K. Riegel and J. Meacham, 1974.

Raphael, D. *The Tender Gift: Breastfeeding*. Englewood Cliffs, N.J.: Prentice-Hall, 1973.

Rappoport, L. "The State of Crisis: Some Theoretical Considerations." In *Crisis Intervention*, edited by H. J. Parad. New York: Family Service Association, 1965.

Ringler, N. M.; Kennell, J. H.; Jarvella, R.; Navojosky, B.; and Klaus, M. H. "Mother-to-Child Speech at Two Years: Effects of Early Postnatal Contacts." *Behavioral Pediatrics* 86 (1975): 141-144.

Robson, K. "The Role of Eye-to-Eye Contact in Maternal-Infant Attachment." *Journal of Child Psychology and Psychiatry* 8 (1967): 13-25.

Roskies, E. *Abnormality and Normality: The Mothering of Thalidomide Children*. New York: Cornell University Press, 1972.

Rubin, R. "Maternal Touch." *Nursing Outlook*, November 1963, pp. 828-831.

Sackett, G. P., and Ruppenthal, G. G. "Some Factors Influencing the Attraction of Adult Female Macaque Monkeys to Neonates." In *The Effect of the Infant on Its*

Caregiver, edited by M. Lewis and L. Rosenblum. New York: John Wiley & Sons, 1974.

Schneirla, T.; Rosenblatt, J.; and Tobach, E. "Maternal Behavior in the Cat." In *Maternal Behavior in Mammals,* edited by J. Rheingold. New York: John Wiley & Sons, 1963.

Shaheen, E.; Alexander, D.; Truskowsky, M.; and Barbero, G. "Failure to Thrive in a Retrospective Profile." *Clinical Pediatrics* 7 (1968): 225.

Skinner, A., and Castle, R. "Seventy-Eight Battered Children: A Retrospective Study." Report by the National Society for the Prevention of Cruelty to Children, 1969.

Solnit, A. J., and Stark, M. H. "Mourning and the Birth of a Defective Child." *Psychoanalytic Study of the Child* 16 (1961): 523.

Sousa, P. L. R.; Baros, F. C.; Cazalle, R. V.; Begéres, R. M.; Pinheiro, G. N.; Menezes, S. T.; and Arruda, L. A. "Attachment and Lactation." Presented at *Pediatria XIV: Nutrition, Taxicology and Pharmacology,* Buenos Aires, Argentina, 1974.

Spitz, R. *The First Year of Life*. New York: International Universities Press, 1965.

Stern, D. "A Micro-Analysis of Mother-Infant Interaction." *Journal of the American Academy of Child Psychiatry* 10 (1971): 510-517.

Waterman, J. H. "Psychogenic Factors in Parental Acceptance of Feeble-Minded Children." *Diseases of the Nervous System* 9 (1948): 184.

Winters, M. "The Relationship of Time of Initial Breastfeeding to Success of Breastfeeding." Master's thesis, University of Washington, 1973.

Zuk, G. H. "Religious Factor and the Role of Guilt in Parental Acceptance of the Retarded Child." *American Journal of Mental Deficiency* 64 (1959): 145.

Patricia Teague Ashton

2 The Role of the Attachment Bond in Effective Parenting

The concept of attachment has recently received considerable attention in the theoretical and research literature in social development (Ainsworth 1973). The term *attachment* first appeared in the work of Bowlby (1958) to refer to the affectional bond between the infant and mother. Current research (Bowlby 1969; Ainsworth and Bell 1974) suggests that development of a strong attachment bond between mother and infant may be a prerequisite for children's development of social competence. There is also evidence to suggest that the quality of the parent-child attachment is related to later cognitive development (Bell 1970).

The purpose of this chapter is to review the research on attachment, extracting information that could lead to more effective parenting.

Impact of Attachment on Development

Current interest in the study of attachment is motivated partly by the assumption that a strong mother-child attachment bond is critical for subsequent development. In early efforts to alert professionals to the importance of the attachment bond, Bowlby (1965) cited studies suggesting that early maternal deprivation resulted in the development of an affectionless character, a pathogenic individual incapable of forming and maintaining deep and lasting affectional ties. In the case of severe deprivation, Bowlby concluded that children were likely to appear retarded in cognitive and social functioning.

Subsequent research indicates that the relationship between attachment and development is more complex than originally conceived by Bowlby. Wide individual differences in vulnerability to deprivation have been noted, in addition to differential effects on various aspects of psychological functioning (Ainsworth 1965). The evidence, however, is consistent in supporting the importance of attachment bonding for both cognitive and social development.

Development of object permanence is typically considered a milestone in children's cognitive development (Piaget 1954). When children recognize that an object out of sight still exists, they are capable of internal representation of the object— the first evidence of the ability to think abstractly. In a study of 33 infants between eight-and-one-half and eleven months of age, Bell (1970) found that development of a harmonious attachment to the mother facilitated the development of object permanence, and thus concluded that the quality of the infant-mother relationship is a crucial environmental factor affecting cognitive development.

Lewis and Goldberg (1969) also reported a significant relationship between mother-infant attachment and perceptual-cognitive development. They concluded that the experience of a consistent, predictable relationship is essential to the development of the generalized expectancy of control which underlies the later development of competence.

Evidence indicating the relationship between attachment and compliance with maternal demands has been provided by Stayton, Hogan, and Ainsworth (1971). Mothers who developed warm, harmonious relationships with their infants were more likely to have compliant infants at twelve months of age. Ainsworth, Bell, and Stayton (1974) therefore proposed that, given an environment in which adults are responsive to infants' needs, children will develop mature social values of adult society without concentrated attempts by the parents.

Ainsworth and Bell (1970) suggested that one of the major roles of the attachment bond is in providing children with a basic sense of security. Once the parent is accepted as a secure base, children are able to explore the environment and develop cognitively and socially from these explorations. Ainsworth and Bell (1974) emphasized that a secure attachment bond does not imply that an infant continuously seeks proximity to mother and is reluctant to leave her side. On the contrary, children feel free to initiate interactions with objects and people in the environment and to explore the surroundings as long as their mothers remain present; attachment tends to be evidenced in children's occasional glances at their mothers to verify continued presence. Exploratory behavior tends to decline when the mother is absent (Ainsworth and Wittig 1969).

Further research has confirmed the link between exploratory behavior and cognitive development. In a study of 33 Black, low socioeconomic status (SES) children, Bell (1970) found that freedom to explore was highly related to scores on the Griffiths Mental Development Scale and measures of object relations at eight and eleven months of age. Beckwith (1971), in a study of 24 adopted infants living in middle SES families, found that high maternal restrictiveness of exploration significantly lowered intelligence scores on the Cattell Infant Intelligence Scale. A secure attachment bond seems to facilitate cognitive development by enabling the child to explore the environment. In addition, infants with a secure attachment are freer to explore interpersonal relationships, as evidenced by their willingness to approach strangers when in the presence of their mothers (Ainsworth 1973).

In summary, the evidence suggests that the affectional tie between parents and children has a significant impact on children's development in a number of crucial areas.

The Paternal Bond

Bowlby's emphasis on the mother-child relationship as the prototype of all subsequent attachments led researchers to focus on mothers and children. In the last few years, however, a number of investigators have included fathers in their research (see Part II of this book). Recognition of the significance of the father's role in child development has emerged from these studies. The data indicate that children attach to their fathers as well as their mothers in early childhood (Cohen and Campos 1974; Lamb 1976a; Willemsen, Flaherty, Heaton, and Ritchey 1974). Lamb (1976a) reported that as early as eight months of age, children preferred to play with their fathers rather than their mothers. He concluded that infants appear to relate to their mothers primarily as sources of security, while fathers act not only as attachment figures, but are preferred over mothers for affiliative interaction, especially play. Smiling, vocalizing, looking, and laughing occurred more often with the father than with the mother. Lamb suggested that children's preference for their fathers may be due to qualitative differences in the ways parents relate to their children; for example, mothers are more likely to hold their infants for caregiving purposes, while fathers are more likely to hold their infants in order to play. While mothers and fathers relate to their children differently (Lewis and Weinraub 1974), children typically form attachments to both parents (Kotelchuck 1972).

Research has consistently demonstrated that the father has a significant impact upon children's cognitive (Radin 1976), moral (Greif 1976), and psychosexual (Biller 1971) development. Lamb (1976) argued that the father's impact on the child is qualitatively different from the mother's, and that the influence of *both* father and mother is critical for the child's optimal development.

Parenting Behaviors Related to Attachment

The single most important contribution to the development of attachment is most likely the quality of interaction between parent and child. Studies consistently have demonstrated that quantity of interaction does not predict strength of attachment. Pedersen and Robson

(1969) found little relationship between the amount of time fathers spent playing with their infants and the strength of attachment as measured by the intensity of the child's greeting of father when reunited after a separation. Similarly, Schaffer and Emerson (1964) reported that the strength of a child's protest at separation was not related to the amount of time mother and child spent together.

The quality of the interaction (as evidenced in the sensitivity of the parent's response to the child's needs) and the emotional intensity of the interaction seem to be critical factors in the development of attachment. A number of studies have demonstrated the crucial role of parental responsiveness in the development of social responsiveness in infants. For example, Rheingold, Gewirtz, and Ross (1959) and Wolff (1969) reported that parental response to the infant's vocalizing or smiling increased the frequency of these behaviors. Clarke-Stewart (1973) reported that the infant's attachment to the mother was highly related to the frequency of her social behavior—looking, talking, playing. In addition, infants' scores on the Bayley Scale of Mental Development were highly related to the responsiveness of mothers to their children's social behaviors. Eye contact between mother and infant has been reported to be related to a strong attachment bond, as well as to social and cognitive development (Ainsworth 1973; Goldberg and Lewis 1969; Moss and Robson 1967; Wolff 1969). Gentle, firm, close, and relatively frequent handling is related to the infant's early cognitive and motor development and to the development of an attachment bond (Ainsworth et al. 1974; Lewis and Goldberg 1969).

Contingent Responsiveness

Recent studies have revealed the importance of *contingent* responsiveness (responses elicited by the infant). The data indicate that infants develop a generalized expectancy of control of the environment when parents respond promptly and consistently to infants' signals (Ainsworth et al. 1974; Clarke-Stewart 1973; Lewis and Goldberg 1969). This early development of expectancy of control may be the foundation for developing cognitive and social competence (Clarke-Stewart 1973). Considering the evidence supporting the importance of expectancy of control (Phares 1976) for successful lifespan development, further research in this area is strongly urged.

Ainsworth and Bell (1974) and Stayton, Hogan, and Ainsworth (1971) found a significant relationship between maternal sensitivity to infant signals and the infant's scores on the Griffiths and Bayley Scales of Mental Development. In addition, Bell (1970) reported a relationship between maternal responsiveness and the infant's early development of object permanence. Beckwith, Cohen, Kopp, Parmelee, and Marcy (1976) found that sensorimotor development as measured by the Gesell Scale at nine months was associated with mutual caregiver-infant gazing at one month, mutual smiling during gazing and more contingent responses to the infant's cries at three months, and greater responsiveness to vocalizations at eight months; the salience of a particular maternal response varied with the infant's age.

Providing further evidence for this relationship between contingent responsiveness and cognitive development from a study of 41 low SES and 7 middle SES Black infants and mothers, Yarrow, Rubenstein, Pedersen, and Jankowski (1972) reported that the mothers' contingent responses to distress were related to the infants' scores on the Bayley Mental and Motor Scales as well as to indicators of goal-directed behavior on the Bayley Scales at five to six months of age.

Of particular importance for parents is the finding that prompt response to an infant's cries does not increase subsequent crying. Despite traditional beliefs to the contrary, maternal responsiveness to infant distress tends to decrease future infant crying and fretfulness and increase more mature forms of communication (Ainsworth, Bell, and Stayton 1974). There is a delay of about three months, however, before a reduction of infant crying is noted as a result of maternal responsiveness. The investigators concluded that this lag between maternal response and its effect on infant crying is due to the strength of crying as a behavioral system in infancy. They suggested that infants require a fairly long-term experience of consistent responding before being able to delay crying.

Bromwich (1977) suggested that neurological immaturity may account for the infant's inability to inhibit crying. Thus, individual differences in crying in the early months are probably due to differences in the maturity of the neurological mechanisms. As the child matures, the inhibitory mechanisms become more efficient and the child is enabled to limit crying in response to environmental influences, such as maternal responsiveness. Infants whose mothers had been responsive to their crying developed more variety, subtlety, and clarity in their noncrying modes of communication by the last quarter of the first year than infants whose mothers had ignored their crying. In addition, Ainsworth and Bell (1974) reported that mothers who frequently held their infants for extended periods had infants who were content to be put down. These data indicate that maternal responsiveness can significantly alter the initial temperament of the infant.

A number of studies have drawn attention to parents' responses to their infants' needs. In a study of low SES mother-infant pairs, Clarke-Stewart (1973) reported that affectionate maternal behavior was relatively infrequent. Only 5 percent of the infant's waking time from nine to eighteen months of age was spent in affectionate contact with the mother, and playful mother-child interaction was even less frequent (less than one-half hour a day). Similar descriptive data of the home activities of infants from other SES backgrounds are needed to determine if affectionate and playful contact between mother and child occurs infrequently in middle and upper SES homes as well.

Additional evidence that mothers tend to concentrate primarily on caregiving responsibilities with their infants has been provided by Lamb (1976b), who found that infants direct more affiliative behaviors to their fathers than to their mothers and seem to prefer their fathers to their mothers. In this study Lamb found no evidence to suggest that the mother was preferred when the child sought security. He attributes this differential attraction to the fact that fathers' interactions were predominantly novel and vigorously playful, while the nature of mothers' interactions was basically caregiving. (See Chapter 6 for further discussion.)

Ainsworth and Bell (1974) developed a sensitivity-insensitivity scale which classified maternal behavior from a value of 9 (highly sensitive), indicating that the mother perceives and accurately interprets her infant's behavior and responds to it promptly and appropriately, to a value of 1 (highly insensitive), indicating that the mother's behavior is almost exclusively self-centered and her responses to the infant tend to be delayed and inappropriate. In Ainsworth and Bell's (1974) study of White, middle SES women from a large United States city, nearly half of the mothers obtained ratings indicating insensitivity to their infants' needs. This maternal insensitivity tended to result in disturbed attachment relationships.

The importance of paternal interaction with the child in establishing father-infant attachment has also been demonstrated. Kotelchuck (1976) observed that the extent of the father's involvement in caregiving was reflected in the strength of the child's attachment to the father. While noting that the father's play interactions with his child contribute to the development of the attachment bond, Kotelchuck concluded that there seems to be a minimum level of paternal caregiving necessary for a relationship to exist. Kotelchuck observed that the few children who did not relate to their fathers (as indicated by children spending less than 15 seconds with fathers on their arrival) were primarily from families with fathers who were very infrequent caregivers. In addition, the extent to which children interacted and demonstrated preferences for their fathers was partially related to paternal caregiving at home. Ross, Kagan, Zelazo, and Kotelchuck (1975) found a significant relationship between proximity to the father during observation and the number of diapers changed by the father each week. Infants whose fathers assumed an active role in caregiving showed separation protest at a later age and terminated it earlier than infants whose mothers were the primary caregivers.

Further support for the influence of paternal caregiving on the attachment bond was provided by a cross-cultural study. In a comparison of United States and Guatemalan children, Lester, Kotelchuck, Spelke, Sellers, and Klein (1974) found that children were less attached to their fathers in Guatemala, where paternal caregiving is very low.

Rebelsky and Hanks (1971) found that father-infant verbal interaction is minimal in the first three months of life. In their study, the mean number of verbal interactions per day between father and child was 2.7, and the average length of interaction was 37.7 seconds. In addition, fathers tended to spend less time vocalizing to their infants during the last half of the study (8 to 12 weeks of age) than in the first half (2 to 6 weeks of age); this decrease was especially evident for fathers of girls. Additional evidence of the father's minimal role in childrearing has been provided by Kotelchuck (1972). Only 25 percent of the 144 fathers of children nine to twelve months old reported that they had any routine caregiving responsibilities.

Given the demonstrated importance of contingent responsiveness for the development of attachment, it seems critical that parents be provided with information that would sensitize them to the need for increased responsiveness to their infants. Lewis and Weinraub (1974) concluded that the attachment bond to the father is initially weaker than that to the mother, because the father's interactions with the infant are minimal in the early months when caregiving constitutes the major interaction between parent and child. To strengthen the early father-infant attachment, fathers need to be encouraged to assume more caregiving responsibilities.

Development of Reciprocity

To relate to children effectively, parents must be aware of the impact children's behavior has on parental response. Bell (1974) urged that the effect of the infant on the parent be investigated. Unfortunately, researchers have been slow to investigate reciprocal infant-parent effects, despite evidence that infants initiate and terminate behavior more often than adults (Schoggen 1963). Moss and Robson (1967) observed that infants initiated about four out of five interactions during two six-hour periods at one month of age. In his study of eight twin infants at three to four months of age, Stern (1974) reported that the infants initiated and terminated 94 percent of all mutual gazes.

A few pioneering researchers have begun the difficult process of studying reciprocal interactions between infant and parent. Clarke-Stewart (1973) reported that maternal responsiveness to distress and demands increased as a result of the infant's social behaviors; the more often the child looked, smiled, and vocalized to the mother, the more affectionate and attached the mother became. Clarke-Stewart suggests that mother and infant may alternate roles in effecting response; at one point, maternal attention may cause an increase in infant attention, followed by a period in which infant attention increases maternal responsiveness.

These results suggest that parents need to be sensitive to the effects their infants are having on their own behavior. For example, parents may become increasingly less stimulating to a quiet baby because of the infant's lack of initiative and response, or they may become less responsive to a fretful baby because of lack of reinforcing positive response on the part of the infant. Als and Lewis (1975) suggest that a process of mutual adaptation occurs between mother and infant. Ratings on the Brazelton Neonatal Behavioral Assessment Scale indicated that 35 percent of the babies in their sample were well-modulated in the first three days of life in comparison to 70 percent by three months. From observations of mother-infant interaction during this period, Als and Lewis reported that mothers tended to vocalize and smile more at lethargic and overactive babies than to well-modulated ones; they concluded that mothers thus modified their infants' initial temperaments. While Als and Lewis's data suggest that mothers respond naturally to temperamental difference, parents, especially overly anxious or insensitive ones, might profit from instruction designed to help them learn to identify and respond appropriately to their infants' temperamental states.

Thomas, Chess, and Birch (1968) provided evidence of the positive effect that sensitizing parents to the temperamental characteristics of their infants can have on subsequent development. By becoming aware of the unique qualities of their infants and responding to their specific needs, parents were able to help their infants overcome initial temperamental difficulties. Thoman (1975) also described a process for identifying and coping with initial temperamental difficulties.

Recognizing the complex interplay between parent and child behavior, Sameroff (1975) recommended that parents be made aware of the intricate relationships between their behavior and that of their infants. He was especially concerned that mothers be alerted to the discontinuous nature of development, so mothers can adjust their behavior to the ever-changing nature of their children. Maternal behaviors which were appropriate at earlier stages may become obsolete and maladaptive as the child matures (Sander 1969). For example, Clarke-Stewart (1973) indicated that physical contact between mother and child, while quite appropriate for infants, can become overly restrictive at later ages.

Convinced that the interdependence of rhythms between mother and child is the root of attachment, Brazelton, Koslowski, and Main (1974) described the rhythmic, cyclic quality of mother-child interactions. They emphasized the need for both members of the dyad to learn the behavior patterns of the other member. The mother must learn the rules concerning (1) the baby's capacity for attention and nonattention, (2) which of her behaviors activate or deactivate the infant, and (3) the appropriate level of complexity of her modeling for the infant's stage of development. According to Brazelton et al. (1974), failure to learn these rules may seriously affect the attachment bond.

Goldberg (1977) also emphasized the need for balance and coordination between mother and child. To the extent that parent and child behaviors are characterized by readability (possessing distinctive cues regarding intent of behavior), predictability, and responsiveness, feelings of efficacy and mastery will develop in parent and child. Consequently, Goldberg recommended that parents be helped to develop the skills of readability, predictability, and responsiveness. To achieve these ends, Ainsworth (1973) recommended the training of professionals to assess parental-infant attachment and instruct parents in the skills of sensitive parenting. Ainsworth suggested that the essential capacity underlying sensitivity to an infant's signals is empathy, and she encouraged further research to provide the basis for designing intervention strategies which would enable parents to improve their empathic understanding of their infants.

It appears that development of parent-infant attachment is facilitated by the parent's warm, contingent responsiveness to the infant. Through experiences of consistent caregiving and affectionate playfulness, infants become attached to the significant persons in their social world.

Attachment Behaviors

Richards (1974) argued that human infants are genetically preadapted to respond to a social environment. He based his argument on evidence that infants are peculiarly sensitive to social stimuli: to the human face, particularly the eyes, and to the human voice. Richards also cited recent research indicating that infants are able to adapt their behavior to subtle rhythms of social exchange: Infant and adult engage in complex cycles of engagement and withdrawal in which the mother's sensitivity is critical in establishing the appropriate level of stimulation. A number of researchers are currently involved in investigating the cyclical and rhythmic interactions of mother and infant through microanalysis of videotape (Brazelton, Tronick, Adamson, Als, and Wise 1975).

Smiling has been frequently identified as an important attachment behavior, probably because of its power to elicit intense adult response (Ainsworth 1973). Developmental studies have indicated that nondiscriminating social smiling peaks between three to four months of age in home-reared infants (Ambrose 1961) and subsequently declines, to be replaced by differential smiling to familiar others, especially the attachment figure(s).

The onset of separation anxiety at about nine months of age, its peak at about twelve months, and its subsequent decline has been replicated cross-culturally, suggesting that this development may be due primarily to cognitive development rather than to the child's social environment (Kagan et al. 1975). Parents need to be aware that protest at separation when the child is about twelve months old is a typical reaction. However, recent studies (Ainsworth 1973) have indicated wide individual differences in separation behavior and response to strangers, and it has been suggested that neither of these behaviors is an appropriate index of the attachment bond.

While a large number of studies have attempted to identify situations which elicit attachment behavior, results are difficult to interpret. Obviously, children's behaviors are determined by a complex interplay of factors, as indicated by the observation of wide individual differences in attachment behaviors. Given a particular situation, different children will respond differently to their mothers' presence and absence; given another situation, the same children may respond differently than before. Extensive observations and analyses of children's reactions in many differing situations are needed before we can specify the types of reactions that might be expected from children in a particular circumstance. For example, Ainsworth (1973) noted that separation anxiety was not as prevalent in her studies as it had been in earlier studies. Is this finding a consequence of more multiple caregiving, of an earlier onset and decline, or, perhaps, a result of subtle differences in the experimental condition that failed to elicit the separation response?

Behaviors typically considered attachment behaviors, e.g., crying, clinging, smiling, sucking, and following (Bowlby 1969), undergo transformations across the lifespan. The clinging and crying of infants become transformed into other behaviors more appropriate for older children.

From a study of the transformations of attachment during the first two years of life, Lewis and Ban (1971) identified two modes of attachment behavior in describing the changes that occur in children's expressions of attachment during those years: proximal (touching and staying in proximity to the mother) and distal (looking and vocalizing). Lewis and Ban observed that children who touched a great deal at one year of age were likely to look at their mothers more frequently during the second year. They observed that proximal behavior decreased between the first and second year, while distal behavior increased, and they concluded that the proximal behavior of the first year had been transformed into distal behavior during the second year. Maccoby and

Feldman (1972) extended the research to three-year-olds and found a similar trend.

Thus, the evidence suggests that different behaviors will express the attachment bond at different ages. While infants may express attachment by visual pursuit and crying, eighteen-month-old children may express attachment by clinging and following. Longitudinal research is needed to trace the transformations in the attachment relationship throughout the lifespan, since failure to progress to more mature forms of attachment behavior may indicate a need for assistance in fostering the attachment relationship.

While factors contributing to the behavioral transformations of attachment are as yet unknown, Lewis and Weinraub (1974) have conjectured that these changes are due to the emergence of competing motives, like exploration and curiosity, and to changing social demands. They found that boys received more proximal stimulation from mothers than girls in the early months, probably due to the male's tendency to be more fretful and more difficult to calm (Moss 1974). By the time their sons were six months old, however, mothers decreased the quantity of their physical interactions, so that by one year of age, girls received more proximal stimulation than boys. A similar transformation occurred in both boys' and girls' relationships with their fathers. Lewis and Weinraub (1974) hypothesized that the reductions in proximal stimulation in father-son, mother-son, and father-daughter dyads are in response to some cultural expectations. The proximal behavior between mother and daughter undergoes no transformation because proximal behaviors among females are relatively acceptable. Also, mothers and fathers may reduce their proximal response to encourage early autonomy in sons.

Day Care and Infant Attachment

An important concern for today's parent is the effect of day care on child development, since approximately seven million children in the United States under the age of five are enrolled in some type of day care (Committee on the Infant and Preschool Child 1975). Traditional beliefs regarding the negative effects of day care and the child's need for mother at home have created serious conflict and uncertainty in the minds of many parents.

Recent research has indicated that day care is not necessarily detrimental to the parent-child bond or other aspects of child development. A particularly well-designed longitudinal study of the psychological effects of day care was conducted by Kagan, Kearsley, and Zelazo (1975). Chinese and Caucasian working and middle SES infants who attended a day care center from age three-and-one-half months to thirty months were compared with a home-reared group of infants matched for ethnicity, SES, and sex. Using the standard procedure for assessment of attachment, these investigators observed an overwhelming preference for the mother in all children when they were bored or distressed, even when the familiar day center caregiver was present. The ratio of preference for mother over the other familiar adult was 7 to 1 for all children. The researchers also found no differences in separation protest in the groups. They did observe more proximity and touching of the mother in the Chinese groups (both day care and home-reared) than in the Caucasian groups, and from this concluded that home experience is more important than day care attendance in influencing psychological attachment to the mother.

One interesting finding of this study was that while the day care children were more comfortable playing with an unfamiliar peer than the home-reared children at twenty months of age, this difference had disappeared by twenty-nine months of age. This observation emphasizes the need to be cautious in generalizing from a single assessment; initial differences may change with time.

According to Kagan et al., day care does not dilute the emotional bond between mother and infant; it is the salience and affectively charged quality of the home experience that is critical to the development of the mother-infant bond. Further support for this position has been provided by Maccoby and Feldman (1972). In their comparison of kibbutz-reared Israeli children and United States children of the same age, Maccoby and Feldman found that the children's attachment behaviors toward their mothers were very similar, despite widely different rearing conditions. While the Israeli infants spent the majority of each day with other children and a substitute caregiver, they still demonstrated typical attachment behaviors to their mothers, indicating that it is the quality of the psychological interaction between mother and child which influences the development of the attachment bond— not the amount of time spent together.

In a comparison of 18 thirty-month-old children who had been placed in a day care setting between six and fifteen months of age, and 23 comparable children who had remained at home, Caldwell, Wright, Honig, and Tannenbaum (1970) found no differences in the children's relationships to their mothers, or in their affiliation, nurturance, hostility, happiness, and emotionality. Doyle (1975) also found no evidence of weakened attachment in his study of 24 infants who had attended day care for seven months.

While the Kagan and Caldwell studies have indicated that day care need not be detrimental, it must be recognized that their centers were of unusual quality, with very small child-adult ratios and large expenditures per child. Whether their results can be generalized to more typical centers with fewer and less highly trained caregivers is unknown.

In contrast to the positive results of the preceding studies, Blehar (1974) observed disturbances in the mother-child relationships of two- and three-year-olds who had been enrolled in full-time day care for about five months; those who started at the age of twenty-five months showed avoidant behavior when reunited with their mothers, and those who entered at thirty-five months of age displayed anxious, ambivalent behavior at reunion. These negative findings might be due to the recency of the day care entry and would possibly be overcome with time. Children may have more difficulty adjusting to a daily separation after two or three years at home than if the separation had begun in early infancy, as in the case of the Kagan infants.

In a comparison study of group day care, family day home care, and full parental care, Lippman and Grote (1974) found no evidence to support a weakened attachment bond as a result of day care, though they did report tentative evidence supporting Blehar's (1974) findings that late entry into a center could lead to defensive attachment *in some children*. Lippman and Grote's (1974) results raise the question of whether certain types of children might be more susceptible to harmful effects of day care than other children.

Having found no significant differences in attachment behavior attributable to day care alone, Brookhart and Hock (1976) concluded that the global characterization of early experiences—home-reared versus day care—does not predict social behavior; however, there was some indication of social disturbances in some males as a result of day care experience. Further evidence of greater vulnerability in males than in females was provided by Bronson (1970). In a developmental study of fear of the strange, Bronson found that males who manifested fear of a stranger before age six months were shyer from ten months to four years of age than boys whose fear of a stranger began after six months of age. In addition, Bronson noted that these fearful males were more likely to have insensitive mothers, as determined by ratings of the quality of maternal care, than males who were less fearful. These relationships were not found for girls, suggesting that males may be more vulnerable to environmental effects than females. Thus, sex differences need to be considered in determining the effects of day care on psychological functioning. Other child characteristics should also be considered in attempting to account for the wide individual differences that have been noted in attachment behaviors (Ainsworth, Bell, and Stayton 1974), for example, premature versus full-term infants, firstborns versus later-borns, single parent versus two parents, early entry versus late entry.

In a study of 223 London children, Moore (1964; 1969) identified four factors that influenced the effect of day care: the quality of substitute care, its continuity and stability, the developmental level of the child, and the personality of the mother. In an analysis comparing the results of two contradictory studies on day care, McCrae and Herbert-Jackson (1976) concluded that the gross categorization ("day care") is meaningless without specific descriptions of program goals and characteristics. For example, Lippman and Grote (1974) found tentative evidence to suggest that family day care may be superior to group day care in a center or full parental care for developing maternal attachment and independence in infants. A great deal of research is needed to investigate the specific characteristics of different types of day care and their influence on children's development.

The need to be concerned about differential outcomes in evaluating day care has been illustrated by a cross-cultural comparison of polymatric (multiple caregiving) and monomatric (single caregiving) infant care in an East African agricultural village (Leiderman and Leiderman 1974). The polymatric infants appeared more apprehensive in the presence of a stranger than the monomatric group; however, this insecurity was not evident when the infants were with familiar persons. In addition, for the low SES group, mental performance was higher in the polymatric group than in the monomatric group. Thus, single measures of the effect of day care alternatives may fail to reveal specific differential results.

Research to date indicates that quality day care does not harm the parent-infant attachment bond; however, it must be recognized that the measures used to assess attachment may not have been sensitive enough to reveal effects. A significant research effort is needed to identify factors which may influence the effects of day care, for example, sex and temperament of the child, attachment to mother, caregiver-infant ratios, child's age at entry, size of center. Given the large numbers of children now enrolled in day care, this information may be critical for the future development of our children.

Recommendations for Parent and Early Childhood Education

Development of a harmonious, contingently responsive parental relationship is probably more important than any specific stimulation or instructional program in children's early years. Being able to recognize the meaning of children's behavior and respond promptly and appropriately to it, knowing when additional stimulation is warranted and when stimulation needs to be reduced, understanding children's temperament and unique needs, being aware of the effect of children's behavior on oneself, establishing a predictable environment in which infants are encouraged to initiate explorations and interactions and to develop a sense of competence in relation to people and things—these are the competencies that seem to facilitate intellectual and social development in children.

Parent education programs should focus on the development of these skills, especially the ability to empathize with the needs of infants. With an awareness that it is the quality of the relationship not the amount of time spent with children that is important, parents may be able to improve the nature of their interactions with their infants, provided they are sensitized to specific ways in which the relationship can become more reciprocal, i.e., more synchronized and responsive.

Early childhood programs designed with similar goals would seem to be most likely to facilitate child development. Major considerations should include: (1) development of a contingent and affectively-charged relationship between caregiver and child—this objective will necessitate small child-adult ratios to enable the adult to respond appropriately to individual needs; (2) training of caregivers skilled in reading children's behavior, capable of empathizing with children's feelings, and able to recognize what stimulation is appropriate; and (3) development of an atmosphere that encourages children to explore and initiate interaction with objects and with others and rewards children with a sense of competence and control.

The trend in early childhood education in the late 1960s and early 1970s was toward direct stimulation of infant cognitive development. The research on attachment suggests that the primary concern in infancy should be on the development of secure, emotional relationships with significant others, as these relationships form the essential base for cognitive growth.

Bromwich (1976; 1977) described an infant intervention project at the University of California, Los Angeles, that focuses on the development of responsive maternal behaviors. The maternal behaviors include: (1) the mother's enjoyment of her infant and (2) her sensitive responsiveness to the infant's cues and signals. The assumption underlying this program is that significant increases in cognitive development are dependent on a secure mother-infant attachment; consequently, the primary objective of the UCLA project is the maintenance of a positive attachment bond between mother and child. Bromwich cautioned, however, that this goal is not easily attained. It requires sensitive and subtle encouragement rather than direct intervention. The mother's self-confidence must not be threatened, nor should her adequacy as a mother be questioned, if she is to continue to enjoy her relationship with her infant.

Conclusion

Research on the parent-child attachment bond provides useful insights into the processes of child development. A warm, affectionate, predictable relationship between parent and child is associated with fostering intellectual, social, emotional, and moral development in the child. Techniques can be developed to help parents read their children's behavior, become sensitive to the need to match their behavior to their children's unique rhythms and cycles, and be consistently responsive to their infants' needs.

Further research into the processes by which attachment develops could be helpful in formulating policy and practice in childrearing. Investigations of the effect of alternative child care practices could help specify conditions which facilitate optimal child development; variations of specific dimensions (e.g., infants' ages when placed in day care, length of daily separations, number of different caregivers, frequency of change in caregivers, ratio of children to caregivers) could help determine more precisely the effects of differential child care alternatives.

Inquiry into the issues of parent-child attachment has yielded greater understanding not only of the origins of social behavior but also of the broader area of human competence in general. Continued interest in the study of the child's development of social relationships should provide information helpful in facilitating the optimal development of both parent and child.

References

Ainsworth, M. D. S. "The Development of Infant-Mother Attachment." In *Review of Child Development Research,* vol. 3, edited by B. M. Caldwell and H. N. Ricciuti. Chicago: University of Chicago Press, 1973.

Ainsworth, M. D. S. "Further Research into the Adverse Effects of Maternal Deprivation." In *Child Care and the Growth of Love,* edited by J. Bowlby. Baltimore: Penguin Books, 1965.

Ainsworth, M. D. S., and Bell, S. M. "Attachment, Exploration, and Separation: Illustrated by the Behavior of One-Year-Olds in a Strange Situation." *Child Development* 41 (1970): 49-67.

Ainsworth, M. D. S., and Bell, S. M. "Mother-Infant Interaction and the Development of Competence." In *The Growth of Competence,* edited by K. Connolly and J. Bruner. London: Academic Press, 1974.

Ainsworth, M. D. S.; Bell, S. M.; and Stayton, D. J. "Infant-Mother Attachment and Social Development: 'Socialisation' as a Product of Reciprocal Responsiveness to Signals." In *The Integration of a Child into a Social World,* edited by M. P. M. Richards. New York: Cambridge University Press, 1974.

Ainsworth, M. D. S., and Wittig, B. A. "Attachment and Exploratory Behavior of One-Year-Olds in a Strange Situation." In *Determinants of Infant Behavior,* vol. 4, edited by B. M. Foss. London: Methuen, 1969.

Als, H., and Lewis, M. "The Contribution of the Infant to the Interaction of His Mother." Paper presented at the Society for Research in Child Development meeting, Denver, Colo., April 1975.

Ambrose, J. A. "The Development of the Smiling Response in Early Infancy." In *Determinants of Infant Behavior,* vol. 1, edited by B. M. Foss. London: Methuen, 1961.
Beckwith, L. "Relationships Between Attributes of Mothers and Their Infants' IQ Scores." *Child Development* 42 (1971): 1083-1097.
Beckwith, L.; Cohen, S. E.; Kopp, C. B.; Parmelee, A. H.; and Marcy, T. G. "Caregiver-Infant Interaction and Early Cognitive Development in Preterm Infants." *Child Development* 47 (1976): 579-587.
Bell, R. Q. "Contributions of Human Infants to Caregiving and Social Interaction." In *The Effect of the Infant on Its Caregiver,* edited by M. Lewis and L. A. Rosenblum. New York: John Wiley & Sons, 1974.
Bell, S. "The Development of the Concept of Object as Related to Infant-Mother Attachment." *Child Development* 41 (1970): 291-311.
Bell, S. M., and Ainsworth, M. D. S. "Infant Crying and Maternal Responsiveness." *Child Development* 43 (1972): 1171-1190.
Biller, H. B. *Father, Child, and Sex Role.* Lexington, Mass.: D. C. Heath, 1971.
Blehar, M. C. "Anxious Attachment and Defensive Reactions Associated with Day Care." *Child Development* 45 (1974): 683-692.
Bowlby, J. *Attachment and Loss,* vol 1. London: Hogarth Press, 1969.
Bowlby, J., ed. *Child Care and the Growth of Love.* Baltimore: Penguin Books, 1965.
Bowlby, J. "The Nature of the Child's Tie to His Mother." *International Journal of Psychoanalysis* 39 (1958): 350-373.
Brazelton, T. B.; Koslowski, B.; and Main, M. "The Origins of Reciprocity: The Early Mother-Infant Interaction." In *The Effect of the Infant on its Caregiver,* edited by M. Lewis and L. A. Rosenblum. New York: John Wiley & Sons, 1974.
Brazelton, T. B.; Tronick, E.; Adamson, L.; Als, H.; and Wise, S. "Early Mother-Infant Reciprocity." In *Parent-Infant Interaction, Ciba Foundation Symposium 33.* New York: American Elsevier, 1975.
Bromwich, R. M. "Focus on Maternal Behavior in Infant Intervention." *American Journal of Orthopsychiatry* 46 (1976): 439-446.
Bromwich, R. M. "Stimulation in the First Year of Life? A Perspective on Infant Development." *Young Children* 32, no. 2 (January 1977): 71-84.
Bronson, G. W. "Fear of Visual Novelty: Developmental Patterns in Males and Females." *Developmental Psychology* 2 (1970): 33-40.
Brookhart, J., and Hock, E. "The Effects of Experimental Context and Experiential Background on Infants' Behavior Toward Their Mother and a Stranger." *Child Development* 47 (1976): 333-340.
Caldwell, B. M.; Wright, C. M.; Honig, A. S.; and Tannenbaum, J. "Infant Day Care and Attachment." *American Journal of Orthopsychiatry* 40 (1970): 397-412.
Clarke-Stewart, K. A. "Interactions Between Mothers and Their Young Children: Characteristics and Consequences." *Monographs of the Society for Research in Child Development* 38, nos. 6-7 (1973): whole no. 153.
Cohen, L. J., and Campos, J. J. "Father, Mother and Stranger as Elicitors of Attachment Behaviors in Infancy." *Developmental Psychology* 10 (1974): 146-154.
Committee on the Infant and Preschool Child. "Statement on Day Care." *Pediatrics* 56 (1975): 484.
Doyle, A. B. "Infant Development in Day Care." *Developmental Psychology* 11 (1975): 655-656.
Goldberg, S. "Social Competence in Infancy: A Model of Parent-Infant Interaction." *Merrill-Palmer Quarterly,* in press.
Goldberg, S., and Lewis, M. "Play Behavior in the Year-Old Infant: Early Sex Differences." *Child Development* 40 (1969): 21-31.
Greif, E. B. "Fathers, Children, and Moral Development." In *The Role of the Father in Child Development,* edited by M. E. Lamb, New York: John Wiley & Sons, 1976.

Hales, D.; Kennell, J.; and Sosa, R. "How Early is Early Contact? Defining the Limits of the Sensitive Period." Paper presented at the American Pediatric Society and the Society for Pediatric Research annual meeting, St. Louis, Mo., April 1976.

Kagan, J.; Kearsley, R. B.; and Zelazo, P. R. "The Effects of Infant Day Care on Psychological Development." Paper presented at the American Association for the Advancement of Science meeting, Boston, February 1975. (ERIC Document Reproduction Service No. ED 122 946.)

Klaus, M., and Kennell, J. *Maternal-Infant Bonding*. St. Louis, Mo.: C. V. Mosby, 1976.

Kotelchuck, M. "The Infant's Relationship to the Father: Experimental Evidence." In *The Role of the Father In Child Development*, edited by M. E. Lamb. New York: John Wiley & Sons, 1976.

Kotelchuck, M. "The Nature of a Child's Tie to His Father." Doctoral dissertation, Harvard University, 1972.

Lamb, M. E. "Fathers: Forgotten Contributors to Child Development." *Human Development* 18 (1975): 245-266.

Lamb, M. E. "Interactions Between Eight-Month-Old Children and Their Fathers and Mothers." In *The Role of the Father in Child Development*, edited by M. E. Lamb. New York: John Wiley & Sons, 1976a.

Lamb, M. E. "Twelve-Month-Olds and Their Parents: Interaction in a Laboratory Playroom." *Developmental Psychology* 12 (1976b): 237-244.

Leiderman, P. H., and Leiderman, G. F. "Affective and Cognitive Consequences of Polymatric Infant Care in the East African Highlands." In *Minnesota Symposia on Child Psychology*, vol. 8, edited by A. Pick. Minneapolis: University of Minnesota Press, 1974.

Leifer, A.; Leiderman, P.; Barnett, C.; and Williams, J. A. "Effects of Mother-Infant Separation on Maternal Attachment Behavior." *Child Development* 43 (1972): 1203-1218.

Lester, B. M.; Kotelchuck, M.; Spelke, E.; Sellers, M. J.; and Klein, R. E. "Separation Protest in Guatemalan Infants: Cross-Cultural and Cognitive Findings." *Developmental Psychology* 10 (1974): 79-85.

Lewis, M., and Ban, P. "Stability of Attachment Behavior: A Transformational Analysis." Paper presented at symposium entitled "Attachment: Studies in Stability and Change," at the Society for Research in Child Development meeting, Minneapolis, April 1971.

Lewis, M., and Goldberg, S. "Perceptual-Cognitive Development in Infancy: A Generalized Expectancy Model as a Function of the Mother-Infant Interaction." *Merrill-Palmer Quarterly* 15 (1969): 81-101.

Lewis, M., and Weinraub, M. "Sex of Parent x Sex of Child: Socioemotional Development." In *Sex Differences in Behavior*, edited by R. C. Friedman, R. M. Richart, and R. L. Van de Wiele. New York: John Wiley & Sons, 1974.

Lippman, M. Z., and Grote, B. H. "Social-Emotional Effects of Daycare." National Institute of Education Final Report, June 1974. (ERIC Document Reproduction Service No. ED 013 371.)

Maccoby, E., and Feldman, S. "Mother-Attachment and Stranger-Reactions in the Third Year of Life." *Monographs of the Society for Research in Child Development* 37, no. 1 (1972): serial no. 146.

McCrae, J., and Herbert-Jackson, E. "Are Behavioral Effects of Infant Day Care Programs Specific?" *Developmental Psychology* 12 (1976): 269-270.

Moore, T. "Children of Full-Time and Part-Time Mothers." *International Journal of Social Psychiatry* 2 (1964): 1-10.

Moore, T. "Stress in Normal Childhood." *Human Relations* 22 (1969): 235-250.

Moss, H. A. "Early Sex Differences and Mother-Infant Interaction." In *Sex Differences in Behavior*, edited by R. C. Friedman, R. M. Richart, and R. L. Van de

Wiele. New York: John Wiley & Sons, 1974.
Moss, H. A., and Robson, K. S. "Maternal Influences in Early Social Visual Behavior." *American Journal of Orthopsychiatry* 37 (1967): 394-395.
Murphy, L., and Moriarty, A. *Vulnerability, Coping and Growth from Infancy to Adolescence*. New Haven, Conn.: Yale University Press, 1976.
Pedersen, F. A., and Robson, K. S. "Father Participation in Infancy." *American Journal of Orthopsychiatry* 39 (1969): 466-472.
Phares, J. *Locus of Control in Personality*. New York: General Learning Press, 1976.
Piaget, J. *The Construction of Reality in the Child*. New York: Basic Books, 1954.
Radin, N. "The Role of the Father in Cognitive, Academic, and Intellectual Development." In *The Role of the Father in Child Development*, edited by M. E. Lamb. New York: John Wiley & Sons, 1976.
Rebelsky, F., and Hanks, C. "Fathers' Verbal Interaction with Infants in the First Three Months of Life." *Child Development* 42 (1971): 63-68.
Rheingold, H. L.; Gewirtz, J. L.; and Ross, H. W. "Social Conditioning of Vocalizations in the Infant." *Journal of Comparative and Physiological Psychology* 52 (1959): 68-73.
Ricciuti, H. N. "Fear and the Development of Social Attachments in the First Year of Life." In *The Origins of Fear*, edited by M. Lewis and L. A. Rosenblum. New York: John Wiley & Sons, 1974.
Richards, M. P. M., ed. *The Integration of a Child into a Social World*. New York: Cambridge University Press, 1974.
Ringler, N.; Kennell, J.; Klaus, M.; and Navokosky, B. "Mother to Child Speech at Two Years: The Effects of Increased Early Post-Natal Contact." Paper presented at the American Pediatric Society and the Society for Pediatric Research annual meeting, Washington, D.C., May 1974.
Robson, K.S. "The Role of Eye-to-Eye Contact in Maternal Infant Attachment." *Journal of Child Psychology and Psychiatry* 8 (1967): 13-15.
Ross, G.; Kagan, J.; Zelazo, P.; and Kotelchuck, M. "Separation Protest in Infants in Home and Laboratory." *Developmental Psychology* 11 (1975): 256-257.
Sameroff, A. J. "Early Influences on Development: Fact or Fancy?" *Merrill-Palmer Quarterly* 21 (1975): 267-294.
Sander, L. W. "The Longitudinal Course of Early Mother-Child Interaction: Cross-Case Comparison in a Sample of Mother-Child Pairs." In *Determinants of Infant Behavior*, vol. 4, edited by B. M. Foss. London: Methuen, 1969.
Schaffer, H. R., and Emerson, P. E. "The Development of Social Attachments in Infancy." *Monographs of the Society for Research in Child Development* 29, no. 3 (1964): serial no. 94.
Schoggen, P. "Environmental Forces in the Everyday Lives of Children." In *The Stream of Behavior: Explorations of Its Structure and Content*, edited by R. G. Barker. New York: Appleton-Century-Crofts, 1963.
Stayton, D.; Hogan, R.; and Ainsworth, M. D. S. "Infant Obedience and Maternal Behavior: Origins of Socialization Reconsidered." *Child Development* 42 (1971): 1057-1069.
Stern, D. N. "Mother and Infant at Play: The Dyadic Interaction Involving Facial, Vocal and Gaze Behaviors." In *The Effect of the Infant on Its Caregiver*, edited by M. Lewis and L. A. Rosenblum. New York: John Wiley & Sons, 1974.
Thoman, E. "How a Rejecting Baby May Affect Mother-Infant Synchrony." In *Parent-Infant Interaction, Ciba Foundation Symposium 33*. New York: American Elsevier, 1975.
Thomas, A.; Chess, S.; and Birch, H. G. *Temperament and Behavior Disorders in Children*. New York: New York University Press, 1968.
Willemsen, E.; Flaherty, D.; Heaton, C.; and Ritchey, G. "Attachment Behavior of One-Year-Olds as a Function of Mother vs. Father, Sex of Child, Session, and

Toys." *Genetic Psychology Monographs* 90 (1974): 305-324.

Wolff, P. H. "The Natural History of Crying and Other Vocalizations in Early Infancy." In *Determinants of Infant Behavior,* vol. 4, edited by B. M. Foss. London: Methuen, 1969.

Yarrow, L. J.; Rubenstein, J. L.; Pedersen, F. A.; and Jankowski, J. J. "Dimensions of Early Stimulation: Differential Effects on Infant Development." *Merrill-Palmer Quarterly* 18 (1972): 205-218.

Michael L. Hanes and Sandra Kanu Dunn

3 Maternal Attitudes and the Development of Mothers and Children

Emerging from the protective womb of the mother, each infant begins the lifelong process of learning the intricacies of human relationships. In this chapter we will artificially dissect the developmental span by focusing on two particular periods, early child development and the less well-defined period of beginning parenthood.

Becoming a parent is a process which demands a series of behavioral adaptations as the child and parent develop individually. Maternal attitudes and behaviors may have a significant influence on the child's development. Since there is little agreement on what should be included within the area of attitudinal research (Thurstone 1937; Smith and Hudgins 1964; Gildea, Glidewell, and Kantor 1961), we have attempted to provide a representative sampling of studies which offer insights on three questions:

- How does the mother view the maternal role, and are differing views consistently related to stable differences in maternal behavior?
- Are there distinct behavioral variations in mother-child relationships which can be related to the mother's verbalized attitudes?
- Which attitudinal variables are related to the development of the child?

Most studies of maternal attitudes suffer from methodological problems; we have included quasi-experimental and clinical studies since they are thought-provoking. However, the reader must be cautious in generalizing results of particular studies to new samples.

Maternal Attitudes about the Maternal Role

How does the mother view the maternal role, and are differing views consistently related to stable differences in maternal behavior?

The literature on mothering over the past fifty years reflects the impact of social trends on the definitions of the maternal role in child and family development. Research in the 1930s and 1940s focused primarily on the problems of childrearing confronting the mother (Senn 1949). While similar concerns have been expressed recently, there appears to be an expanded view of both the factors influencing maternal competence and the societal and familial roles of men and women. Shifting role definitions have generated an intense research interest in the biological and psychological functioning of men and women in relation to parental roles (Lamb 1976; Wortis 1971). Thus, it seems particularly pertinent to examine those attitudes that reflect mothers' self-perceptions as women as well as attitudes that reflect mothers' views of the maternal role.

Only a few studies have attempted to examine the complex relationships between mothers' self-perceptions in their maternal and nonmaternal roles. Most research has focused on the relationships between mothers' perceptions of self-esteem and competencies, maternal employment, and maternal childrearing behaviors. Baruch (1973) reported that women who rated themselves highly on competence-related traits also evidenced higher self-esteem scores. In addition, high self-esteem and competence were reported for those women whose mothers had a demonstrated preference for a career, while there was no significant effect noted toward higher self-esteem for those women whose mothers were employed but did not prefer to be.

Self-esteem seems to be closely equated with satisfaction with a given role in society. Ferree (1976) found that role dissatisfaction was reported by 26 percent of the full-time homemakers in her sample, while only 14 percent of the employed mothers expressed dissatisfaction in their roles. In addition, over half of the full-time homemakers felt that they were not very good at housework, while all of the employed mothers considered themselves good or extremely good at their paid jobs. Interestingly, all of the mothers had minimal schooling, and the employed mothers had unskilled or semiskilled jobs.

While these studies tend to suggest that role satisfaction and self-esteem are related to self-ratings of competence, they also raise questions about factors which may contribute to a mother's perceptions of herself, the consistency of such perceptions, and their expression in behavior.

The complexity of reciprocating influences which may affect development and consistency of self-perceptions is particularly evident in studies of maternal employment (Poznanski, Maxey, and Marsden 1970). Poznanski et al. concluded from their review of the literature on maternal employment and child outcomes that family stability was relatively more important than the simple distinction of whether or not the mother was employed.

Hoffman (1961) reported differences in childrearing behaviors between satisfied and dissatisfied working mothers. Mothers who enjoyed working were relatively high on positive affect toward their children, used mild discipline, and tended to avoid assigning household tasks to their children. In contrast, mothers who disliked working appeared less involved with their children, obtained children's help with household tasks, and had children who were relatively more assertive and hostile. No distinction was made, however, between those working mothers who accepted the maternal role and those who did not.

The detailed findings of Yarrow et al. (1962) support the position that role satisfaction in mothering and nonmothering roles is related to childrearing behaviors. These investigators reported that role satisfaction was related to consistency and control factors in the mother-child relationship. The dissatisfied working mothers tended to view their children as dependent; they tended to use more verbal pressure toward independent behavior and to assign more responsibilities to their children. Dissatisfied nonworking mothers also exhibited generally inferior mothering behaviors and lower adequacy in mothering ratings. Yarrow et al. concluded that the mother's fulfillment or frustration in nonmothering roles was related to consistency and control factors in the mother-child relationship.

While dissatisfaction in a work role seems to be one factor related to behavior in the maternal role, additional factors may affect a mother's acceptance of the mothering role. Zuckerman and Oltean (1959), for example, advanced the position that mothering role conflict may be the source of low self-acceptance. They based their position on the fact that low self-acceptance scores were related to maternal attitudes of hostility or rejection as measured by the Parent Attitude Research Instrument. To determine the effect of psychological stability on maternal role functioning, Cohler et al. (1970; 1974) studied mothers who had been hospitalized for psychiatric care. Former patients generally tended to deny childrearing concerns and to believe that mother-child responsiveness was unimportant. Cohler et al. reported that impaired maternal role performance was most frequently associated with social withdrawal. These findings suggest that maternal role functioning is altered when basic psychological functioning is disturbed.

Maternal Attitudes and Behaviors

Are there distinct behavioral variations in mother-child relationships which can be related to the mother's verbalized attitudes?

The consistency between maternal attitudes and maternal behaviors has only partially been explained by research, most of which has focused primarily on the infancy period. Tulkin and Cohler (1973) examined maternal attitudes related to appropriate control, encouragement of reciprocity, appropriate closeness, acceptance of emotional complexity, and comfort in perceiving infant needs. Studies of low socioeconomic status (SES) and middle SES mothers indicated significantly higher attitude scores for middle SES mothers on all attitudes except appropriate closeness, which yielded nonsignificant differences between the samples. Tulkin and Cohler also observed both samples in a mother-infant interaction situation. The most consistent relationships between maternal behaviors and attitudes were observed in the middle SES sample. Middle SES mothers who expressed positive attitudes toward encouragement of reciprocity also spent more time face to face with their infants, responded to and initiated infant vocalization, gave the infants toys, and responded to the infants' fretting. Tulkin and Cohler were unable to find significant relationships between any of the maternal attitudes and maternal behavior for the low SES mothers. In contrast, Zunich (1971), using different instruments, reported significant relationships between maternal attitudes toward family life and maternal behaviors within a sample of low SES mothers. In some cases, then, maternal attitudes can be related to differences in maternal behavior.

Additional research has examined the acceptance of specific aspects of role acceptance over time. Moss (1967) interviewed mothers prior to their children's birth and then observed the mother-child dyad when the infants were three weeks old. Moss reported that a measure of acceptance of the nurturant role obtained from the interviews was directly related to observed maternal responsiveness. Similar studies (Moss, Robson, and Pedersen 1969; Robson, Pedersen, and Moss 1969) reported relationships between prenatal attitudes of mothers and maternal behavior shortly after birth. Robson et al. found that a prenatal measure of interest in affectionate contact was correlated with the frequency of mother-infant mutual gazing at one month postpartum. Moss et al. reported that ratings of animation in the mother's voice during pregnancy correlated with the amount of stimulation the mother provided the infant at one and three months of age. Maternal behavior may indeed be reflective of attitudes the mother has expressed prior to the child's birth.

Recent studies and position statements on the developmental process of mothering provide a conceptual framework for examining variables which may contribute to the stability or change in maternal attitudes. For example, socioeconomic status has been commonly associated with developmental variations in maternal behaviors and attitudes which presumably result from variations in social and economic conditions (Havighurst 1972; Sears, Maccoby, and Levin 1957). Wandersman (1973) concluded from a review of the literature on socialization, however, that there are a small number of consistent SES differences in maternal behaviors. Wandersman noted trends which indicate stylistic differences in mother-child interactions. In general, low SES mothers interact using more authoritative, coercive, and physically assertive techniques, while middle SES mothers interact using more egalitarian, guiding, and verbally orienting techniques. Martin (1975) also cited studies which support Wandersman's general conclusions. Deutsch's (1973) extensive literature review identifies mediating variables that have been related to SES differences in child development and points out the need to elaborate on these variables which are embedded within SES categorizations.

Studies of maternal stress provide excellent opportunities to explore the development of maternal attitudes and their relationship with maternal behavior. Grimm (1969) reported that psychological tension increased in the last half of the last trimester of pregnancy. Stress was most commonly expressed in relation to fears involving death or injury to the mother or child, abnormality of the child, and difficulty in delivery. Grimm also reported that mothers who had a history of favorable life experiences and positive attitudes toward other areas of female functioning tended to have favorable attitudes toward pregnancy. Additional studies suggest that emotional stability before birth is predictive of emotional stability postpartum (Grimm and Venet 1966); mothers who are able to remain relaxed during childbirth (i.e., cope with stress) are more likely to be pleased with their infants at first sight (Newton and Newton 1962).

Richards and Bernal (1972) and Storr (1974) suggest that a major source of stress is the unrealistic expectations that primiparous parents may develop as a result of inadequate knowledge of parenting. Levy and McGee (1975) investigated the relationship between expectations and the subjective outcomes of childbirth. Primiparous mothers answered questions before labor and after birth. The mother's evaluation of childbirth as favorable or unfavorable was related directly to whether the experience was rated better or worse than her expectation. Anticipation of labor and delivery was positively related to a woman's perception of her own mother's experience in childbirth, but anticipation was not related to a woman's evaluation of her actual delivery experience. Women receiving extreme communications (e.g., frightening stories concerning labor and delivery) or no information from their mothers reported poorer evaluations of childbirth than women who had received moderate communications. The limited data available indicate that accurate information about childbirth may directly affect a mother's evaluation of the experience. Unfortunately, the effects of positive or negative evaluations of childbirth have not been related to child development characteristics and/or the mother's attitudes about the child.

The lack of knowledge and the physical stress of childbirth have been considered sources of postpartum depression (Kosdilsky and Banet 1972). Postpartum depression frequently involves extreme irritability and moodiness and, in some cases, refusal of food. Supporting the position that postpartum depression is the result of pregnancy-related stress, and not lack of knowledge, Grimm and Venet (1966) reported nonsignificant differences in the occurrence of postpartum depression between primiparous and multiparous mothers. Interestingly, Broussard and Hartner (1971) reported that mothers who experienced postpartum depression were more likely to evaluate their babies as below average in development.

One mediating variable which may reflect the effect social and economic conditions have on the mother's attitudes about childbearing and childrearing is the mother's expressed desire for pregnancy. Grimm and Venet (1966) reported that the desire for pregnancy related positively to social class and negatively to parity. That is, women of higher social class status, based on income, education, and occupation, were more favorably disposed to pregnancy. Also, the fewer number of children in the family, the greater the enthusiasm for the pregnancy. Desire for pregnancy obtained during the third month of pregnancy did not relate to somatic symptoms during pregnancy or to ease of labor and delivery. Desire for pregnancy was significantly related to the degree of enthusiasm for the infant at birth (rated independently by the obstetrician), to the lack of depression postpartum and to greater warmth in handling the infant. The work by Kennell et al. (1970) also suggests that positive views of pregnancy lead to stronger attachment with the infant.

The desire for pregnancy appears to change during pregnancy. Cameron (1969) studied a sample of 225 mothers who were asked how they felt, retrospectively, about their desire for children at three different points in time: upon knowledge of the pregnancy, at quickening (first felt fetal movements), and at birth. The results indicated that at the initial point 18 percent were distressed and 28 percent were pleased about the pregnancy. These results are not nearly as positive as those reported by Sears et al. (1957) who reported that 62 percent of the mothers of firstborn children were pleased when they learned of the pregnancy. Cameron (1969) reported that maternal desire for the child increased at quickening, and again at birth. These findings are consistent with the preliminary results of the Matejcek et al. (1972) study of unwanted pregnancies. Few postpartum differences existed in the conscious attitudes of mothers who had previously not desired a child and a control group of mothers who had wanted to become pregnant.

Study of the relationship between women's verbalized attitudes toward the maternal role with behavioral differences has raised many questions and provided few answers. The following starting points are offered for future research:

- Maternal role performance appears to be affected by the mother's perception of herself and satisfaction in the nonmaternal role, as well as by her perception of herself as a woman.
- Maternal behavior seems to be consistent with attitudes expressed prior to the birth of the child.
- Maternal stress appears to be a psychological variable which influences a mother's perceptions toward both her maternal experiences and her infant.

Maternal Attitudes and the Mother-Child Relationship

Which attitudinal variables are related to the development of the child?

As the previous discussion indicates, the relationship between mothers' attitudes and their behavior has not been clearly delineated in the research literature. Similarly, the relationship between maternal attitudes and child outcomes is relatively unexplored. In the following section, studies of the behavioral characteristics of mother-child relationships form the bases for examining those maternal behaviors and related attitudes that may affect the child's development.

A number of investigators have emphasized the interactive, developmental nature of the mother-child relationship (Bell 1968; Gewirtz 1969; Gordon 1974; Greenfield 1972; Rheingold 1969). The mother not only initiates behavior with the child, but also responds to the child's behavior. Positive relationships have been found between the child's language development and the mother's verbal stimulation; the child's skill with objects and the mother's presentation of play materials; and mother's and child's positive social behaviors (Clarke-Stewart 1973). Positive relationships have been found between mother and child attentiveness behaviors (Osofsky and Danzger 1973).

More recently, investigators have suggested that the mother and child not only employ reciprocating influences in their relationship but also modify the nature of their interactive behavior as both become competent (Sander 1976). Blank (1976) suggested that even though the mother may maintain stable characteristics, any given maternal behavior may be appropriate at one point in the developmental span and inappropriate at another. There may be some characteristics of the mother-child interaction which do not change over time, although Bronson (1974) reported that such wide variation exists in mothers' behavioral responses to their children's requests for attention that there is no way to predict the specific content of the maternal response. Nevertheless, some consistency in maternal response can probably be identified, and that most likely is related to the mothers' attitudinal repertoire. Situational variations may affect the content of the interaction, while mothers' attitudes may affect the extent to which content and expression are consistent. For example, a mother may express negative attitudes about the amount of attention a child requires during early infancy. The same mother may respond to the infant's demands for attention with positive behaviors in a social context and negative behaviors in the home. Obviously different maternal behaviors may not be directly related to different maternal attitudes about mothering, as Karnes and Zehrbach (1975) point out in their discussion of maternal behaviors and attitudes.

The early work of Brody (1956) attempted to identify the dimensions underlying mother-child interaction. Brody delineated four groups of mothers based on laboratory observations of 32 mothers and their infants:

Group A—Sensitive, consistent, and attentive mothers.

Group B—Less sensitive, less consistent, and somewhat overactive or overattentive mothers.

Group C—Insufficiently sensitive, moderately inconsistent, but adequately attentive mothers.

Group D—Hypersensitive, very inconsistent, and hyperactive mothers.

Differentiation of the four groups was dependent on the examination of all three dimensions; subtle variations on one dimension, when combined with variations on a second dimension, resulted in a distinctly different interaction style. Obviously, the most difficult problem is defining consistency, sensitivity, and attentiveness behaviorally, so that the relationships between verbalized attitudes, behavioral content, and infant response can be examined.

Investigations which link infant behavioral outcomes to maternal responsiveness, infant stimulation, and mutual gazing provide some tentative hypotheses about the relationship between early maternal attitudes and infant development. Schaffer and Emerson (1964) reported a positive relationship between maternal responsiveness to infant crying, total amount of stimulation, and infant attachment at eighteen months. Ainsworth and Bell (1969) also reported that maternal responsiveness was predictive of infant exploratory behavior and attachment at one year of age.

Beckwith (1972) suggested that responsiveness seems to be more important than the amount of time the mother is available to the infant. Maternal involvement and stimulation have been correlated positively with the child's social responsiveness to the mother (Beckwith 1972; Bell 1970; Stern, Caldwell, Hersher, Lipton, and Richmond 1969). Work by Stayton, Hogan, and Ainsworth (1971) and Gordon's (1974) in-depth analysis of mother-child interaction suggest that the mother's awareness of the child's needs and her willingness to respond to these needs are significant influences on the child's attainment of competency. Gordon (1977) concluded, however, that maternal stimulation was most predictive of the child's cognitive development when the mother modified her stimulation to match the infant's needs.

Each of the cited studies implies a certain level of maternal emotional involvement in the relationship. Emotional involvement appears to be a significant influence in the development of social initiative in the child. Yarrow (1963) reported that the level of positive emotional expression in comparison with maternal stimulation was highly related to an infant's social initiative. Mothers who developed a close personally satisfying relationship with their children were more likely to be emotionally involved with their children. Studies of mother-infant interaction have indicated that mutual gazing, which can signify emotional involvement, is positively related to infant development (Gordon 1977).

Since it appears that infant response to maternal stimulation begins almost immediately after birth (Condon and Sander 1974), it is not surprising that mother-child interaction patterns appear to be established very early in the child's life (Gordon 1977). The assertion that the infant plays an important role in the development of interaction patterns, however, is relatively recent (Bell 1968; Korner and Grobstein 1976; Moss 1967).

The clearest relationship between infant differences and parental behavior concerns sex differences. Lewis (1972) reported that attachment behaviors in the infant appeared to be a function of the sex of the parent and the child. Mothers tended to use proximal attachment modes with infants while fathers tended to use distal modes of interaction. Gordon (1974) found that mothers interact differently with male infants than with female infants.

Current interest in infant temperament and the effect of the infant on the parent is reflected in an investigation by Duchowny (1974), suggesting that alert neonates with a heightened capacity to respond to stimuli, both visual and auditory, favorably influenced the mother's self-image at one month postpartum. The measure of self-image included the mother's confidence, emotional involvement with the infant, and the extent to which the mother was able to view the infant as a unique individual.

Two related studies have examined the effects of premature infants on mothers' attitudes. Smith et al. (1969) conducted psychiatric interviews with a sample of mothers of premature infants and a comparison sample of mothers of full-term infants. They reported no significant differences in the mothers' emotional moods, concern for the infant, and acceptance of pregnancy and the baby. Seashore et al. (1973) suggested that early separation of the premature infant and mother was related to a lower self-rating on confidence, especially for primiparous mothers. In addition, Seashore et al. reported that self-ratings of confidence predicted skill in diapering, bathing, and feeding one week after the infant was discharged from the hospital.

There is a growing interest in situational variables as they affect the early development of the mother-infant relationship. In a general sense, the mother's environment during pregnancy will undoubtedly affect the mother's attitudes about childrearing; as Lambie, Bond, and Weikart (1974) point out, a mother's attitudes toward her children are not independent of social and economic conditions. Similarly, the presence or absence of a father may affect the mother's attitude about both the child and herself, depending on how the mother views the father's absence (Anastasiow and Hanes 1975; Marsella, Dubanoski, and Mohs 1974). Kohn (1959) suggested that SES may affect the mother-child relationship through the role definitions of the parents. Ramey and Campbell (1976) reported distinct SES differences in mother's locus of control as measured by Rotter's Internal-External Locus of Control Scale. That is, low SES mothers felt their future was controlled primarily by external sources, while middle SES mothers felt internal control of their futures. Gildea et al. (1961) reported similar distinctions between low and middle SES mothers in their perceptions of responsibility and potency in childrearing. Because of the multitude of possible environmental influences and reciprocating influences, Schaefer (1975) suggested that additional work examining all family members as well as community variables needs to be done before we can begin to understand the full impact of environmental variables on the mother-child relationship.

Extensive reviews of research by Caldwell (1964), Becker (1964), and Martin (1975) reflect the vast amount of data accumulated on parent-child interaction. Little information is available, however, about possible attitudinal bases which may explain variations in behavior and enduring behavior patterns. While attitudes undoubtedly influence maternal behavior, few studies of young children have examined the relationships between verbalized attitudes, maternal behavior, and child behavior. Tentative conclusions which can be drawn include:

- Maternal responsivity and sensitivity to the child appear to be interrelated in affecting the child's social and cognitive growth.
- Emotional involvement on the part of the mother appears to be related to social growth in the infant.
- Mother-child interaction patterns usually are established very early in the child's life.
- The mother-child relationship is generally seen as an interactive system with a number of possible reciprocating influences.

Implications for Research

Perhaps the greatest need at the present time is for an extensive review of the literature, accompanied by a conceptual synthesis of maternal attitudes and early child development. A number of methodological and theoretical issues need to be discussed to clarify the questions for future research; Jacoby (1969) may be a useful example.

In 1964, Caldwell pointed out the need for studies that examine the total interaction of verbalized attitude, maternal behavior, and child response. The past decade has produced few such studies, and the need remains. At the same time, we lack instrumentation for measuring affective areas of development (Gordon 1977) in both the mother and the child; undoubtedly there will be a continued emphasis on observational instruments. Lytton's (1971) review will be helpful to the researcher interested in observation techniques.

There also appears to be a renewed interest in case studies and longitudinal analyses, such as those reported by Brody (1956), Foster and Anderson (1930), and Werner (1971). Despite the time and effort required to conduct well-designed longitudinal research, the results of previous studies have provided valuable data for understanding child development. Longitudinal research is needed to enhance understanding of the relationship between mothers' attitudes and children's development.

Implications for Programs in Parent Education

> Within the last decade there has developed in this country a tremendous interest in the young child and in the much more neglected subject of training for parenthood.... There has been an increasing recognition of the fact that the mere being a father or a mother is not in itself sufficient to prepare the individual for the complex and difficult task of rearing children.
> The interest that originally concerned itself with the young child as an entity has developed into a study of the child in his home situation, that is, in relation to his parents. (Foster and Anderson 1930, p. 1)

Our concern remains the same today: How can we facilitate the development of parents and children? Any discussion of effective parenting leads to a number of questions related to adequate caregiving, developing competence in the child and parent, providing support systems, and, more recently, social values. Parenting programs have frequently failed to assess adequately the cognitive, affective, and behavioral needs of the target population prior to the design and implementation of the program. The lack of needs assessment can be based, in part, on the false assumption that empirical evidence exists which clearly identifies the characteristics of a population, the characteristics of a competent parent, and effective means of assisting parents in becoming competent. Program designers need to learn as much as possible about the expressed needs of parents to avoid grossly inappropriate and/or ineffective programming.

While some programs have stated goals that related to attitudes, a basic problem is the lack of instruments to assess the affective needs of parents (Gordon, Hanes, Lamme, and Schlenker 1975). Despite the methodological flaws inherent in some procedures, carefully designed questionnaires, interviews, and observational strategies can provide useful information for programming. Karnes and Zehrbach (1975), using Fishbein's (1967) model, have provided an interesting discussion of the ways in which attitudes about personal behavior may interact with the normative attitudes of the community.

As program designers begin to examine the attitudes of mothers and women approaching parenthood, they may discover that mothers are most receptive to new information during pregnancy and the neonatal period, since a number of psychological changes occur in the mother during these times (Brazelton 1973; Caplan 1960; Klaus and Kennell 1976).

Perhaps the most significant research implication for parenting programs is the acceptance of attitudes as a valid aspect of the mother's (or caregiver's) functioning (Lally 1977). Our task is to facilitate the development of the mother within the constraints she defines.

> We are unable to do much about some of the factors which make having a baby so critical and difficult an experience. We can, however, scrutinize our own attitudes and the implications of such principles of baby care as we are willing to put into practice, to make sure that they do not imply too severe demands upon the mother or any intolerance of need or of acknowledged difficulty on her part. (Escalona 1949, p. 51)

Michael L. Hanes and Sandra Kanu Dunn prepared this chapter while he was Associate Professor of Early Childhood Education at the University of Florida, Gainesville, Florida.

References

Ainsworth, M. D. S., and Bell, S. M. "Some Contemporary Patterns of Mother-Infant Interaction in the Feeding Situation." In *Stimulation in Early Infancy,* edited by J. A. Ambrose. London: Academic Press, 1969.

Anastasiow, N. J., and Hanes, M. L. "Identification and Sex Role." In *The Application of Child Development Research to Exceptional Children,* edited by J. Gallagher. Reston, Va.: Council for Exceptional Children, 1975.

Appleton, T.; Clifton, R.; and Grotberg, S. "The Development of Behavioral Competence in Infancy." In *Review of Child Development Research,* vol. 4, edited by F. D. Horowitz. Chicago: University of Chicago Press, 1975.

Baruch, G. K. "Feminine Self-Esteem, Self-Ratings of Competence and Maternal Career Commitment." *Journal of Counseling Psychology* 20 (1973): 487-488.

Becker, W. "Consequences of Different Kinds of Parental Discipline." In *Review of Child Development Research,* vol. 1, edited by M. L. Hoffman and L. W. Hoffman. New York: Russell Sage, 1964.

Beckwith, L. "Relationships Between Infants' Social Behavior and Their Mothers' Behavior." *Child Development* 43 (1972): 397-411.

Bell, R. Q. "A Reinterpretation of the Direction of Effects in Studies of Socialization." *Psychological Review* 75 (1968): 81-95.

Bell, S. M. " The Development of the Concept of Object as Related to Infant-Mother Attachment." *Child Development* 41 (1970): 291-311.

Blank, M. "The Mother's Role in Infant Development." In *Infant Psychiatry,* edited by E. Rexford, L. Sander, and T. Shapiro. New Haven, Conn.: Yale University Press, 1976.

Brazelton, T. B. "Effect of Maternal Expectations on Early Infant Behavior." *Early Child Development and Care* 2 (1973): 259-273.

Brody, S. *Patterns of Mothering.* New York: International Universities Press, 1956.

Bronson, W. C. "Mother-Father Interaction: A Perspective on Studying Development of Competence." *Merrill-Palmer Quarterly* 20 (1974): 275-301.

Broussard, E. R., and Hartner, M. S. S. "Further Consideration Regarding Maternal Perception of the First Born." In *Exceptional Infant: Studies in Abnormalities,* vol. 2, edited by J. Hellmuth. New York: Brunner/Mazel, 1971.

Caldwell, B. M. "The Effects of Infant Care." In *Review of Child Development Research,* vol. 1, edited by M. L. Hoffman and L. W. Hoffman. New York: Russell Sage, 1964.

Cameron, P. "How Much Do Mothers Love Their Children?" Urbana, Ill.: ERIC Clearinghouse on Early Childhood Education, 1969. (ERIC Document Reproduction Service No. ED 081 485).

Caplan, G. "Patterns of Parental Response to the Crisis of Premature Birth." *Psychiatry* 23 (1960): 365-374.

Clarke-Stewart, K. A. "Interactions Between Mothers and Their Young Children: Characteristics and Consequences." *Monographs of the Society for Research in Child Development* 38 (1973): nos. 6-7 serial no. 153.

Cohler, B. J., et al. "Social Relations, Stress, and Psychiatric Hospitalization among Mothers of Young Children." *Social Psychiatry* 9 (1974): 7-12.

Cohler, B. J.; Weiss, J. L.; and Greenbaum, H. U. " Child Care Attitudes and Emotional Disturbance among Mothers of Young Children." *Genetic Psychology Monographs* 82 (1970): 3-47.

Condon, W. S., and Sander, L. W. "Neonate Movement Is Synchronized with Adult Speech: Interactional Participation and Language Acquisition." *Science* 183 (1974): 99-101.

Deutsch, C. P. "Social Class and Child Development." In *Review of Child Development Research,* vol. 3, edited by B. M. Caldwell and H. N. Ricciuti. Chicago: University of Chicago Press, 1973.

Duchowny, M. S. "Interactional Influence of Infant Characteristics and Postpartum Maternal Self-Image." Urbana, Ill.: ERIC Clearinghouse on Early Childhood Education, 1974. (ERIC Document Reproduction Service No. ED 104 556.)

Escalona, S. K. "The Psychological Situation of Mother and Child upon Return Home from the Hospital." In *Problems of Infancy and Childhood,* edited by M. J. E. Senn. New York: Josiah Macy, Jr., 1949.

Ferree, M. M. "The Confused American Housewife." *Psychology Today* 10, no. 4 (1976): 76-80.

Fishbein, M. "Attitude and the Prediction of Behavior." In *Readings in Attitude Theory and Measurement,* edited by M. Fishbein. New York: John Wiley & Sons, 1967.

Foster, J. C., and Anderson, J. E. *The Young Child and His Parents.* Minneapolis: University of Minnesota Press, 1930.

Gewirtz, J. L. "Levels of Conceptual Analysis in Environmental-Infant Interaction Research." *Merrill-Palmer Quarterly* 15 (1969): 7-47.

Gildea, M. C.; Glidewell, J. C.; and Kantor, M. B. "Maternal Attitudes and General Adjustment in School Children." In *Maternal Attitudes and Child Behavior,* edited by J. C. Glidewell. Springfield, Ill.: Charles C. Thomas, 1961.

Gordon, I. J. *The Infant Experience.* Columbus, Ohio: Charles E. Merrill, 1975.

Gordon, I. J. *An Investigation into the Social Roots of Competence.* Final Report to National Institute of Mental Health, Department of Health, Education, and Welfare, October 1974.

Gordon, I. J. "Significant Factors in Effective Parenting." Paper presented at "Effective Parenting" conference sponsored by Bilingual Children's Television, Inc., New Orleans, La., March 31-April 2, 1977.

Gordon, I. J.; Hanes, M. L.; Lamme, L. L.; and Schlenker, P. *Research Report of Parent Oriented Home-Based Early Childhood Education Programs.* South Carolina Department of Education as fiscal agent for USOE, Region IV, Atlanta, Ga., May 30, 1975.

Greenberg, M.; Rosenberg, I.; and Lind, J. "First Mothers Rooming-In with Their Newborns: Its Impact upon the Mother." *American Journal of Orthopsychiatry* 43 (1973): 783-788.

Greenfield, P. M. "Cross-Cultural Studies of Mother-Infant Interaction: Towards a Structural-Functional Approach." *Human Development* 15 (1972): 131-138.

Grimm, E. E. "Women's Attitudes and Reactions to Child Bearing." In *Modern Woman: Her Psychology and Sexuality,* edited by G. D. Goldman and D. S. Milnor. Springfield, Ill.: Charles C. Thomas, 1969.

Grimm, E. R., and Venet, W. R. "The Relationship of Emotional Adjustment and Attitudes to the Course and Outcome of Pregnancy." *Psychosomatic Medicine* 28 (1966): 34-49.

Havighurst, R. J. "Social Class and Human Development." In *Determinants of Behavioral Development,* edited by F. J. Monks, W. W. Hartup, and J. deWit. New York: Academic Press, 1972.

Hoffman, L. W. "Effects of Maternal Employment on the Child." *Child Development* 32 (1961): 187-197.

Hubert, J. "Belief and Reality: Social Factors in Pregnancy and Childbirth." In *The Integration of the Child into a Social World,* edited by M. P. M. Richards. New York: Cambridge University Press, 1974.

Jacoby, A. P. "Transition to Parenthood: A Reassessment." *Journal of Marriage and the Family* 31 (1969): 720-727.

Karnes, M. B., and Zehrbach, R. R. "Parental Attitudes and Education in the Culture of Poverty." *Journal of Research and Development in Education* 8 (1975): 44-53.

Kennell, J. H.; Slyter, H.; and Klaus, M. H. "The Mourning Response of Parents to the Death of a Newborn Infant." *New England Journal of Medicine* 283 (1970): 344-349.

Klaus, M. H., and Kennell, J. H., eds. *Maternal-Infant Bonding.* St. Louis, Mo.: C. V. Mosby, 1976.

Kohn, M. L. "Social Class and Parental Values." *American Journal of Sociology* 64 (1959): 337-351.

Korner, A. F., and Grobstein, R. "Individual Differences at Birth: Implications for Mother-Infant Relationship and Later Development." In *Infant Psychiatry*, edited by E. Rexford, L. Sander, and T. Shapiro. New Haven, Conn.: Yale University Press, 1976.

Kosdilsky, M. L., and Banet, B. *What Now? A Handbook for Couples (Especially Women) Postpartum.* Washington, D.C.: Daily, 1972.

Lally, R. "Creating Effective Group Learning Environments for Infants." In *Update: The First Ten Years of Life*, edited by M. L. Hanes, I. J. Gordon, and W. Breivogel. Gainesville, Fla.: University of Florida, 1977.

Lamb, M. E. "The Role of the Father: An Overview." In *The Role of the Father in Child Development*, edited by M.E. Lamb. New York: John Wiley & Sons, 1976.

Lambie, D.; Bond, J. T.; and Weikart, D. *Home Teaching with Mothers and Infants.* Ypsilanti, Mich.: High/Scope Educational Research Foundation, 1974.

Levy, J. M., and McGee, R. K. "Childbirth as a Crisis: A Test of Janis' Theory of Communication and Stress Resolution." *Journal of Personality and Social Psychology* 31 (1975): 171-179.

Lewis, M. "Mothers and Fathers, Girls and Boys: Attachment Behavior in the One-Year-Old." In *Determinants of Behavioral Development*, edited by F. J. Monks, W. W. Hartup, and J. deWit. New York: Academic Press, 1972.

Lewis, M., and Rosenblum, L. A., eds. *The Effect of the Infant on Its Caregiver.* New York: John Wiley & Sons, 1974.

Lytton, H. "Observation Studies of Parent-Child Interaction: A Methodological Review." *Child Development* 42 (1971): 651-684.

Marsella, A. J.; Dubanoski, R. A.; and Mohs, K. "The Effects of Father Presence and Absence Upon Maternal Attitudes." *Journal of Genetic Psychology* 125 (1974): 257-263.

Martin, B. "Parent-Child Relations." In *Review of Child Development Research*, vol. 4, edited by F. D. Horowitz. Chicago: University of Chicago Press, 1975.

Matejcek, Z.; David, P. H.; Stupkova, E.; Schuller, V.; Dytrych, Z.; and Jelinkova, V. "Prague Study on Children Born from Unwanted Pregnancies." In *Determinants of Behavioral Development*, edited by F. J. Monks, W. W. Hartup, and J. deWit. New York: Academic Press, 1972.

Moss, H. A. "Sex, Age and State as Determinants of Mother-Infant Interaction." *Merrill-Palmer Quarterly* 13 (1967): 19-36.

Moss, H. A.; Robson, K. S.; and Pedersen, F. "Determinants of Maternal Stimulation of Infants and Consequences of Treatment for Later Reactions to Strangers." *Developmental Psychology* 1 (1969): 239-246.

Newton, N., and Newton, M. "Mothers' Reactions to Their Newborn Babies." *Journal of the American Medical Association* 181 (1962): 206-211.

Osofsky, J. D., and Danzger, B. "Relationships Between Mother-Infant Interaction." Urbana, Ill.: ERIC Clearinghouse on Early Childhood Education, 1973. (ERIC Document Reproduction Service No. ED 086 323.)

Poznanski, F.; Maxey, A.; and Marsden, G. "Clinical Implications of Maternal Employment: A Review of Research." *Journal of the American Academy of Child Psychiatry* 9 (1970): 741-746.

Ramey, C. T., and Campbell, F. A. "Parental Attitudes and Poverty." *Journal of Genetic Psychology* 128 (1976): 3-6.

Rheingold, H. L. "The Social and Socializing Infant." In *Handbook of Socialization Theory and Research*, edited by D. A. Guslin. Chicago: Rand McNally, 1969.

Richards, M. P. M., and Bernal, J. B. "An Observational Study of Mother-Infant Interaction." In *Ethological Studies of Child Behavior*, edited by N. J. B. Jones. London: Cambridge University Press, 1972.

Robson, K. S.; Pedersen, F. A.; and Moss, H. A. "Developmental Observations of Dyadic Gazing in Relation to the Fear of Strangers and Social Approach Behavior." *Child Development* 40, no. 2 (1969): 619-627.

Sander, L. W. "Issues in Early Mother-Child Interaction." In *Infant Psychiatry*, edited by E. Rexford, L. Sander, and T. Shapiro. New Haven, Conn.: Yale University Press, 1976.

Schaefer, E. S. "Family Relationships." In *The Application of Child Development Research to Exceptional Children*, edited by J. Gallagher. Reston, Va.: Council for Exceptional Children, 1975.

Schaffer, H. R., and Emerson, P. E. "The Development of Social Attachments in Infancy." *Monographs of the Society for Research in Child Development* 29, no. 3, (1964): serial no. 94.

Sears, R. R.; Maccoby, E. E.; and Levin, H. *Patterns of Child Rearing*. Evanston, Ill.: Row, Peterson, 1957.

Seashore, M. H.; Leifer, A. D.; Barnett, C. R.; and Leiderman, P. H. "The Effect of Denial of Early Mother-Infant Interaction on Maternal Self-Confidence." *Journal of Personality and Social Psychology* 26 (1973): 369-378.

Senn, M. J. E. *Problems of Infancy and Childhood*. New York: Josiah Macy, Jr., 1949.

Smith, L. M., and Hudgins, B. B. *Educational Psychology: An Application of Social and Behavioral Theory*. New York: Alfred A. Knopf, 1964.

Smith, N., et al. "Mother's Psychological Reactions to Premature and Full-Size Newborns." *Archives of General Psychiatry* 21, no. 2 (1969): 177-181.

Standley, K. "Parental and Perinatal Correlates of Neonatal Behaviors." Urbana, Ill.: ERIC Clearinghouse on Early Childhood Education, 1974. (ERIC Document Reproduction Service No. ED 104 554.)

Stayton, D. J.; Hogan, R.; and Ainsworth, M. D. S. "Infant Obedience and Maternal Behavior: The Origins of Socialization Reconsidered." *Child Development* 42 (1971): 1057-1069.

Stern, G.; Caldwell, B.; Hersher, L.; Lipton, E.; and Richmond, J. "A Factor Analytic Study of the Mother-Infant Dyad." *Child Development* 40 (1969): 163-181.

Storr, C. "Freud and the Concept of Parental Guilt." In *Intimacy, Family and Society*, edited by A. Skolnick and J. Skolnick. Boston: Little, Brown, 1974.

Thurstone, L. L. *The Measurement of Attitude*. Chicago: University of Chicago Press, 1937.

Tulkin, S. R., and Cohler, B. J. "Child Rearing Attitudes and Mother-Child Interactions in the First Year of Life." *Merrill-Palmer Quarterly* 19 (1973): 95-106.

Wandersman, L. P. "Stylistic Differences in Mother-Child Interactions: A Review and Re-Evaluation of the Social Class and Socialization Research." *Cornell Journal of Social Relations* 8 (1973): 197-218.

Werner, E. E. *Children of Kaui*. Honolulu: University of Hawaii Press, 1971.

Wortis, R. P. "The Acceptance of the Concept of the Maternal Role by Behavioral Scientists: Its Effects on Women." *American Journal of Orthopsychiatry* 41 (1971): 733-746.

Yarrow, L. J. "Research in Dimensions of Early Maternal Care." *Merrill-Palmer Quarterly* 9 (1963): 101-114.

Yarrow, M. R.; Scott, P.; DeLeeuw, L.; and Heinig, C. "Child-Rearing in Families of Working and Nonworking Mothers." *Sociometry* 25 (1962): 122-140.

Zuckerman, M., and Oltean, M. "Some Relationships Between Maternal Attitude Factors and Authoritarianism, Personality Needs, Psychopathology, and Self-Acceptance." *Child Development* 30 (1959): 27-36.

Zunich, M. "Lower Class Mothers' Behavior and Attitudes Toward Child Rearing." *Psychological Reports* 29 (1971): 1051-1058.

Ervin Staub

4 Socialization by Parents and Peers and Experiential Learning of Prosocial Behavior

How do children learn to be kind, considerate, and helpful to other people? What factors contribute to a tendency to behave positively toward others? After decades of nearly complete neglect, these questions have caught the imagination of psychologists and have led to the intensive study of positive social behavior, its origins, and the manner in which it develops. This interest may partially reflect current concern with these questions in our culture.

Before I discuss some of the childrearing practices, parental behaviors, and circumstances of children's lives that might contribute to prosocial behavior, a few general issues seem important to consider. First, most parents, particularly with their first child, probably start out without a clear conception of what kind of person they would like their child to become. They might know that they want the child to be happy and successful, but they might have thought little about which of the many characteristics of human beings they would like their child to possess. Often, we rear our children in a trial and error fashion. Seeing that something is not quite what we would like, we try something different, but we do not think a great deal about the kinds of values we want to induce in our children, and the kinds of behaviors we would like them to exhibit later in life.

Certainly most people have *some* conception of what values and characteristics are desirable, since it is almost impossible to live in a culture without acquiring such a conception. But many people do not have a self-conscious awareness of what they personally believe are desirable characteristics they want to promote. In fact, many parents who think of themselves as liberated and enlightened may balk at the idea that they either want to or actually do "promote" any characteristics. Rather, they prefer to believe that they simply allow their children to grow and develop, unimpeded by limitations they place on them.

© 1978, Ervin Staub

This is certainly a misconception. By their example and guidance, or lack of it, parents and teachers inevitably shape children's learning and development.

Even if people know what kind of person they want their children to be, few are well informed about how to accomplish such goals: how to relate to children, how to discipline or talk to them, what to do to help them develop into certain kinds of persons. Given the lack of both clear goals and the knowledge to accomplish them, it is not surprising that children sometimes show unintended characteristics, and sometimes characteristics that we certainly do not wish them to have.

I would like to mention one example of this from my own research. We found that older children who are exposed to sounds of distress coming from another room are more likely than younger children to attempt to help in some manner, up to a certain age. Somewhere between the second and fourth grades, the frequency of help begins to decline. Sixth grade children help about as frequently as kindergarten children, and substantially less frequently than second and fourth grade children, whether they heard the sounds of distress alone or in the company of another child (Staub 1970). Why should this happen? Since an older child is more competent, and presumably has learned to a greater degree that it is desirable to help others, one would expect older children to help more. We talked with our participants after they had the opportunity to help, and sixth grade children often told us that they thought they were not supposed to go into the strange room. Some said they thought somebody would get mad if they did. When the adult experimenter asked, "Who?" some children answered, "You."

To explore the possibility that the children were inhibited from initiating helpful action because they felt that it was inappropriate for them to enter a strange room, and consequently they feared disapproval, or even punishment for doing so, we conducted some other experiments (Staub 1971a). In one of them, we told the children, each of whom was drawing alone in a room, that if they needed more drawing pencils they could go into the other room to get them. In another condition, the experimenter said nothing before leaving the room. Then, children heard a crash and sounds of distress from the adjoining room. The children who had received permission to enter the other room helped more than children who had not received permission. But still, only about 50 percent of the children helped, which was the same frequency as helping by the second grade children in the previous study. There were several clues to indicate that our participants, who were seventh grade children, might still have been inhibited from going into the adjoining room. One of these clues was particularly dramatic. A girl, immobile for some time listening to the sounds of distress, suddenly picked up one of her drawing pencils, broke its edge on the table, picked up the second one, broke it too, and ran into the adjoining room. Like this child, some of the children may have felt that they were only allowed to go into the other room if they had a good reason—such as really needing a drawing pencil.

We conducted another experiment with seventh grade girls in which the permission to go into the other room was more global and general. Children working on a questionnaire were told that they could play with toys in the other room while taking a break or when they had finished their task. Other children were told nothing. Still others were told not to go into the other room because they were working on the same task as the child in that room and we did not want them to exchange information. Of the children who received permission to go into the other room, 10 out of 11 actively helped, while only 3 out of 11 children who were told nothing and 4 out of 11 children who were told not to enter the room actively helped. Other research replicated the findings that permission and prohibition to enter other rooms affect children's helping (Weissbrod 1977).

The behavior of the children seemed to have been inhibited by rules of socially appropriate behavior, which apparently included the prohibition against entering strange rooms in strange places, and perhaps also the prohibition of interrupting work on a task. By teaching children to obey varied rules that are relevant or applicable to many everyday circumstances, we seem unintentionally to inhibit their willingness to initiate help for others. It seems that we do not adequately teach our children to discriminate situations in which polite, proper social behavior is desirable from other situations in which such rules should be disregarded to do something that benefits another person.

This leads to another issue. Many of us feel conflict over whether we want our children to be helpful and kind and to behave positively toward others. We may think that concern with others' welfare is associated with a lack of sufficient concern for oneself, with a lack of proper self-assertion. It seems, from tangential information at least, that this need not be so at all. On the one hand, self-confidence, high self-esteem, and, probably, the willingness and ability to assert oneself, are likely to contribute to positive social behavior (Staub, forthcoming). Considering it the other way around, one of the sources of self-esteem for many people is how morally good they judge themselves to be (Epstein 1973). Another such source is their judgment of their own competence. People who are helpful toward others in an effective manner may, therefore, think of themselves as both moral and competent, and hold themselves in esteem. Finally, sensitivity to others in everyday interactions is likely to contribute significantly to positive relationships with people and to good personal adjustment (Staub, forthcoming).

Socialization Practices and Prosocial Behavior

What kind of interaction between parents and children might be expected to contribute to children's positive orientation toward other people, to their kindness and helpfulness? In the following discussion, I will focus on parent-child interactions that seem most important.

Parental Warmth, Nurturance, and Affection

A warm, nurturant, affectionate relationship between children and parents, in contrast to a cold, indifferent, distant relationship, seems to contribute to the development of positive tendencies (Staub 1975a; forthcoming). Parents' warmth and affection have several consequences. First, they create an atmosphere in the home in which children are more likely to learn whatever parents teach them, verbally or through their example. Second, an affectionate, warm relationship with a parent is likely to make children want to be like their parents and adopt parents' values and behaviors to a greater degree; it is likely to lead children to identify with the parents and adopt or internalize their values. Third, having the experience of a benevolent environment, one that treats them well, children are more likely to be benevolently oriented toward their environment and people in it, to assume that other people are kind rather than unkind, to desire contact with others rather than to avoid them. Last, warmth and affection are likely to make children regard themselves better, make them more confident of their actions and less concerned about the potential negative consequences of what they might do.

There is research evidence that even a relatively brief interaction with a person who relates to a child in a warm, rewarding fashion, in contrast to a person who relates to a child in a matter-of-fact, relatively impersonal way, has different effects on behavior. Following a ten-minute warm interaction, kindergarten children who heard sounds of distress of a child coming from another room were more likely to enter in an attempt to investigate what happened and, presumably, to help (Staub 1971b; Weissbrod 1976).

Other research showed that nurturance affects children's learning. In this investigation, groups of nursery school children were supervised on repeated occasions by a person who treated them either in a warm, affectionate manner or in a straightforward, indifferent manner. The children received one of two kinds of training. Some played with toy figures and were shown helpful reactions the toy figures could make to the needs of others. The adult supervising the children also described and explained the reactions. Other children had the same experiences and in addition were exposed to the examples of the adult caregiver, who at various times engaged in helpful activities in front of the children. The children who experienced the latter, more extensive training and were supervised by a warm, affectionate adult, later acted more helpfully than children who received the same training, but who had an indifferent adult supervisor. These children were also more helpful than children who received only the less extensive training (Yarrow, Scott, and Waxler 1973).

In another experimental project with similar supervision of groups of children by a warm or an indifferent adult, children observed the adult enact scenes with small doll figures. Children supervised by the warm adult remembered more of the helpful, positive behaviors that the adult made the figures perform, while children supervised by the indifferent adult imitated more of the negative, aggressive behaviors performed with the figures (Yarrow and Scott 1972). The findings suggest the important possibility that affection, warmth, or nurturance by an adult can create a context which affects the nature and meaning of the child's experiences and results in selective learning.

In these studies researchers exposed children to selected experiences for a limited time period and evaluated some consequences of these experiences. In other kinds of research, the practices of parents in rearing children were evaluated by asking the parents and/or the child to describe how the parents would discipline the child under various circumstances. The child's peers were also asked to indicate whether they viewed the child as considerate. These studies indicated that parental affection is associated with moral values and with other children's perceptions of the child as considerate (Hoffman 1975, 1977; Hoffman and Saltzstein 1967).

Parental Control

Another basic aspect of parents' orientation toward children is the exercise of effective control over children's behavior. This is likely to be important in the effective socialization of children, both in general and in the domain of positive social behavior. The term *control* refers to the parents' insistence that children carry out important directives and adhere to rules the parents consider important. Affection and warmth, without a reasonable degree of control, are as likely to lead to license as to socialized positive behavior. The manner of control is highly important. Obviously, violent means of control are discrepant from, and seem incongruent with, an otherwise affectionate environment. There is strong evidence that the frequent use of physical punishment by parents results in children's aggression, hostility, and resistance (Aronfreed 1968; Eron, Walder, and Lefkowitz 1971). Other less violent modes of control are necessary if children are to develop positive social tendencies.

The importance of control in the domain of prosocial behavior is suggested by several experiments which show that when children interact with nurturant persons, as opposed to either neutral or relatively cold and distant persons, for a relatively brief period, they are either unaffected by nurturance, or less willing to sacrifice material rewards they previously gained, to benefit other children (Rosenhan and White 1967; Weissbrod 1976). Children are probably unwilling to deprive themselves of things they desire if they believe there will be no negative consequences because the adult supervising them is accepting and affectionate.

More generally, the importance of control has been shown by Baumrind (1967, 1971, 1975). In several studies, four-year-old nursery school children's behaviors in the nursery school were observed and coded. Parental childrearing practices were evaluated through questionnaires administered to parents and a limited amount of home observation. "Firm enforcement" of rules was an apparently important aspect of the pattern of practices employed by parents whose children showed positive and effective social behavior in school. Reasoning by parents and warmth are other aspects of this pattern, which Baumrind called authoritative.

In addition to demonstrating the importance of control, these findings call attention to the importance of considering patterns of practices, rather than separate dimensions of childrearing. Similarly, Coopersmith (1967) found that it was beneficial for parents to set firm standards of conduct for children. Combined with other parental behaviors, such as clear indications of interest in children's (ten- to eleven-year-old boys) well-being, the setting of firm standards was related to high self-esteem in children.

Reasoning and Induction by Parents

A third important influence on learning to be prosocial is reasoning by parents with children—explaining why children should behave in certain ways and not in other ways. There is, however, a discrepancy in research findings. When parents are asked to describe how they treat their children, or when children are asked to describe how parents treat them, reports of the use of induction (parents pointing out to children the negative consequences of undesirable behaviors on other people) are associated with positive behavior by children (Dlugokinski and Firestone 1973, 1974; Hoffman 1963, 1975; Hoffman and Saltzstein 1967). In most existing studies this positive behavior was not directly observed; it was determined by other children's descriptions of children as concerned about others' welfare, considerate, and helpful. Experimental studies, in contrast, have shown that an adult telling children that sharing is good, a nice thing to do, etc., has relatively little effect on children's willingness to donate (Bryan 1975; Bryan and Walbeck 1970a, b; Rushton 1975, 1976).

There are many differences between the two kinds of studies. Induction by the parent may be moderately correlated with other practices. In addition, when measurement of positive behavior involves ratings by children of how helpful other children are, the ratings are likely to be based on behaviors quite different from donating things for (unknown) others, which is the usual measure in experimental studies. Rather, ratings of positive behavior may be based on children's willingness to do things for others, to express sympathy and affection, etc. Another difference is that a parent has continuing control over the child. A parent who reasons with the child may often imply insistence that the child behave in a manner consistent with what the parent says. In contrast, in most experimental studies it is implied that the adult will have little more to do with the child after the verbal communication.

There are two kinds of verbal communications that have been found effective in experimental studies. One is a communication that explicitly tells children what is expected of them, that states a behavioral rule or norm (Grusec 1972; Grusec and Skubicki 1970; White 1972); children tend to abide by that. The other is "positive" induction, or communication that points to the positive consequences for others of children's behavior. I will describe later the evidence that such induction, when it accompanies children's actual participation in prosocial behavior, increases subsequent prosocial behavior.

Modeling and Other Types of Socialization Experiences

As in other domains, modeling seems to influence children's prosocial behavior. There is extensive research to show that children who observe generous models are more likely to donate various possessions than children who do not observe models or who observe selfish models (Bryan and Walbeck 1970a, 1970b; Grusec 1972; Rushton 1975). My analysis (Staub, forthcoming) of the influence of modeling suggests that when observers attribute to models positive motives and intentions, unselfishness, and the desire to benefit others, they are likely to imitate the models. When circumstances lead people to attribute selfish purposes or intentions, models are less likely to be imitated. These generalizations are based primarily on research with adults (Hornstein 1970), and it is possible that young children are less affected by differences in models' motives, particularly if such differences are subtly communicated. However, children are likely to imitate models because the models' behavior defines expectations, sets standards, and communicates appropriate actions.

In addition to modeling, role playing of prosocial behavior by children has been found to increase their later prosocial behavior. In a sense, this is an example of experiential learning, which will be discussed below. Pairs of kindergarten children in one study (Staub

1971c) engaged in role playing prosocial acts. One child enacted a need for help and the other responded helpfully, then the children exchanged roles. Role playing increased the frequency of girls' responses to sounds of distress coming from an adjoining room. It also increased the amount of candy boys donated to a child whose parents presumably could not give him anything for his birthday. Since children did not role play sharing at all, this generalization, which was also apparent a week after the experimental session, suggests that role playing may have provided the opportunity for role taking, for considering another child's needs from the other child's perspective. That role playing can serve such functions has been shown by Chandler's (1973) study, in which participation in extensive role playing experiences increased delinquent children's role taking capacity and decreased their antisocial behaviors over an 18-month period.

Although I have discussed modeling here only to a limited degree, modeling in the broadest sense may have tremendous significance. What children see in their own environment, on television, and in other places; the kind of understanding they acquire about the world; the conceptions they come to have about dealing with events are of substantial importance. For example, do they feel that conflict should be resolved by discussion and compromise, or by aggression? The structure of children's environments educates them about options they have and reasonable plans for action, and it communicates values to them. Indirectly, this reasoning is supported by findings of Friedrich and Stein (1973) who repeatedly exposed nursery school children to prosocial television programs. There was an increase in the interactive prosocial behaviors of those children who tended to watch primarily aggressive television programs at home. Such children may have learned new, prosocial strategies through exposure to prosocial television programs, which they could then try out in their interactions in the nursery school.

Natural Socialization: Learning by Doing

An important source of learning or development is children's experience, including the kinds of behaviors they themselves engage in. Cognitive developmental theory has long focused on children's experience, particularly their experience in role taking in their interactions with peers, as a source of development. Whether the term *experience* refers to anything beyond role taking that is different from what other theories focus on is unclear. Possibly, an important meaning of "experience" is that it focuses on events as they appear to the child. I have suggested elsewhere that a particular type of experience—children's participation in positive behavior—is likely to increase their later positive actions (Staub 1975a, 1975b, 1976, forthcoming). Focusing responsibility on children to behave positively may lead to their understanding that such behavior is desirable and expected by other people. However, the focusing of responsibility is likely to lead to meaningful learning, as the discussion of control suggests, only if children actually engage in prosocial behavior.

A variety of studies had findings which implied the importance of participation in prosocial behavior. In a cross-cultural study, Whiting and Whiting (1975) found a relationship between the extent to which children have important responsibilities for the maintenance of the family and their tendency to make responsible suggestions to others, to offer help, and to engage in helpful behavior. The children's responsibilities primarily took the form of tending animals or taking care of younger siblings. From a description by Bossard and Boll (1956) of large families, it again seems that children, usually the oldest in the family, who have extensive responsibilities for taking care of younger siblings and other household tasks, frequently become responsible and helpful individuals. In several of my studies, firstborn children, particularly from large families, tended to respond more to sounds of distress and to engage in attempts to help than later-born children (Staub 1970, 1971b, 1971c). Youngest siblings tended to be least helpful (Staub 1970). Bronfenbrenner's (1970) account of practices in Russian schools suggests that when children are made responsible for each others' conduct, they tend to show a great deal of responsibility.

The kinds of demands that are put on children, the guidance that leads them to different kinds of activities, and the kinds of behaviors they engage in as a result must influence the kinds of people they will become. When children engage in various forms of positive behavior, and they do so repeatedly over time, they are likely to make self-attributions about the reasons for their behavior. They are likely to come to consider themselves as helpful or to consider behavior that benefits others as important, and others' welfare as their responsibility.

A number of experiments with adults showed that prior participation in positive behavior increases later positive behavior. This has been found even when people are induced to engage in a single prosocial act and the effect of this single act on a later prosocial act is evaluated (Staub, forthcoming). It is likely that self-attribution and the learning of prosocial values and/or responsibility for others' welfare will follow when children are directed by other people to behave prosocially or responsibly. However, it is also likely that self-attribution will follow only when children are not directed in an extremely forceful way to participate in prosocial acts, or even if originally some force is exerted, the application of pressure is not continued on later occasions.

In a number of studies, mainly with fifth and sixth grade children as subjects, my associates and I have explored the influence of participation in prosocial behavior on children's later prosocial behavior, sometimes by itself, sometimes in conjunction with induction. In one study (Staub and Fotta, in Staub 1975b), we had children participate in four 40-minute sessions, either making toys for hospitalized children or engaging in a neutral activity. Girls who engaged in the prosocial behavior and who had the positive consequences of this behavior pointed out to them expressed greater intentions for later helpful acts and wrote more letters to hospitalized children then either boys or girls in other experimental groups.

In another study (Staub, Levy, and Shortsleeves, in Staub 1975b), girls who taught a younger girl either first aid skills or how to make a puzzle subsequently wrote more letters to hospitalized children than girls who learned the same activities and practiced them but did not teach them.

Staub and Feinberg (1976a; in Staub, forthcoming) also found that participation in certain prosocial activities, or teaching those activities to other children, had comparable effects. In one group, boys and girls either taught a younger child to make toys or made toys themselves to find out what kinds of toys children like and thereby help the art teacher select appropriate materials for classes. Later, these children donated more of their gift certificates for poor, hospitalized children than subjects in a control group or subjects in other experimental groups. The children in the control group made the toys without any special reason being stated. Participation in another experimental group had different effects on boys and girls. Children either made toys for poor, hospitalized children or taught younger children to make toys for poor, hospitalized children, and the positive consequences of their behavior was pointed out to them. In fact, a list of these positive consequences was drawn up together by the child and the experimenter, so that the children participated in thinking about the positive consequences. Induction significantly increased the amount of work that girls later expended in making toys for hospitalized children in comparison to control or prosocial action without induction subjects, but somewhat decreased toymaking by boys.

In fact, in all of our experimental studies using induction, as well as in most other research in which verbal communications were directed at children (Staub, forthcoming), boys were unaffected or negatively affected by verbal communications. My belief is that this is the result of opposition—a feeling of limitation of freedom and the desire to go contrary to the directions received—that is evoked in boys. Since boys in our culture are trained for independence and self-reliance, and sometimes thought to resist authority, they may be resistant to orders, directions, or verbal communications that can be interpreted as attempts to influence their behavior. An oppositional tendency may be quite widespread and may modify the influence of many socialization practices directed at children, in both home and school, but we know extremely little about it.

My belief in the appropriateness of interpreting the data by invoking an oppositional tendency is increased by two findings. First, in a study with kindergarten children induction did not affect children's behavior on two later measures of prosocial action, but decreased the number of paper clips (dropped by an experimenter) that children picked up (Staub 1971c). A second finding comes from Staub and Feinberg 1976a; in Staub, forthcoming). Induction combined with participation or teaching resulted in very little toymaking by boys two or three days after the experimental session. However, induction resulted in a substantial amount of toymaking by boys about two weeks later—slightly more than in the other experimental groups. Opposition may have diminished over time, while some of the inductive reasons may have been remembered.

Peer Socialization

Finally, I would like to discuss briefly an important form of socialization of children that has been rather neglected in theory and research: the socialization children receive in their interactions with peers. There is extensive evidence that interaction among peers is guided by both reciprocity and complementarity (Staub, forthcoming). Reciprocity refers to the tendency of children to be recipients of the kinds of behaviors they direct toward others. Children who behave aggressively tend to have aggressive behavior directed at them; children who behave positively tend to receive positive behaviors. Complementarity refers to the fact that children's behavior fits with or matches behavior directed toward them. For example, children who are generally responsive to others, but who tend not to provide specific help, are the recipients of generally positive behavior, but they receive no request for help. The child's behavior and the behavior directed toward the child complement each other (Staub and Feinberg 1976b; in Staub, forthcoming).

The apparent significance of peer socialization is enhanced if we consider that some children may develop consistent negative patterns of interaction with others, which are likely to affect how they think about themselves (as being disliked or incompetent in social interactions), and how they think about and feel toward others (as being hostile, unpleasant, negative, difficult to interact with, maybe not worth the trouble). Habitual patterns that children develop in approaching and interacting with others may also be affected. Thus, children's long term adjustment may be affected (Cowen, Pederson, Babigan, Izzo, and Frost 1973; Roff, Sells, and Golden 1972).

It seems important to study socialization experiences of children at home and in the schools, as well as the kinds of behavior they engage in, experiences they have and their peer interactions, in conjunction with one another. These three types of socialization are likely to interact and jointly determine how children develop and the kinds of personalities they form, including their values, beliefs, orientation toward others, and prosocial behavior.

References

Aronfreed, J. *Conduct and Conscience*. New York: Academic Press, 1968.
Baumrind, D. "Child Care Practices Anteceding Three Patterns of Preschool Behavior." *Genetic Psychological Monographs* 75 (1967): 43-88.
Baumrind, D. "Current Patterns of Parental Authority." *Developmental Psychology* 4 (1971): 1-101.
Baumrind, D. *Early Socialization and the Discipline Controversy*. Morristown, N.J.: General Learning Press, 1975.
Bossard, J. H. S., and Boll, E. S. *The Large Family System*. Philadelphia: University of Pennsylvania Press, 1956.
Bronfenbrenner, U. *Two Worlds of Childhood*. New York: Russell Sage, 1970.
Bryan, J. "Children's Cooperation and Helping Behaviors." In *Review of Child Development Research*, edited by E. M. Hetherington. Chicago: University of Chicago Press, 1975.
Bryan, J., and Walbeck, N. "Preaching and Practicing Generosity: Children's Actions and Reactions." *Child Development* 41 (1970a): 329-354.
Bryan, J. and Walbeck, N. "The Impact of Words and Deeds Concerning Altruism upon Children." *Child Development* 41 (1970b) 747-757.
Chandler, M. J. "Egocentrism and Antisocial Behavior: The Assessment and Training of Social Perspective—Talking Skills." *Developmental Psychology* 9 (1973): 326-332.
Coopersmith, S. *Antecedents of Self Esteem*. San Francisco: Fremont, 1967.
Cowen, E. L.; Pederson, A.; Babigan, H.; Izzo, L. D.; and Frost, M. A. "Long-Term Follow-Up of Early Detected Vulnerable Children." *Journal of Consulting and Clinical Psychology* 41 (1973): 438-446.
Dlugokinski, E., and Firestone, I. J. "Congruence Among Four Methods of Measuring Other-Centeredness." *Child Development* 44 (1973): 304-308.
Dlugokinski, E. L., and Firestone, I. J. "Other Centeredness and Susceptibility to Charitable Appeals: Effects of Perceived Discipline." *Developmental Psychology* 10 (1974): 21-28.
Epstein, S. "The Self-Concept Revisited. Or a Theory of a Theory." *American Psychologist* 28 (1973): 404-416.
Eron, L.; Walder, L. O.; and Lefkowitz, M. M. *Learning of Aggression in Children*. Boston: Little, Brown, 1971.
Friedrich, L. K.; and Stein, A. H. "Aggressive and Prosocial Television Programs and the Natural Behavior of Preschool Children." *Monographs of the Society for Research in Child Development* 38, serial no. 151 (1973): 1-64.
Grusec. J. E. "Demand Characteristics of the Modeling Experiment: Altruism as a

Function of Age and Aggression." *Journal of Personality and Social Psychology* 22 (1972): 139-148.
Grusec, J. E.; and Skubicki, L. "Model Nurturance Demand Characteristics of the Modeling Experiment and Altruism." *Journal of Personality and Social Psychology* 14 (1970): 352-359.
Hoffman, M. L. "Parent Discipline and the Child's Consideration for Others." *Child Development* 34 (1963): 573-588.
Hoffman, M. L. "Sex Differences in Moral Internalization and Values." *Journal of Personality and Social Psychology* 32 (1975): 720-729.
Hoffman, M. L. "Personality and Social Development." *Annual Review of Psychology* 28 (1977): 295-321.
Hoffman, M. L., and Saltzstein, H. D. "Parent Discipline and the Child's Moral Development." *Journal of Personality and Social Psychology* 5 (1967): 45-57.
Hornstein, H. A. "The Influence of Social Models on Helping." In *Altruism and Helping Behavior,* edited by J. Macauley and L. Berkowitz. New York: Academic Press, 1970.
Roff, M.; Sells, B.; and Golden, M. M. *Social Adjustment and Personality Development in Children*. Minneapolis: University of Minnesota Press, 1972.
Rosenhan, D., and White, G. "Observation and Rehearsal as Determinants of Prosocial Behavior." *Journal of Personality and Social Psychology* 5 (1967): 424-431.
Rushton, J. P. "Generosity in Children: Immediate and Long-Term Effects of Modeling, Preaching, and Moral Judgment." *Journal of Personality and Social Psychology* 31 (1975): 459-466.
Rushton, J. P. "Socialization and the Altruistic Behavior of Children." *Psychology Bulletin* 83 (1976): 898-915.
Staub, E. "A Child in Distress: The Influence of Age and Number of Witnesses on Children's Attempts to Help." *Journal of Personality and Social Psychology* 14 (1970): 130-140.
Staub, E. "Helping a Person in Distress: The Influence of Implicit and Explicit 'Rules' of Conduct of Children and Adults." *Journal of Personality and Social Psychology* 17 (1971a): 137-145.
Staub, E. "A Child in Distress: The Influence of Modeling and Nurturance on Children's Attempts to Help." *Developmental Psychology* 5 (1971b): 124-133.
Staub, E. "The Use of Role Playing and Induction in Children's Learning of Helping and Sharing Behavior." *Child Development* 42 (1971c): 805-817.
Staub, E. *The Development of Prosocial Behavior in Children*. Morristown, N.J.: General Learning Press, 1975a.
Staub, E. "To Rear a Prosocial Child: Reasoning, Learning by Doing, and Learning by Teaching Others." In *Moral Development: Current Theory and Research,* edited by D. DePalma and J. Folley. Hillsdale, N.J.: Lawrence Erilbaum Associates, 1975b.
Staub, E. "The Development of Prosocial Behavior: Directions for Future Research and Applications to Education." Paper presented at Moral Citizenship/Education Conference, June 1976, Philadelphia.
Staub, E. *Positive Social Behavior and Morality*. New York: Academic Press, forthcoming.
Staub, E., and Feinberg, H. "Experiential Learning and Induction as Means of Developing Prosocial Conduct." Unpublished research, University of Massachusetts, Amherst, 1976a.
Staub, E., and Feinberg, H. "Positive and Negative Peer Interaction and Some of Their Correlates." Unpublished research, University of Massachusetts, Amherst, 1976b.
Staub, E., and Fotta, M. "Participation in Prosocial Behavior and Positive Induction as Means of Children Learning to be Helpful." Unpublished research, University of

Massachusetts, Amherst, 1975.
Staub, E.; Levy. R.; and Shortsleeves, J. "Teaching Others as a Means of Learning to Be Helpful." Unpublished research, University of Massachusetts, Amherst, 1974.
Weissbrod, C. "Noncontingent Warmth Induction, Cognitive Style, and Children's
Weissbrod, C. "Noncontingent Warmth Induction, Cognitive Style, and Children's Imitative Donation and Rescue Effort Behaviors." *Journal of Personality and Social Psychology* 34 (1976): 274-281.
Weissbrod, C. "The Effect of Adult Warmth and Rules on Male and Female Children's Rescue Latency." Paper presented at the Society for Research in Child Development meeting, March 1977, New Orleans.
White, G. M. "Immediate and Deferred Effects of Model Observation and Guided and Unguided Rehearsal on Donating and Stealing." *Journal of Personality and Social Psychology* 21 (1972): 139-148.
Whiting, B. B., and Whiting, J. M. W. *Children in Six Cultures: A Psychocultural Analysis*. Cambridge, Mass.: University Press, 1975.
Yarrow, M. R., and Scott, P. M. "Imitation of Nurturant and Nonnurturant Models." *Journal of Personality and Social Psychology* 23 (1972): 259-270.
Yarrow, M. R.; Scott, P. M.; and Waxler, C. Z. "Learning Concern for Others." *Developmental Psychology* 8 (1973): 240-261.

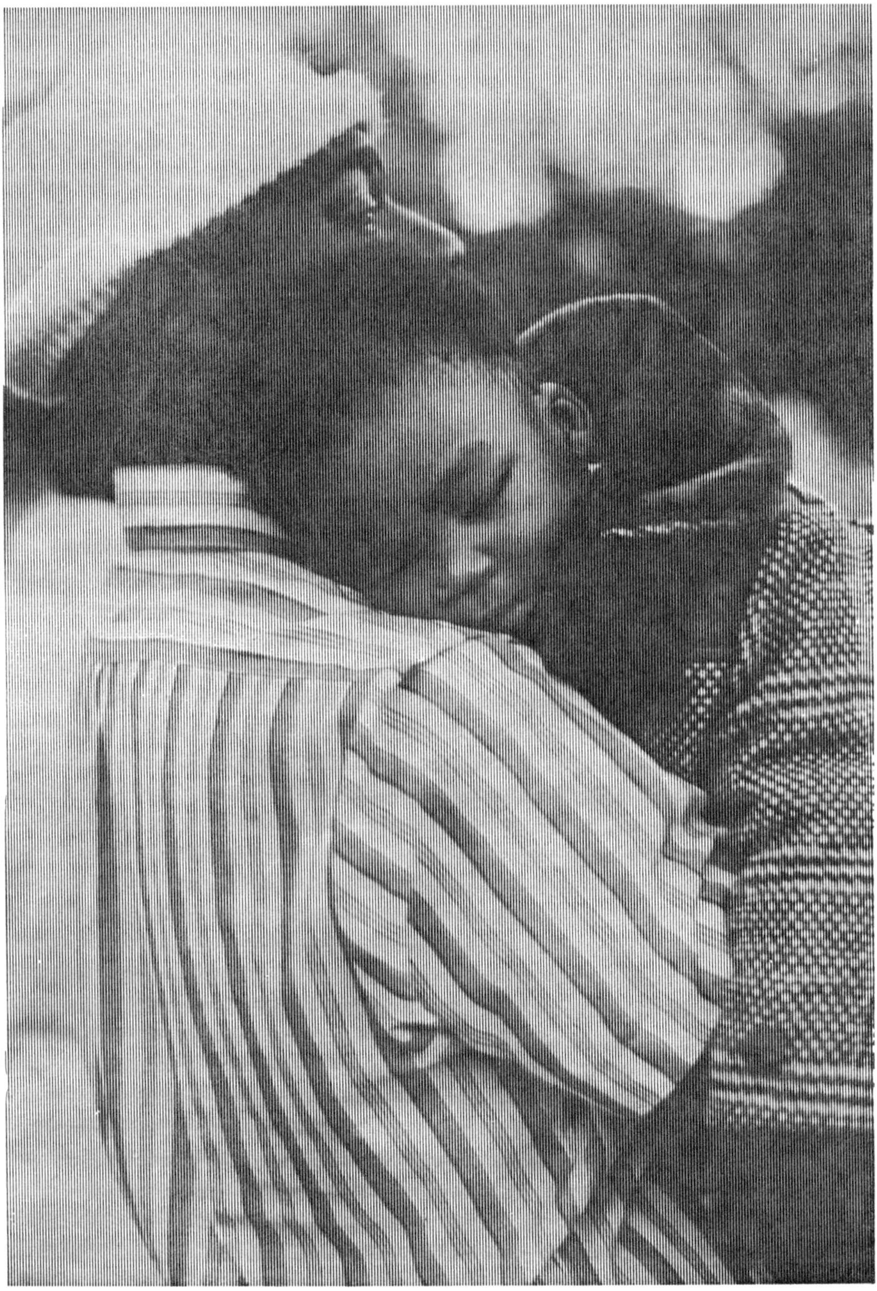

II

How Does the Father Influence Development?

Researchers can no longer ignore the father when studying young children's development in the family. Several factors have stimulated this new interest in the father's role. Political and social assaults on sex-role stereotyping; increased numbers of working mothers, especially those who are heads of households; divorced/widowed fathers rearing their children virtually alone; and changes of roles and responsibilities within the nuclear family are bringing about fundamental changes in how fathers affect children's development. The lack of substantial data about the effect of the father's presence on development is not totally due to the researcher's myopia. There are also logistical problems. Fathers are often less accessible as research subjects. They may be reluctant to participate in studies of childrearing as rearing children has been viewed as an aspect of the maternal rather than the paternal role, and as an area about which men are judged to have little expertise. Lamb reviews research which documents that the father-infant relationship during the first two years is a significant one; and that infants establish enduring relationships with fathers who exhibit responsive, sensitive behavior even though they may not devote much time to caregiving activities.

Weinraub makes a strong case that the father's impact is that of another parent. While fathers in general do not appear to be frequently available to children for caregiving, they have a significant impact on the development of children's cognitive skills, their achievement orientation, and their sex-role development. The nature of this influence is both direct and indirect and is in part moderated by the mother. Mother-father relationships have appeared to influence the quality of the interaction between the child and either parent. Young and Hamilton present an apologia on the father's role in development. Their call for a redefinition of the role of the father has a sound foundation in the research they cite and in that reviewed by Lamb and Weinraub.

Michael E. Lamb

5 The Father's Role in the Infant's Social World

A half-dozen years ago, it would have been impossible to write a review of substantive research under the above title. Until that time, developmental psychologists had been content to assume that the sole relationship enjoyed by young infants was that with their mothers. Only two studies had considered infant-father relations at all, and though their findings were revealing, little attention was paid to them (Pedersen and Robson 1969; Schaffer and Emerson 1964). Interestingly, neither group of researchers observed or interviewed fathers—both relied upon mothers as their primary sources of information!

In the 1970s, by contrast, research on father-infant relations has mushroomed. Indeed, developmental research involving fathers is currently very much in vogue. Fads are not new to social science, but they have a depressing tendency to be self-destructive, not only because they foster unreasonable expectations, but also because they often foster theoretical perspectives that are no less narrow than the "outmoded" frameworks they usurp. Ironically, then, just a few years after the first limited acknowledgement that fathers may indeed play a socially salient role in their infants' lives, I feel constrained to open with a warning that we must *add* fathers to the hypothetical infant social world, rather than *replace* mothers by fathers at the center of a new and uncomfortably unrealistic view of the infant's environment. My aim in this chapter is not to champion the role of fathers, but simply to urge that we appreciate, in our theoretical models as well as in the conduct of research, that infants may have significant relationships with their mothers *as well as with* their fathers *as well as with* siblings (where these exist). In short, I shall argue that significant progress toward understanding early socioemotional development at the very least requires us to acknowledge that infants are socialized in the context of a complex, multidimensional social system.

Demonstrating the validity of such a perspective has involved addressing two types of questions about infant behavior. Because it was (and may still be) traditionally presumed that mothers were especially, if not uniquely, significant to young infants, most of the initial studies were directed toward several basic questions:

- Whether infants were attached to their fathers at all, and if so, whether infants became attached to their mothers sooner;
- Whether they consistently preferred their mothers; and
- Whether the nature of the mother-infant relationship determined the nature and development of the father-infant bond.

All major theories of sociopersonality development (the social learning, the psychoanalytic, and the ethological) implicitly or explicitly propose that the answers to all these questions would assuredly be affirmative—that is, if infants had relationships with their fathers at all (Ainsworth 1969; Gewirtz 1972; Maccoby and Masters 1970). Their many differences notwithstanding, the major theorists all appear to approve of Freud's (1948) famous dictum that "the mother-infant relationship is unique, without parallel, established unalterably as the prototype of all later love relations" (p. 45).

The second major issue concerns the types of relationships infants have with their mothers and fathers. As far as personality development is concerned, the major issue is probably not *whether* a relationship exists, but *what type* of relationship it is—with what types of (formative) experiences does the relationship provide the young infant. In the long run, then, the significance of fathers relative to mothers can be determined not simply by demonstrating that infants have relationships with both parents, but by clarifying the salient characteristics of the mother-infant and father-infant relationships, thereby identifying the formative roles that mothers and fathers play in the lives of their infants.

Parental Attachments and Preferences

The earliest studies of paternal attachment provided us with provocative (indeed surprising) results, although certain methodological and conceptual confounds made researchers wary in their interpretations and conclusions. The first investigation of father-infant relations was reported in 1964 by two Scottish researchers, Schaffer and Emerson. To their great surprise, they found that most of the infant subjects were attached to both their mothers and fathers by nine months of age, and by eighteen months, 80 percent of the infants were attached to both parents; only 50 percent showed preferences for their mothers. Internal analyses further revealed that infants commonly became attached to individuals who played no role in their physical care.

This confirmed the findings of some experimental research involving rhesus monkeys from which Harlow (1961; Harlow and Zimmerman 1959) concluded that the provision of physiological gratification (e.g., feeding) played an insignificant role in the process of mother-infant bonding. The results of research involving both humans and monkeys, then, called into question the drive reduction notions which underlay the presumption of maternal preeminence (Ainsworth 1969; Dollard and Miller 1950). Unfortunately, however, we may not have learned a great deal about father-infant attachments from Schaffer and Emerson since their sole measure of attachment was the reported probability that the baby would cry or protest in response to brief everyday separations from specific individuals, and as we shall note presently, this is not a very sensitive measure of attachment (Cohen and Campos 1974; Lamb 1975). In addition, all the data were derived from *maternal* reports, which may not be a reliable source of information concerning parent-infant (especially *father*-infant) relations.

Pedersen and Robson (1969) also obtained information exclusively from maternal interviews. Their focus was somewhat different, though, for they sought information only about the infants' responses to their fathers, and they focused mainly on reunion or greeting responses. Clearly, most infants were delighted to see their fathers— they were said to greet them warmly. Interpretation of this finding is difficult, however, because in the absence of reliable comparisons with the infants' style of greeting their mothers, babysitters, or strangers, it is not possible to say much about the relative importance or salience of fathers.

The first observational study of father-infant relations was reported by Kotelchuck in 1972. In subsequent years, Kotelchuck has reported on several similar studies, all of which have been conducted as experiments involving a series of separations from and reunions with the child's mother, father, and a stranger. The primary measures of attachment have been indexes of separation protest (crying, disruption of play), and tabulations of the frequency of interactive behaviors such as smiling. One consistent finding emerges from Kotelchuck's research: Twelve- to twenty-one-month-old children show no preference for either parent, whether observed at home or in unfamiliar laboratory sessions (Kotelchuck 1972, 1976; Kotelchuck, Zelazo, Kagan, and Spelke 1975; Ross, Kagan, Zelazo, and Kotelchuck 1975; Spelke, Zelazo, Kagan, and Kotelchuck 1973).

Because these findings were not predicted by any of the major social-developmental theories, they were accorded great attention by both professionals and laypersons. Unfortunately, however, the results of these studies are less convincing than they might have been had Kotelchuck and his colleagues chosen different measures of attachment. Several studies, as well as recent theoretical discussions, have shown that behaviors such as smiling occur frequently in interaction with persons to whom infants are clearly not attached (Lamb 1976b, 1977c). Furthermore, the frequency with which they occur in interaction with any individual appears to be a function of the relative sociability or activity of the interactive partner (Lamb 1976e, 1977c). In other words, tabulating the occurrence of these affiliative behaviors may tell us little (if anything) about infants' enduring preferences or affective relationships. Consequently, conclusions based on such measures are equivocal.

The results of a study conducted by Cohen and Campos (1974) lead us to question the separation protest measure as well. In a somewhat stressful procedure involving disruptions of the infants' behavior every minute, Cohen and Campos (1974) found that several measures of proximity-seeking showed preferences for mothers over fathers, whereas separation protest did not. Likewise, Stayton, Ainsworth, and Main (1973), in a study of mother-infant relations, found separation protest to be an insensitive measure of whether infants were attached to particular persons or not. While there is reason to question the measures used in the studies conducted by Kotelchuck and Schaffer, it is significant to note that all the studies performed by Kotelchuck and his colleagues support Kotelchuck's initial conclusion that infants are clearly attached to both parents. Even Cohen and Campos (1974), who found children's preferences for mothers over fathers, found clear preferences for fathers over unfamiliar individuals.

Besides the measurement difficulties, another problem prevented researchers from reaching definitive conclusions regarding the onset of parental attachments from the results of these studies. This was the failure or inability of researchers to obtain useful information in laboratory settings from infants under ten months of age (the age of Cohen and Campos's youngest subjects). Since most researchers and theorists agree that infants form their first attachment relationships around seven months of age, we knew nothing until 1975 about father-infant relations in the first three months following the onset of this discriminant attachment phase of social development. Consequently, as recently as 1975, it was impossible to state whether mother-infant relationships indeed formed earlier than father-infant bonds (as most theories predict), or whether infants showed initial preferences for their mothers—preferences which subsequently disappeared (which would be compatible with the data).

Kotelchuck (1972) had, in fact, attempted to study six- and nine-month-old children, but had found both his experimental procedure and his separation protest indexes to be inappropriate for such young infants. Consequently, my major study in this area involved observations of infants in naturalistic home settings, rather than in artificially-structured laboratory experiments. Because of the measurement problems alluded to earlier, I recorded the incidence of infant affiliative (e.g., wanting to be held by or fussing to a person) behaviors, as well as separation- and reunion-related behavior. To learn something of the earliest phases of mother-infant and father-infant attachment, the infants were observed in their homes from seven months of age. All observations took place at times when both parents were present; each lasted one-and-a-half to two hours. As in all the studies we have described, the infants came from intact, traditional, White families. Unlike most studies, however, a wide range of social class backgrounds was represented.

Despite the fact that we recorded a number of measures (the attachment behavior indexes) that should have revealed preferences had they existed, our conclusions were remarkably similar to Kotelchuck's. From the time infants were first able to form relationships through thirteen months of age, they were attached to both parents and showed no consistent preference for either parent over the other (Lamb 1976b, 1977e). The same conclusion was supported even when we controlled statistically for the relative activity or salience of the parents in the immediate situation (Lamb 1977e). Analysis of the infants' responses to brief, naturally-occurring separations and reunions, meanwhile, also showed no preference for either parent (Lamb 1975). Because most of our criterial measures had demonstrable validity, inasmuch as they showed clear preferences for both parents over a relatively unfamiliar female stranger, our data strongly suggested that seven- to thirteen-month-olds were attached to both their mothers and their fathers. In the stress-free and undisturbed home environment, furthermore, there was no indication that either parent could be described as a primary or preferred attachment figure.

Another research grant made it possible to study 14 of the original 20 infants as well as 6 additional subjects for another year—that is, until they reached their second birthdays. The procedure and the measures were similar, and the analyses were again revealing. Across the second year of life, we found significant preferences for the *fathers* in the display of attachment behaviors (Lamb 1977b). These preferences remained significant even after we took the relative activity of the adults into account by way of covariant analyses.

Internal analyses revealed that these preferences only occurred among the boys, most of whom came to demonstrate preferences for their fathers over the course of the year. In fact, by the end of the second year, all but one of the boys in the sample were showing consistent preferences for their fathers over their mothers on our attachment behavior measures (Lamb 1977c). The girls, by contrast, were much less consistent—some preferred their mothers, some their fathers, and some neither parent.

What accounted for these dramatic preferences on the part of the boys? One possible reason immediately came to mind: Perhaps the fathers were making themselves especially attractive to their sons, and the infants were simply responding to the relative salience of their parents. This may indeed have been the case, for we found that fathers were twice as active in interaction with sons as were mothers, and half as active in interaction with daughters as with sons (Lamb 1977b,c). Thus it seemed that the parents were behaving in such a way as to maximize the salience of the same-sex parent in the infant's life, and that the sex-differentiating behavior of the fathers was most significant.

There is some reason to believe that this early "channeling" may play an important role in the establishment of gender identity in male children. Money and Ehrhardt (1972) have argued convincingly on the basis of extensive clinical evidence that gender identity must be established within the first two to three years of the child's life if adjustment difficulties are to be avoided. Most studies have found that boys whose fathers are absent during the first few years of their lives are far more likely to have gender role and gender identity problems than boys whose fathers are absent later (Biller 1971, 1974; Hetherington and Deur 1971). Several studies (mostly involving interviews) have also concluded that fathers are more concerned than mothers about the establishment of sex-appropriate behavior in their children—especially their sons—and that sex-stereotyping begins earlier and with greater intensity among boys (Bronfenbrenner 1961; Brown 1956, 1957, 1958; Cava and Rausch 1952; Goodenough 1957). Clearly, then, there is every reason to believe that fathers may be playing an especially important role in the personality development of their children (particularly sons) from early in the first years of the children's lives.

Viewed together, the data I have presented in this section strongly suggest that:

- Infants become attached to their mothers and fathers at about the same time;
- They do not show the predicted preferences for their mothers during the first year; and
- Male infants generally develop preferences for their fathers in the second year of life.

Needless to say, none of these findings was predicted by any of the traditional theories of social development. Indisputably, however, the weight of the evidence left little doubt that infants had significant relationships with their fathers as well as with their mothers. Clearly, one might argue, if contemporary theorists are to give an adequate and veridical account of the determinants and course of sociopersonality development in infancy, it is surely necessary that they acknowledge the multidimensionality of the infant's social world. Or is it?

The Characteristics of Parent-Infant Relationships

The immediate response to my findings concerning parent-infant attachment in the first year and to the results of Kotelchuck's experimental investigations of older infants was more cautious than the conclusion to the preceding section might suggest. Theorists such as Ainsworth (personal communication) argued that whereas infants might indeed have relationships with their fathers as well as with their mothers, the father-infant relationships were insignificant and essentially redundant. In other words, the mother-infant bond was viewed as critically formative—its absence could be devastating. By contrast, the father-infant attachment could be present or absent without having any major consequences for the child's development.

My analyses of the types of interaction that took place between fathers and infants and between mothers and infants, consequently, appear especially relevant, for in these analyses I aimed to determine whether the mother-infant and father-infant relationships involved different types of experiences for the infants. Evidence that they did would indicate that the father-infant relationship was not redundant, that it embodied characteristic types of interaction. This would mean that mothers and fathers provided different experiences for their infants, and hence that they made differentiable contributions to their children's development.

The analyses of play and physical contact interaction confirmed that the mother-infant and father-infant relationships involved different types of interaction (Lamb 1976b, 1977e). As indicated in Figures 1 and 2, fathers were more likely to engage their infants in physically stimulating and unpredictable or idiosyncratic types of play. The mothers, meanwhile, were more likely to initiate conventional games (like peek-a-boo and pat-a-cake) and toy-mediated play. Some of these differences were fairly consistent across time; unfortunately, our predetermined categories proved inadequate for describing the more complex forms of play that became increasingly common toward the end of the first year of life.

While one might regard the findings of our play interaction analyses as somewhat equivocal, there can be little question about the robustness of our findings concerning physical contact or holding. The mothers, we found, were far more likely to pick up their babies for caretaker purposes or to move them away from forbidden activities than were the fathers. Fathers most often held their infants to play with them, or because the infants simply wanted to be held. The differences are evident in Figures 3 and 4.

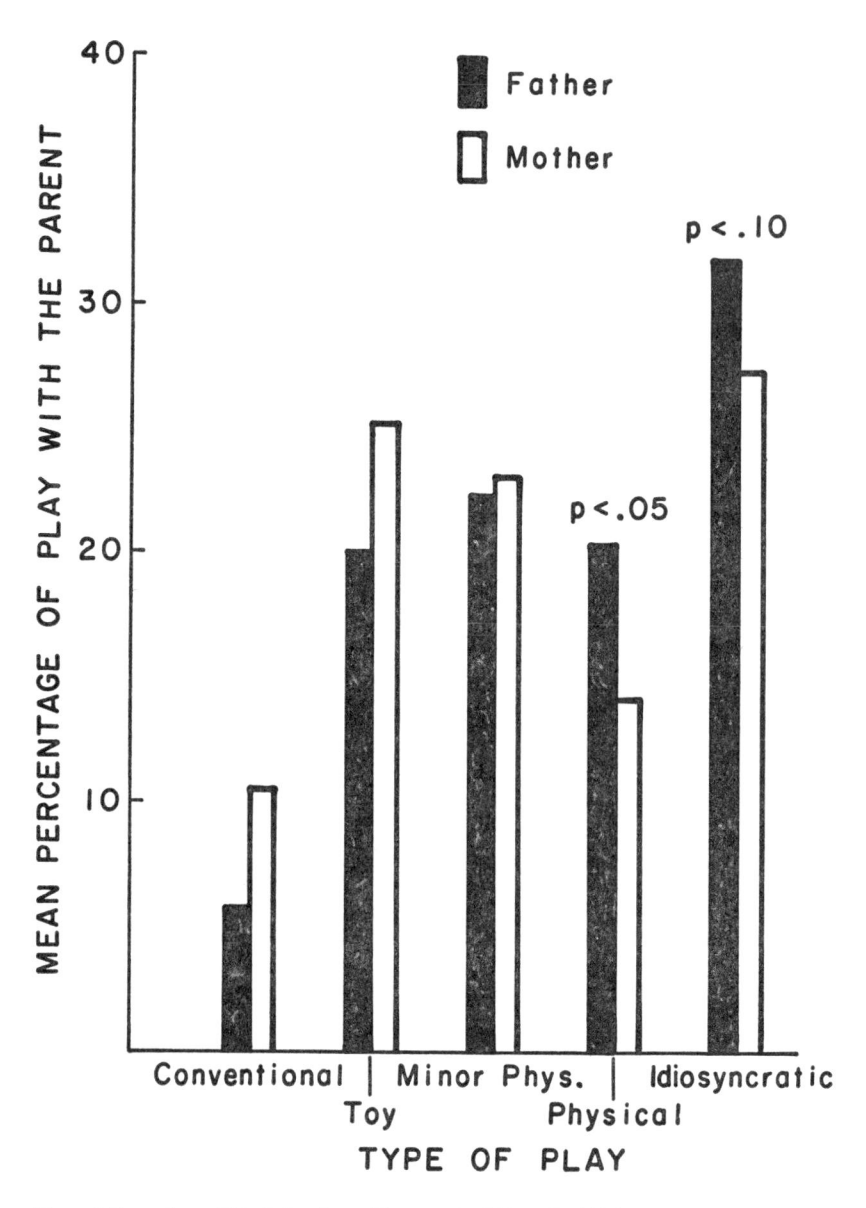

Figure 1. Types of parent-infant play observed in seven- to eight-month-old infants. Reprinted with permission from Lamb, M. E., ed., *The Role of the Father in Child Development.* Copyright© John Wiley & Sons, New York, 1976.

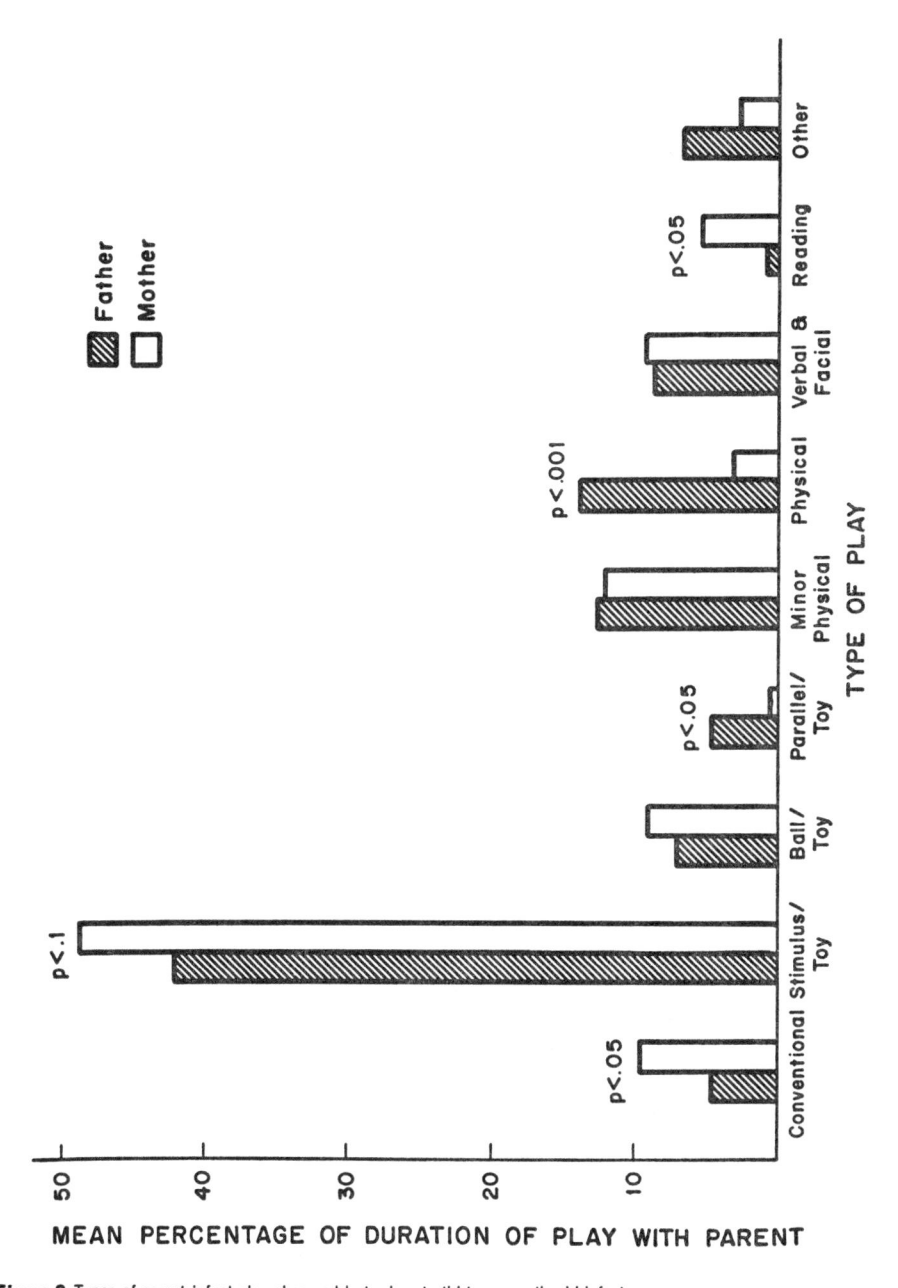

Figure 2. Types of parent-infant play observed in twelve- to thirteen-month-old infants.

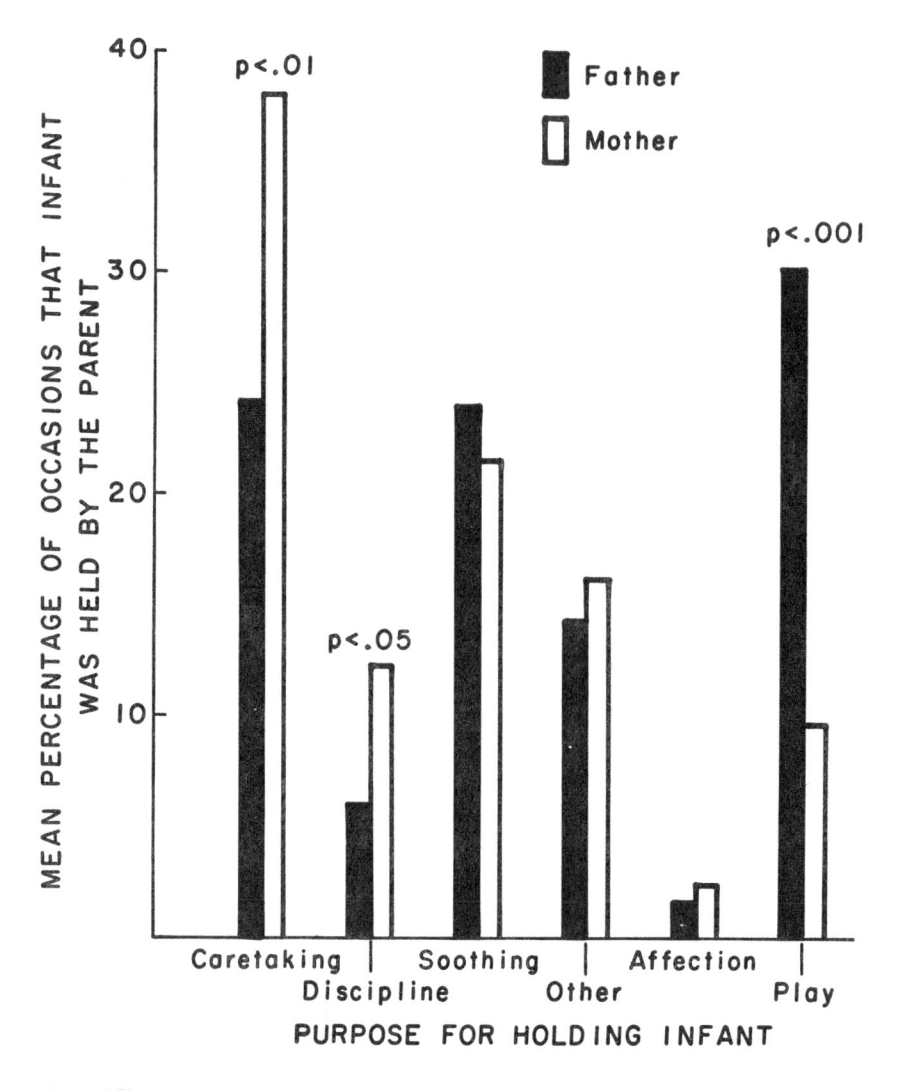

Figure 3. The reason why mothers and fathers picked up their infants at seven to eight months of age. Reprinted with permission from Lamb, M. E., ed., *The Role of the Father in Child Development.* Copyright© John Wiley & Sons, New York, 1976.

The Father's Role

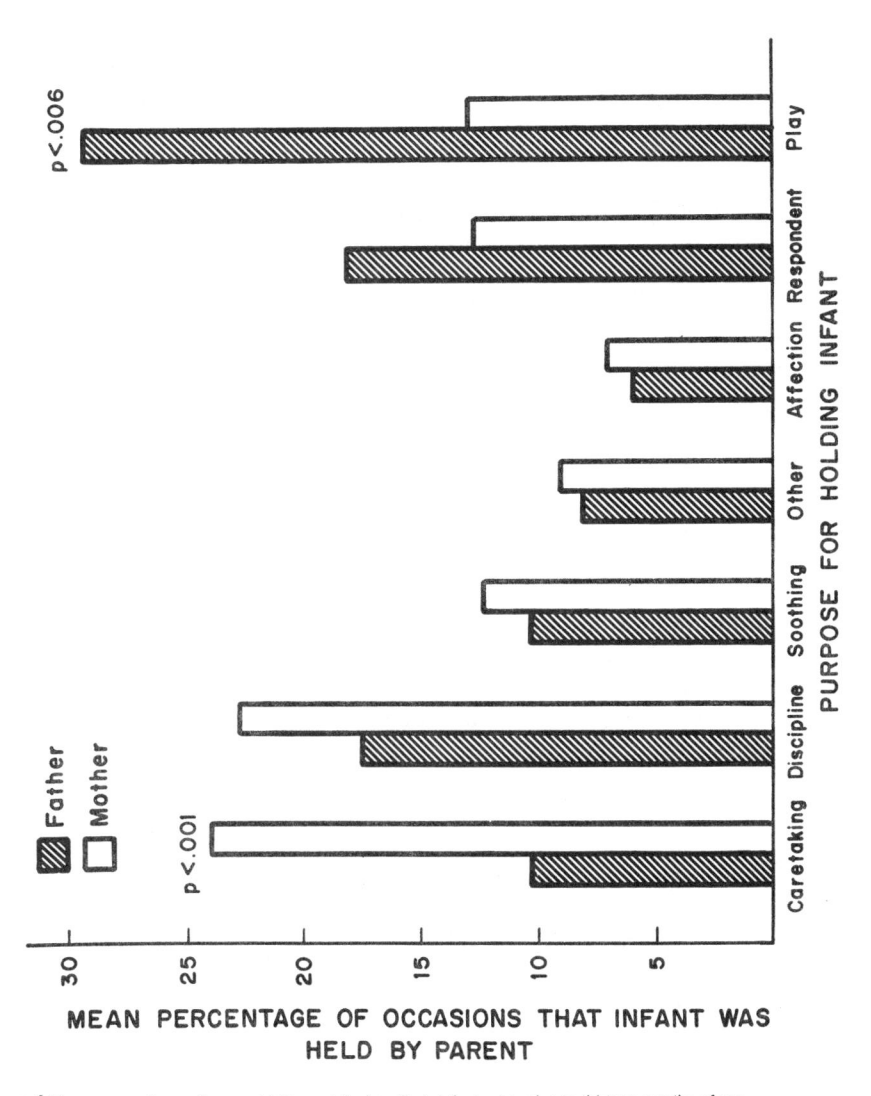

Figure 4. The reason why mothers and fathers picked up their infants at twelve to thirteen months of age.

The specific differences we found are clearly related to the sex roles and occupational roles (i.e., caretaker, breadwinner) of the parents; presumably, some would not have been evident had the fathers, say, been primary caretakers, while their wives worked. Nevertheless, there is clear evidence that within traditional nuclear families, the mother-infant and father-infant relationships are not only salient, but they are also *qualitatively different.* More recently, Yogman (1977; Yogman, Dixon, Tronick, Adamson, Als, and Brazelton 1976) has suggested that these qualitative differences may emerge in the first few months of the infant's life. Both Yogman's and my own findings underline the need for researchers and theorists to consider the significance of both mother-infant and father-infant relationships in their formulations.

In the course of the longitudinal study described earlier in this chapter (Lamb 1976b, 1977b, e), I explored Freud's proposal (one that has been adopted implicitly by subsequent theorists) that the mother-infant relationship serves as "the prototype for all later love relations" (Freud 1948, p.45). Contrary to this hypothesis, time-lagged correlational analyses gave no indication that the mother-infant relationship in any way determined the course of development of the father-infant relationship (Lamb 1975).

Actually, the analyses conducted in that first study were neither appropriate nor convincing since frequency counts of the occurrence of attachment behaviors are unsuitable indexes of the qualitative or temporally consistent aspects of either the mother-infant or father-infant relationships. We attempted to explore the proposition more thoroughly in a later study in which we used a procedure known as the "strange situation." This procedure was developed by Ainsworth (Ainsworth and Bell 1970; Ainsworth and Wittig 1969) in order to permit the assessment of the quality of mother-infant attachment and has been employed extensively by Ainsworth and her colleagues (Ainsworth, Blehar, Waters, and Wall, forthcoming). Despite the more sensitive and appropriate measures, this later study, too, yielded no support for the notion that the character of the mother-infant relation in any way predicted or determined the quality or character of the father-infant relationship (Lamb 1978c).

Although findings of "no evidence" are always difficult to interpret definitively, we can at least say that there is more reason to believe that the mother-infant and father-infant relationships develop independently than to suggest that the development of the father-infant relationship is predicated upon the nature and extent of an earlier mother-infant bond.

The Effects of Stress on Infant Parental Preferences

Having established that infants are indeed attached to both their parents from the time they are first able to form relationships, we shall return now to the question of infant preferences. You may recall that during home observations, seven- to thirteen-month-old infants showed no preference for either parent. During the second year of life, most boys showed preferences for their fathers while daughters, on the whole, showed no preference for either parent. From the perspective of ethological attachment theory, there is one problem with these estimates of preference—they are based solely upon observations of infants in stress-free situations. Attachment theorists such as Bowlby (1969) and Ainsworth (1972; Ainsworth et al. forthcoming) argue that "true" preferences may be obscured in such settings because the babies feel sufficiently secure to interact generally. When they are distressed, however, infants should reduce the amount of interaction they have with nonattachment figures and subsidiary/secondary (i.e., nonpreferred) attachment figures, while increasing the display of attachment behavior toward their primary attachment figures. These two tendencies should serve to accentuate any relative preferences that may not be evident in stress-free circumstances.

In order to investigate the effects of stress on infant preferences, we observed the infant subjects of our longitudinal study in laboratory settings when they were eight, twelve, and eighteen months of age (Lamb 1976a,d,f). Another sample of twenty-four-month-olds had been observed previously in an even more stressful procedure (Lamb 1976c). These experiments involved observation of the infants in increasingly stressful circumstances, and our findings were convincingly clear. In stress-free episodes in the laboratory, the infants either showed no preferences for either parent, or slight preferences for their fathers. When moderately distressed, the infants increased the display of attachment behavior to the available parent regardless of whether mother or father was present. When both parents were available, however, twelve- and eighteen-month-old infants sought comfort from their mothers preferentially (Lamb 1976a,f). Interestingly, eight- and twenty-four-month-old children did not show preferences for their mothers, even when the children were distressed (Lamb 1976c,d). Notwithstanding the findings of our home observations, therefore, there was unambiguous evidence that mothers were the primary attachment figures of infants at least over a relatively narrow period during the second year of life.

These findings concerning the effects of stress on infant preferences allow us to make our findings compatible with the major theories of social development (which predict that infants will show preferences for their primary caretakers), and also permit us to explain a number of apparent inconsistencies that have emerged among the results of several recent investigations of infant parental preferences (Feldman and Ingham 1975; Lamb 1976a,f; Willemsen, Flaherty, Heaton, and Ritchie 1974). Most of the "inconsistencies" disappear when one takes into account the stressfulness of the situation, and the social ecology—that is, whether the infant was able to choose between the two parents in the test situation instead of being observed with one parent at a time.

The Determinants of Attachment

Thus far, we have been concerned with determining—

- Whether infants form attachments to both their parents;
- What types of relationships they form; and
- Whether young infants show preferences for either parent.

Now I want to give explicit consideration to the question: What determines whether or not an infant will become attached to the father? As one might expect, the same things that account for the development of mother-infant attachments appear to be involved in the development of father-infant attachments.

First, contrary to the predictions of psychoanalysts like Freud (Mächtlinger 1976) and drive-reduction learning theorists like Dollard and Miller (1950), extensive involvement in the physical care of the baby does not seem to be necessary. The limitations of their data-gathering procedures notwithstanding, Schaffer and Emerson (1964) found that many of their infant subjects formed attachments to adults (not only fathers, but also grandparents, relatives, etc.) who played no role whatsoever in their care. In addition, many of the fathers involved in my longitudinal study seldom assumed responsibility for the infants' care, especially during the first year.

Second, there is general agreement that beyond some undetermined threshold level, the sheer amount of time that a parent and his/her infant spend together is also a poor predictor of whether or not a relationship will be formed (Feldman 1973, 1974; Pedersen and Robson 1969; Schaffer and Emerson 1964). Thus infants enrolled in day care may form attachments to their mothers that are indistinguishable from those formed between home-reared infants and their mothers (Doyle 1975; Doyle and Somers 1975; Feldman 1973; Ragozin 1975; Ricciuti and Poresky 1973; but see Blehar 1974). It is the *quality* of the interaction when parent and infant are together that seems to be most important. Specifically, parents who respond contingently and appropriately to the infant's signals or initiatives and who initiate interaction that is appropriate given the baby's current state, needs, and abilities are most likely to facilitate the development of secure parent-infant attachments (Ainsworth, Bell, and Stayton 1971, 1972, 1974; Schaffer and Emerson 1964). Parke's sensitive observations of mothers, fathers, and infants in the neonatal period and in the first months of the infants' lives indicate that most fathers are keen to interact with their infants, and that they do so affectionately, sensitively, and competently (Parke and O'Leary 1975; Parke and Sawin 1976, 1977).

Infants, then, become attached not simply to those who interact a great deal with them, but to those who interact with them in a sensitive manner. Although involvement in the infant's physical care is not necessary for the development of an infant-adult attachment, caring for an infant may be one way in which parents learn about infants and develop sensitivity to them. It is especially likely that fathers who have had little experience with infants during their own childhood and adolescence may develop sensitivity to infants most easily through interacting with and caring for one. Parenthetically we might note that on psychophysiological and observational measures, the mothers and fathers of young infants are equivalently sensitive to infant signals (Frodi, Lamb, Leavitt, and Donovan 1978; Parke and Sawin 1976, 1977). We do not yet know to what extent experience with infants (e.g., parenthood, babysitting) is necessary for this sensitivity to develop, nor whether there is a sex difference in this regard.

Following Spelke et al.'s (1973) finding that protest at separation from fathers was more likely to occur when the fathers had been involved in caretaking, Kotelchuck (1975; Zelazo, Kotelchuck, Barber, and David 1977) conducted two experimental "intervention" studies aimed at determining whether it was possible to facilitate father-infant bonding by encouraging fathers to take a greater role in the care of and in interaction with their infants. Both studies yielded the same result: After the intervention period, babies who were initially unfazed by separation from their fathers began to respond with distress when their fathers left them. It is impossible, of course, to say what played the critical role in these cases: It might have been involvement in caretaking, increased sensitivity, or simply the greater amount of time spent by father and baby in interaction with one another. For practical purposes one could argue that it does not really matter as these three things are likely to occur together.

"Second Order" or Indirect Effects

As theorists have come to appreciate that the infant's social world is a complex multidimensional system, they have come to emphasize that any member of the child's social network can influence the child either directly (i.e., through interaction) or indirectly (i.e., via the member's effect on other individuals who interact with the child). Thus, fathers may influence their children through their direct interactions with them, or they may affect their wives' attitudes or parenting styles which in turn influence the infant (Bronfenbrenner 1976; Lewis and Feiring, forthcoming; Lewis and Weinraub 1976).

One area in which indirect effects may be important, for example, is in the interpretation of research on the effects of father-absence (Herzog and Sudia 1973). Initially, most theorists assumed that children raised without fathers were adversely affected because they were deprived of a major role model and disciplinary agent (Biller 1971). While these factors may indeed be important, any effect they have is surely supplemented by the emotional and economic strains under which the estranged wives and their children must live (Herzog and Sudia 1973). Herzog and Sudia (1973) and Lewis and Weinraub (1976) have gone so far as to argue that *most* of the influence fathers have on their children is indirectly mediated.

The bulk of the experimental research on second-order effects has been directed toward understanding how the presence of one parent/spouse influences the interaction between the infant and the other parent. We have already discussed how this parameter influences the behavior of infants who are distressed: Recall that distressed twelve- and eighteen-month-old children show preferences for their mothers when both parents are available whereas when either parent alone is present, they organize their attachment behavior indistinguishably around their mothers and fathers (Lamb 1976a,f).

When infants are not distressed, the transformation of a dyadic (parent and infant) into a triadic (both parents and infant) situation consistently results in reduced levels of interaction between the two persons who were part of the initial dyad (Lamb 1976a, 1977a,b,d, 1978a,b). The same thing happens, incidentally, when a child joins the parents (Rosenblatt 1974) or when any family member joins a group of confamilials (Cleaves and Rosenblatt 1977). The reason appears to be simple: Each person has alternative social partners in the larger group, and each will tend to distribute attention among available interactants. At least two factors influence the baby's behavior: (a) the tendency to interact with both mother and father when the two are available, rather than with one of them exclusively, and (b) the reduced social salience of each parent (i.e., they are interacting with one another as well as with the infant which means that each elicits or initiates less interaction with the baby). Interestingly, there is no correlation between the social activity of parents and one-year-olds in these situations, suggesting that one-year-olds are insensitive to social cues. Their behavior seems to be influenced solely by the number of parents available for interaction (Lamb 1977a, 1978a). By contrast, eighteen- and twenty-four-month-old infants are affected by both of these social cues (Lamb 1976a, 1977b).

Most of the relevant studies have shown that the father's (mother's) presence indeed influences the mother-infant (father-infant) interaction. Thus far, however, all studies show effects only on the absolute amounts of interaction; the types of interaction that occur are similar (Lamb 1977d). If we wished to compare the relative activity of mothers and fathers in interaction with their children, therefore, it would be important to ensure that the behavior of each was observed in a similar social setting. On the other hand, if we were interested in determining what kinds of interactional experiences mothers and fathers provide for their infants, it may not be so important to pay attention to the context. Actually, at this stage, we should probably add a cautionary qualifier to this statement. There may be subtle effects on the types of interaction which are not being reflected on the gross measures we employ. Only fine-grained research will indicate whether and under what circumstances second-order effects are important considerations when we are interpreting research on father-infant relationships.

Alternative ways of viewing indirect effects are exemplified by the research of Pedersen (1975; Pedersen, Anderson, and Cain 1977) and Clarke-Stewart (1977). Pedersen and his colleagues collected attitudinal information from the parents by interview, observed them interacting with their babies, and assessed the neonates' behavioral performance on the Brazelton (1973) scale. They then computed correlations among the many variables. They have reported some interesting relations between neonatal characteristics and paternal (or maternal) attitudes which are in turn correlated with indexes of the other parents' interactional style. These findings suggest that indirect effects may be important, but a coherent overall pattern has not emerged from the data analyzed thus far. Clarke-Stewart (1977), meanwhile, reported that any significant impact of fathers on the competence of their infants was mediated via their wives—that is, the influence was wholly indirect. This is certainly a provocative finding, although Clarke-Stewart's use of statistical procedures that are not really appropriate for small samples (only 14 babies were studied) and the probability that some "findings" may emerge spuriously when a large number of computations are performed lead me to caution that further details regarding Clarke-Stewart's analyses must be presented before her conclusions can be evaluated. As always, the best way to lend credence to unexpected findings is to replicate them with a new sample.

Conclusion

Happily, all the findings we have reviewed in this chapter can be interpreted in such a way that they extend the major theories rather than usurp them. It is clear that the infant's primary caretaker—the mother in the "traditional," largely middle-class, White families with which we have been concerned—becomes the most affectively salient person in the infant's life, and must surely play an important role in shaping the child's personality. This does not mean, however, that the child's mother is uniquely or solely important; from the time infants are first able to form relationships, most appear to be attached to both their mothers and their fathers. The two parent-infant relationships, furthermore, are qualitatively different—they involve different types of experiences for the infant. Neither relationship, then, is redundant: Both may make independent and important contributions to the sociopersonality development of the child. This implies that we need to take both into account when discussing the nature of social development in infancy.

At this stage, we know little about the long-term implications of the father-infant and mother-infant attachments. There is suggestive circumstantial evidence that the father-infant relationship may be especially important for the first stages of psychosexual development. As we noted earlier, gender identity is typically established in the first few years of life. Fathers appear to play a particularly important role in shaping the sex-stereotyped behavior of their sons and establishing themselves as salient models in the eyes of their children. This intriguing finding notwithstanding, it is clear that further research is needed to clarify the process of gender identity adoption in girls, and, more generally, to explore the association between the quality and characteristics of parent-infant relationships and the child's later personality.

Thus far, developmental psychologists have been dismally unsuccessful in their attempts to understand the role of early experiences in psychosocial development (Caldwell 1964). The absence of demonstrable associations between early experiences and later personality may indicate not that parent-infant relationships are formatively insignificant, but that researchers have clung to a narrowly unrealistic conception of the breadth of the infant's social world, and so have failed to represent early experiences realistically. When formulating propositions concerning early experience-outcome associations, therefore, future researchers will have to acknowledge not only that there are a number of significant individuals in the infant's environment whose influence must be considered, but also that each of these may affect the infant directly as well as indirectly—via relationships with one another

(Pedersen 1977). Only when we come to appreciate the multidimensionality and complexity of the infant's social world are we likely to advance our understanding of the determinants of infant personality development (Lamb 1977f).

References

Ainsworth, M. D. S. "Attachment and Dependency: A Comparison." In *Attachment and Dependency*, edited by J. L. Gewirtz. Washington, D.C.: Winston, 1972.

Ainsworth, M. D. S. "Object Relations, Dependency, and Attachment: A Theoretical Review of the Infant-Mother Relationship." *Child Development* 40 (1969): 969-1025.

Ainsworth, M. D. S., and Bell, S. M. "Attachment, Exploration, and Separation: Illustrated by the Behavior of One-Year-Olds in a Strange Situation." *Child Development* 41 (1970): 49-67.

Ainsworth, M. D. S.; Bell, S. M.; and Stayton, D. J. "Individual Differences in the Development of Some Attachment Behaviors." *Merrill-Palmer Quarterly* 18 (1972): 123-145.

Ainsworth, M. D. S.; Bell, S. M.; and Stayton, D. J. "Individual Differences in Strange Situation Behavior of One-Year-Olds." In *The Origins of Human Social Relations*, edited by H. R. Schaffer. London: Academic Press, 1971.

Ainsworth, M. D. S.; Bell, S. M.; and Stayton, D. J. "Infant Mother Attachment and Social Development: Socialization as a Product of Reciprocal Responsiveness to Signals." In *The Integration of a Child into a Social World*, edited by M. P. M. Richards. New York: Cambridge University Press, 1974.

Ainsworth, M. D. S.; Blehar, M. C.; Waters, E. C.; and Wall, S. N. *The Strange Situation*. Hillsdale, N.J.: Lawrence Erlbaum Associates, forthcoming.

Ainsworth, M. D. S., and Wittig, B. A. "Attachment and Exploratory Behavior of One-Year-Olds in a Strange Situation." In *Determinants of Infant Behavior*, vol. IV, edited by B. M. Foss. London: Methuen, 1969.

Biller, H. B. *Father, Child, and Sex Role*. Lexington, Mass.: D. C. Heath, 1971.

Biller, H. B. *Paternal Deprivation: Family, School, Sexuality and Society*. Lexington, Mass.: D. C. Heath, 1974.

Blehar, M. C. "Anxious Attachment and Defensive Reactions Associated with Day Care." *Child Development* 45 (1974): 683-692.

Bowlby, J. *Attachment*. Attachment and Loss, vol. I. New York: Basic Books, 1969.

Brazelton, T. B. *Neonatal Behavioral Assessment Scale*. Philadelphia: J. B. Lippincott, 1973.

Bronfenbrenner, U. "The Changing American Child—A Speculative Analysis." *Journal of Social Issues* 17 (1961): 6-18.

Bronfenbrenner, U. "The Experimental Ecology of Education." *Educational Researcher* 5 (1976): 5-15.

Brown, D. C. "Masculinity-Femininity Development in Children." *Journal of Consulting Psychology* 21 (1957): 197-203.

Brown, D. G. "Sex Role Development in a Changing Culture." *Psychological Bulletin* 55 (1958): 232-242.

Brown, D. G. "Sex Role Preference in Young Children." *Psychological Monographs* 70 (1956): 1-19.

Caldwell, B. M. "The Effects of Infant Care." In *Review of Child Development Research,* vol. I, edited by M.L. Hoffman and L.W. Hoffman. New York: Russell Sage, 1964.

Cava, E. L., and Rausch, H. L. "Identification and the Adolescent Boy's Perception of His Father." *Journal of Abnormal and Social Psychology* 47 (1952): 855-856.

Clarke-Stewart, K. A. "The Father's Impact on Mother and Child." Paper presented at the Society for Research in Child Development meeting, New Orleans, March 1977.

Cleaves, W. T., and Rosenblatt, P. C. "Intimacy Between Adults and Children in Public Places." Paper presented at the Society for Research in Child Development meeting, New Orleans, March 1977.

Cohen, L. J., and Campos, J. J. "Father, Mother, and Stranger as Elicitors of Attachment Behaviors in Infancy." *Developmental Psychology* 10 (1974): 146-154.

Dollard, J., and Miller, N. E. *Personality and Psychotherapy.* New York: McGraw-Hill, 1950.

Doyle, A. B. "Infant Development in Day Care." *Developmental Psychology* 11 (1975): 655-656.

Doyle, A. B., and Somers, K. "The Effect of Group and Individual Day Care on Infant Development." Paper presented at the Canadian Psychological Association meeting, Quebec, June 1975.

Feldman, S. S. "The Impact of Day Care on One Aspect of Children's Social-Emotional Behavior." Paper presented at the American Association for the Advancement of Science meeting, San Francisco, February 1974.

Feldman, S. S. "Some Possible Antecedents of Attachment Behavior in Two-Year-Old Children." Unpublished manuscript, Stanford University, 1973.

Feldman, S. S., and Ingham, M. E. "Attachment Behavior: A Validation Study in Two Age Groups." *Child Development* 46 (1975): 319-332.

Freud, S. *An Outline of Psychoanalysis.* New York: W.W. Norton, 1948.

Frodi, A. M.; Lamb, M. E.; Leavitt, L. A.; and Donovan, W. L. "Fathers' and Mothers' Responses to Infant Smiles and Cries." *Infant Behavior and Development* 1 (1978): in press.

Gewirtz, J. L., ed. *Attachment and Dependency.* Washington, D.C.: Winston, 1972.

Goodenough, E. W. "Interest in Persons as an Aspect of Sex Differences in the Early Years." *Genetic Psychology Monographs* 55 (1957): 287-323.

Harlow, H. F. "The Development of Affectional Patterns in Infant Monkeys." In *Determinants of Infant Behavior,* vol. I, edited by B. M. Foss. London: Methuen, 1961.

Harlow, H. F., and Zimmerman, R. R. "Affectional Responses in the Infant Monkey." *Science* 130 (1959): 42.

Herzog, E., and Sudia, C. "Children in Fatherless Families." In *Review of Child Development Research,* vol. III, edited by B. M. Caldwell and H. N. Ricciuti. Chicago: University of Chicago Press, 1973.

Hetherington, E. M., and Deur, J. L. "The Effects of Father Absence on Child Development." *Young Children* 26, no. 4 (March 1971): 233-248.

Kotelchuck, M. "Father Caretaking Characteristics and Their Influence on Infant-Father Interaction." Paper presented at the American Psychological Association meeting, Chicago, September 1975.

Kotelchuck, M. "The Infant's Relationship to the Father: Experimental Evidence." In *The Role of the Father in Child Development,* edited by M. E. Lamb. New York: John Wiley & Sons, 1976.

Kotelchuck, M. "The Nature of the Child's Tie to His Father." Doctoral dissertation, Harvard University, 1972.

Kotelchuck, M.; Zelazo, P.; Kagan, J.; and Spelke, E. "Infant Reaction to Parental Separations When Left with Familiar and Unfamiliar Adults." *Journal of Genetic Psychology* 126 (1975): 255-262.

Lamb, M. E. "A Comparison of 'Second Order' Effects Involving Parents and Siblings." Unpublished manuscript, University of Wisconsin—Madison, 1977a.

Lamb, M. E. "The Development of Mother-Infant and Father-Infant Attachments in the Second Year of Life." *Developmental Psychology* 13 (1977b):637-648.

Lamb, M. E. "The Development of Parental Preferences in the First Two Years of Life." *Sex Roles* 3 (1977c): 495-497.

Lamb, M. E. "The Effects of Ecological Variables of Parent-Infant Interaction." Paper presented at the Society for Research in Child Development meeting, New Orleans, March 1977d.

Lamb, M. E. "Effects of Stress and Cohort on Mother- and Father-Infant Interaction." *Developmental Psychology* 12 (1976a): 435-443.

Lamb, M. E. "Father-Infant and Mother-Infant Interaction in the First Year of Life." *Child Development* 48 (1977e): 167-181.

Lamb, M. E. "Infant Social Cognition and 'Second Order' Effects." *Infant Behavior and Development* 1 (1978a): 1-10.

Lamb, M. E. "Interactions Between 18-Month-Olds and Their Preschool-Aged Siblings." *Child Development* 49 (1978b): in press.

Lamb, M. E. "Interactions Between Eight-Month-Old Children and Their Fathers and Mothers." In *The Role of the Father in Child Development*, edited by M. E. Lamb. New York: John Wiley & Sons, 1976b.

Lamb, M. E. "Interactions Between Two-Year-Olds and Their Mothers and Fathers." *Psychological Reports* 38 (1976c): 447-450.

Lamb, M. E. "The One-Year-Old's Interaction with Its Parents." Paper presented at the Eastern Psychological Association meeting, New York, April 1976d.

Lamb, M. E. "Parent-Infant Interaction in Eight-Month-Olds." *Child Psychiatry and Human Development* 7 (1976e): 56-63.

Lamb, M. E. "Qualitative Aspects of Mother- and Father-Infant Relationships." *Infant Behavior and Development* 1 (1978c): in press.

Lamb, M. E. "A Reexamination of the Infant Social World." *Human Development* 20 (1977f): 65-85.

Lamb, M. E. "The Relationships Between Infants and Their Mothers and Fathers." Doctoral dissertation, Yale University, 1975.

Lamb, M. E. "Twelve-Month-Olds and Their Parents: Interaction in a Laboratory Playroom." *Developmental Psychology* 12 (1976f): 237-244.

Lewis, M., and Feiring, C. "The Child's Social World." In *Child Influences on Marital and Family Interaction: A Life-Span Perspective*, edited by R. M. Lerner and G. B. Spanier. New York: Academic Press, forthcoming.

Lewis, M., and Weinraub, M. "The Father's Role in the Child's Social Network." In *The Role of the Father in Child Development*, edited by M. E. Lamb. New York: John Wiley & Sons, 1976.

Maccoby, E. E., and Masters, J. C. "Attachment and Dependency." In *Carmichael's Manual of Child Psychology*, vol. 2, edited by P. H. Mussen, 3rd ed. New York: John Wiley & Sons, 1976.

Mächtlinger, V.J. "Psychoanalytic Theory: Preoedipal and Oedipal Phases with Special Reference to the Father." In *The Role of the Father in Child Development*, edited by M. E. Lamb. New York: John Wiley & Sons, 1976.

Money, J., and Ehrhardt, A. A. *Man and Woman, Boy and Girl.* Baltimore: Johns Hopkins University Press, 1972.

Parke, R. D., and O'Leary, S. "Father-Mother-Infant Interaction in the Newborn Period: Some Findings, Some Observations, and Some Unresolved Issues." In *The Developing Individual in a Changing World*, vol. 2, edited by K. F. Riegel and J. Meacham. The Hague: Mouton, 1975.

Parke, R. D. and Sawin, D. B. "The Family in Early Infancy: Social Interactional and Attitudinal Analyses." Paper presented at the Society for Research in Child Development meeting, New Orleans, March 1977.

Parke, R. D., and Sawin, D. B. "The Father's Role in Infancy: A Re-Evaluation." *The Family Coordinator* 25 (1976): 365-371.

Pedersen, F. A., ed. "The Family System: Networks of Interactions among Mother, Father, and Infant." Unpublished manuscript, 1977.

Pedersen, F. A. "Mother, Father, and Infant as an Interactive System." Paper presented at the American Psychological Association meeting, Chicago, September 1975.

Pedersen, F. A.; Anderson, B. J.; and Cain, R. L. "An Approach to Understanding Linkages Between the Parent-Infant and Spouse Relationships." Paper presented at the Society for Research in Child Development meeting, New Orleans, March 1977.

Pedersen, F. A., and Robson, K. S. "Father Participation in Infancy." *American Journal of Orthopsychiatry* 39 (1969): 466-472.

Ragozin, A. "Attachment in Day Care Children: Field and Laboratory Findings." Paper presented at the Society for Research in Child Development meeting, Denver, April 1975.

Ricciuti, H.N., and Poresky, R.H. "Development of Attachment to Care Givers in an Infant Nursery During the First Year of Life." Paper presented at the Society for Research in Child Development meeting, Philadelphia, March 1973.

Rosenblatt, P.C. "Behavior in Public Places: Comparison of Couples Accompanied by Children." *Journal of Marriage and the Family* 36 (1974): 750-755.

Ross, G.; Kagan, J.; Zelazo, P.; and Kotelchuck, M. "Separation Protest in Infants in Home and Laboratory." *Developmental Psychology* 11 (1975): 256-257.

Schaffer, H.R., and Emerson, P.E. "The Development of Social Attachments in Infancy." *Monographs of the Society for Research in Child Development* 29, no. 3 (1964): serial no. 94.

Spelke, E.; Zelazo, P.; Kagan, J.; and Kotelchuck, M. "Father Interaction and Separation Protest." *Developmental Psychology* 9 (1973): 83-90.

Stayton, D.J.; Ainsworth, M.D.S.; and Main, M.B. "Development of Separation Behavior in the First Year of Life: Protest, Following and Greeting." *Developmental Psychology* 9 (1973): 213-225.

Willemsen, E.; Flaherty, D.; Heaton, C.; and Ritchey, G. "Attachment Behavior of One-Year-Olds as a Function of Mother Vs. Father, Sex of Child, Session, and Toys." *Genetic Psychology Monographs* 90 (1974): 305-324.

Yogman, M.W. "The Goals and Structure of Face-To-Face Interaction Between Infants and Fathers." Paper presented at the Society for Research in Child Development meeting, New Orleans, March 1977.

Yogman, M.W.; Dixon, S.; Tronick, E.; Adamson, L.; Als, H.; and Brazelton, T.B. "Development of Infant Social Interaction with Fathers." Paper presented at the Eastern Psychological Association meeting, New York, April 1976.

Zelazo, P.; Kotelchuck, M.; Barber, L.; and David, J. "The Experimental Facilitation of Attachment Behaviors." Paper presented at the Society for Research in Child Development meeting. New Orleans, March 1977.

Marsha Weinraub

6 Fatherhood: The Myth of the Second-Class Parent

When's daddy coming home?

Daddy's arrival—an event eagerly awaited by some children, morbidly feared by others, but rarely taken for granted by any American children. Yet fathers have been considered second-class parents by educators, counselors, psychologists, and our legal system. With the overemphasis on the importance of the mother-child relationship, particularly during the child's "tender years," the father's contribution to child development has been to some extent ignored, considered more in its absence than its presence. Recently, however, this view has been changing. As a result of (1) ethological observations of children in naturalistic settings, (2) new attitudes toward sex roles, and (3) increasing stresses on the nuclear family and the rise in alternative childrearing situations, students of the family have become more aware that the mother is neither the first nor the only influential individual in the child's development (Kotelchuck 1972; Lamb 1975, 1976; Lewis and Weinraub 1974, 1976). The child exists and grows within a rich and complex social network (Weinraub, Brooks, and Lewis 1977). As a member of this social network, the father plays an important role in influencing the child's development.

This chapter first reviews briefly the major areas in which the father has been assumed to affect the child's social and cognitive development. Next, differences between father-child and mother-child interactions are examined, and then how these sex-of-parent differences might be involved in mediating the father's effect on development is considered. The final section discusses specific mechanisms by which the father contributes to child development. It is argued that the father's contribution to the child's development is a critical one, not because of quantitative or qualitative differences in father-child versus mother-child interactions, but because of direct and indirect effects which accrue as a result of the presence of two parents. As a second parent—that is, as one of two, not as a subordinate or second-class

© 1978, Marsha Weinraub

parent—the father plays a major role in the child's social network. Parenting is a difficult and demanding job; two caregivers are better prepared than one to meet the economic, social, and intellectual needs of children. As co-parent and as complement to the mother, the father makes a substantial contribution to the child's development.

Major Areas of Paternal Influence

Although fathers could be expected to affect development in all areas, research has documented three areas as being critically influenced by fathers: development of sex roles, cognitive abilities, and achievement motivation.

Sex-Role Development

As the child's first male model, the father has been assumed to exert a significant influence on the development of masculinity in boys and, to a lesser extent, the development of femininity in girls. It has been generally assumed that children growing up in families without fathers will have difficulties adopting behaviors, interests, and abilities considered appropriate for their sex. Several studies have reported that father absence in boys is predictive of increased dependency, decreased aggression, and weaker masculine sex-role orientation and preference (Bach 1946; Badaines 1976; Biller 1968, 1969; Hetherington 1966; Phelan 1964; Santrock 1970; Sears, Pintler, and Sears 1946). However, because the differences between father-absent and father-present boys tend to be small in magnitude and inconsistently observed across measures, and because other studies have observed heightened masculinity—termed *compensatory masculinity*—in father-absent boys (Douvan and Adelson 1966; Lynn and Sawrey 1959; McCord, McCord, and Thurber 1962), the effects of father absence may, in fact, be less dramatic and less clear-cut than has been generally assumed. (A full discussion of these and other data is presented by Herzog and Sudia 1973.) Moreover, it is difficult to determine whether differences between father-absent and father-present children can be attributed to the absence of the father per se or to specific attitudes and patterns of behavior characteristic of mothers in father-absent families.

More clearly demonstrating the father's contribution to the child's sex-role development are studies of the relationship between particular characteristics of father-present families and children's sex-role identification. Although neither paternal masculinity nor paternal encouragement for the performance of sex-typed behaviors has been shown to be correlated in and of themselves with sons' masculinity, they do seem to be related to femininity in daughters (Angrilli 1960;

Mussen and Rutherford 1963). Characteristics that are related to both masculinity in sons and femininity in daughters include paternal warmth and affection, understanding, involvement, and dominance within the family (Bronson 1959; Biller 1969; Hetherington 1967; Johnson 1963; Moulton, Burnstein, Liberty, and Altucher 1966; Mussen and Distler 1959, 1960; Mussen and Rutherford 1963; Sears 1953; Sears, Maccoby, and Levin 1957). More important than fathers' masculinity, punitiveness, or limit-setting for the development of children's appropriate sex-role identification are fathers' warmth, affection, and involvement. [See Biller and Borstelmann (1967) for a more complete review of this literature.]

Cognitive Abilities

A variety of studies have shown that children reared in families without fathers do less well on standardized measures of intelligence and are more likely to show feminine styles of performance (verbal scores higher than mathematical scores) than children reared in two-parent families (Biller 1974; Carlsmith 1964; Herzog and Sudia 1973; Lynn 1974). This is more characteristically the case when father absence is caused by divorce or separation than when father absence is caused by death. However, difficulties in adequately controlling socioeconomic status across groups and differences in performance as a function of reasons for father absence suggest once again that the father's contribution may not be the variable accounting for differences between father-absent and father-present children.

Studies of individual differences in children from father-present families demonstrate more clearly the role of the father in influencing cognitive abilities from preschool through adolescence. Most of the data pertain to fathers' effects on sons. Warm and accepting fathers who listen to their children and are involved in their activities without dominating them have brighter, more creative, more flexible, and more imaginative sons (Busse 1969; Cross 1966; Epstein and Radin 1975; Hurley 1965). Boys with high-interacting fathers do better in school (Blanchard and Biller 1971). In particular, paternal nurturance enhances cognitive functioning in middle- and working-class preschool boys; in lower-class boys, paternal restrictiveness hinders cognitive performance (Epstein and Radin 1975). Negative paternal characteristics are correlated with global, as opposed to analytic, approaches to problem solving. Low-interacting fathers and fathers who are perceived as dominating, tyrannical, and rejecting have sons with global cognitive styles (Heilbrun, Harrell, and Gillard 1967; Witkin, Dyk, Faterson, Goodenough, and Karp 1962). Fathers who believe in rigid, absolute standards have sons with less flexible approaches to problem solving (Busse 1969).

The data relating paternal characteristics and cognitive development in daughters are more limited and less consistent. Whereas Hurley (1965) found that paternal acceptance positively predicted intelligence scores for both girls and boys, most other investigators have found sex differences in the predictors of cognitive abilities. Epstein and Radin (1975), for example, were unable to find paternal predictors of cognitive performance in girls. Heilbrun et al. (1967) found that, in contrast to sons, daughters showed more analytic problem-solving ability when they viewed their fathers as less dominant and less nurturant. Lynn (1974) has suggested that some fathers may inhibit their daughters' analytic thinking by encouraging them to be "feminine."

According to Aldous (1975), the relationship between problem solving and parental behavior may be very complex. Aldous found that for girls but not for boys, overall father interaction and fathers' directions in a laboratory problem-solving situation were positively related to originality of children's problem solutions. While mothers and fathers gave highly original daughters approximately the same number of directions, fathers gave low originality daughters *fewer* directions and mothers gave low originality daughters *more* directions. Fathers' affective behaviors during the task situation were not related either to sons' or daughters' originality; mothers' positive affect tended to predict poorer performance for both sons and daughters.

Achievement Motivation

Fathers have an important effect on their children's educational, occupational, and financial aspirations (Mobley 1975). Considerable evidence demonstrates the relationship, if complex, between paternal behavior and achievement motivation in both boys and girls from preschool through college age. In middle- and working-class boys of preschool age, fathers' nurturance enhances motivation; in lower-class boys, fathers' restrictiveness inhibits motivation (Epstein and Radin 1975). Similarly, for fifth grade children, fathers' involvement in academic matters in all areas but mathematics is related to sons' higher achievement motivation (Boerger 1971, in Lynn 1974). However, when fathers are overly involved and controlling—doing their sons' homework, threatening them or being extremely solicitous—sons may clash with their fathers, find it difficult to live up to their fathers' expectations, and withdraw from the achievement arena (Boerger 1971; Cross and Allen 1969).

Surprisingly, fathers may play an even more critical role in influencing daughters' than sons' achievement motivation (Aldous 1975; Bing 1963; Crandall, Dewey, Katkovsky, and Preston 1964; Katkovsky, Crandall, and Good 1967; Ringness 1970). Fathers who are attentive and encouraging of their daughters' achievements without being overwhelmingly affectionate have highly motivated daughters who are willing to take responsibility for their own successes and failures. In both males and females of college age, high achievement appears to be related to perceptions of the father as accepting but not controlling; low achievement appears to be related to perceptions of the father as distant, autocratic, and punitive (Cross and Allen 1969; Teahan 1963). Although fathers may be more influential in sons' than daughters' vocational choice (Werts 1966), fathers may be more critical than mothers in determining daughters' career orientation and vocational choice (Oliver 1975; Walstedt 1974).

Summary. Studies of the relationship between paternal characteristics in father-present families and various aspects of child development leave little doubt that fathers make a valuable contribution to the development of sex roles, cognitive abilities, and achievement motivation. In all three of these areas, characteristics of the father which are most clearly related to aspects of optimal development particularly in boys include paternal warmth, acceptance, and involvement.

Differences in Father-Child and Mother-Child Interactions

Our increased awareness of the significance of the father's contribution to child development has raised questions about the nature of father-child interaction, particularly as it compares to mother-child interaction.

Quantity

It is generally agreed that fathers spend very little time interacting with their children, certainly much less time than mothers. This is most clearly documented in studies of infants. Estimates of the amount of time fathers spend in direct contact with their infants in the first year of life range from less than a minute per day (Rebelsky and Hanks 1971) to slightly more than an hour per day (Pedersen and Robson 1969). Although the amount of time fathers spend with their children probably increases as children grow older (Lewis and Weinraub 1974), the total amount of time fathers spend with their children is limited by the fact that most fathers are employed in full-time jobs. Since a larger proportion of women than men hold part-time jobs (U.S. Department of Commerce 1976), employed mothers are still more likely to have shorter work weeks and more flexible working hours than employed fathers.

However, differences in the quantity of time fathers and mothers spend with their children do not necessarily imply that mothers and fathers will have differential impact on their children. It is increasingly recognized that the amount of time parents interact with or are available to their children (beyond a minimal amount) has very little effect on the quality of their relationship. In particular, the amount of time most fathers spend interacting with their children does not appear to predict children's behavior toward the fathers (Ban and Lewis 1974; Kotelchuck 1972; Pedersen and Robson 1969). Even though mothers spend significantly more time interacting with their infants than fathers, few differences in children's behaviors toward mothers and fathers have been observed, especially after one year of age (Feldman and Ingham 1975; Kotelchuck 1972; Lamb 1976; Lewis and Weinraub 1974; Weinraub and Frankel 1978; Willemsen, Flaherty, Heaton, and Ritchey 1974; also see Chapter 5).

In light of the limited amount of time fathers spend with their children, the father's effects on child development may be realized not as a result of the amount of interaction but as a result of the specific quality of his contribution to the child's social network. These effects may be conceptualized as direct effects—resulting from specific activities and behaviors the father engages in when he is with his child—and indirect effects—resulting from the father's membership in and association with other members of the child's social network. In the following section, parental sex differences in direct effects will be considered.

Quality

Household Activities. One of the most obvious differences between mothers and fathers can be seen in the tasks they engage in around the home. As part of a recent study (Weinraub and Leite 1977), we asked mothers and fathers of two-year-old children which parent assumed responsibility for different household tasks. The results showed that labor was clearly divided in conformity with sex-role stereotypes. Mothers were assigned responsibility for sewing, ironing, washing clothes, washing dishes, vacuuming, and making beds; fathers were assigned responsibility for fixing the car, carpentry, mowing the lawn, and repairing broken appliances. Although between one-fourth and one-third of the parents reported shared responsibilities for grocery shopping, cooking, lifting heavy boxes, taking out the trash, and outdoor housepainting, the majority of parents divided labor along clear sex-typed lines.

As early as three years of age, and possibly even before, children too are aware of sex stereotypic division of household labor (Thompson 1975; Vener and Snyder 1966; Weinraub and Leite 1977). Certainly, by elementary school, children's concepts of parental roles in the home suggest that mothers are seen as engaged in child care and homemaking; fathers are seen as engaged in activities outside the home involving physical strength and endurance (Bronfenbrenner 1961; Hartley 1960).

Caregiving. Not only are fathers less involved than mothers in household duties, they also appear to be less involved in caregiving. Studies of interaction during infancy reveal that fathers take very little responsibility for caregiving in the early years. Of the 144 fathers with children from nine to twelve months old that Kotelchuck (1972) interviewed, only 25 percent reported any regular caregiving activity. Interviewing mothers of one- and four-year-old children, Newson (1963, 1968, in Lamb 1975) found that while 99 percent of the fathers played with their children, many of them were not highly involved in everyday caregiving functions. Only 52 percent of the fathers were considered to take a highly participant part in their children's daily life; the remaining fathers were reported to have no more than a "moderate share" in the children's activities. This meant that they participated in child care only when asked or under very special circumstances. Thus, nearly one-half of these fathers contributed very little to the daily care of their children. For two-year-old children of university-related parents, Fagot (1974) observed that, on the average, mothers did 70 percent and fathers 30 percent of the caregiving. Although reports of fathers' caregiving behaviors with school-age children are not available, all other factors suggest that while fathers' involvement in caregiving may increase as children mature, fathers may still be significantly less involved in caregiving than mothers.

Styles of Childrearing and Children's Perceptions of Parental Characteristics. According to Parsons and Bales (1955), fathers' and mothers' roles, like masculine and feminine roles, are divided along instrumental and expressive lines. The father's role is instrumental, one of competence and mastery. The father is provider, judge, and ultimate disciplinarian. He is the child's model for planning ahead, delaying gratification, and interacting with the world outside the family. The mother, on the other hand, is expressive. She smooths over interpersonal relations and keeps the family functioning as a unit. She is affectionate, solicitous, conciliatory, and emotionally supportive. Though separation of these two modes—the expressive and the instrumental—along sex-role lines is not entirely supported by empirical studies (Maccoby and Jacklin 1974), there is some evidence to support the notion that, at least within the family, fathers play a more instrumental role, linking children to the larger society outside the family, and mothers play a more expressive, nurturant role. Interviews with mothers and fathers conducted by Stolz (1966) have revealed that fathers are more likely to be concerned with children's education, moral values, personal values, and physical safety; mothers are more concerned with children's emotional adjustment, happiness, and freedom from anxiety. Fathers are also more likely to say that socialization agents other than the mother, such as schools and the media, are beneficial to their children.

Interviews and observations of children suggest that children from preschool through high school perceive their mothers as more affectionate and nurturant and their fathers as more punitive and restrictive (Armentrout and Burger 1972; Bronfenbrenner 1961; Emmerich 1959; Fitzgerald 1966; Kagan, Hosken, and Watson 1961; Kagan and Lemkin 1960). Mothers often are seen as more supportive and encouraging of their children, and fathers are seen as bigger and stronger, better able to protect the child from danger, more controlling and more action-oriented. These findings are congruent with Thomes's (1968) observation that elementary school children perceive their fathers' role in the home as teacher, disciplinarian, and protector; and with Stehbens and Carr's (1970) observation that ninth grade children see their fathers as less involved in their lives, less child-centered, and less accepting of them as individuals than their mothers.

Sex-Typing. Although the behaviors by which fathers influence children's sex-role typing are still relatively undefined, data collected over the last three decades suggest that fathers are more actively and personally concerned with sex-role acquisition than mothers (Aberle and Naegele 1952; Block 1973; Goodenough 1957; Lansky 1967; Margolin and Patterson 1975; Sears et al. 1957; Tasch 1952). Fathers have been shown to be particularly opposed to feminine behavior in their two- to four-year-old sons. Goodenough (1957) found that fathers were worried and concerned when their sons appeared unaggressive and unwilling to defend themselves, yet they rarely expressed such concern about unaggressiveness in their daughters (Lansky 1967; Tasch 1952). According to Aberle and Naegele (1952), middle-class fathers were very concerned that their children receive proper sex-role training. Fathers expected their sons to be masculine and to go on to college and a good job; they expected their daughters to be pretty, sweet, and affectionate, and to get married. Whether these attitudes are still more common in fathers than in mothers in the 1970s is hard to say. Nevertheless, several recent studies have observed that fathers are more likely to respond differentially to their children on the basis of gender than mothers (Aldous 1975; Block 1973; Fagot 1974; Margolin and Patterson 1975). Although one study (Fling and Manosevitz 1972) has found greater encouragement of sex-typing in same-sex than opposite-sex parents, most other studies have found fathers more concerned with sex-typing than mothers.

Free Play Behavior. Despite differences in parental roles derived from interviews of parents of children, direct observations of mothers and fathers interacting with their children (from infancy through childhood) have yielded few clear sex-of-parent differences in free play interactions. In fact, the similarities appear more striking than the differences. Parke and O'Leary (1976) observed parents in the hospital room and found that fathers are equally as active as mothers in social interactions with their newborn infants. Fathers look at, talk to, hold, and rock their newborns as often as mothers. Although mothers spent more time in specific caregiving interventions, fathers responded as sensitively and appropriately as mothers.

Studying physical contact and play behaviors with eight-month-old children, Lamb (1976, also see Chapter 5) reported no parental differences in amount of physical contact or play, only differences in styles of play and reasons for physical contact. Although Clarke-Stewart (1977) observed that mothers touched and talked to their fifteen- to thirty-month-old children more than fathers in a home situation, Weinraub and Frankel (1978) observed in a laboratory setting that proximity to the child and talking were complicated by sex-of-parent by sex-of-child interactions. Parents talked to and got down on the floor to play with same-sex more than opposite-sex eighteen-month-olds. Thus, for infants, few differences in father-child versus mother-child free play interactions have been clearly observed. Weinraub and Frankel have suggested that parental differences may be observed not in mean *amounts* of behavior but in *patterns* of behavior. Maternal behaviors may be highly interrelated, while paternal behaviors may be more differentiated.

Observational studies of older children offer confusing and sometimes conflicting findings regarding sex-of-parent differences in parent-child play interactions. Fagot (1974) observed mothers and fathers interacting naturally at home with their two-year-old children. Mothers praised, criticized, and punished their children more than fathers. There were no sex-of-parent differences in the amount of time mothers and fathers spent playing with their children. Osofsky and O'Connell (1972) observed parents with their four- to six-year-old daughters in both structured and unstructured interactions. Fathers tended to be less involved with their daughters than mothers; fathers were also more action-oriented, either jumping into or totally withdrawing from physically helping their daughters with the task, while mothers were more supportive and encouraged their daughters' efforts.

The majority of studies suggest that the sex of the parent may interact with the sex of the child. Rothbart and Maccoby (1966) found that parents were more likely to take the disciplinarian role with same-sex than with opposite-sex children. Presenting parents videotapes of children in a variety of hypothetical situations, they found that parents showed more positive attention and were more permissive toward opposite-sex children than toward same-sex children. These situations included those in which children sought comfort, were dependent, asked to stop a game, or protested the intrusion of a younger sibling.

Observing naturalistically in the home, Baumrind (1971) found congruent results. However, to complicate matters, Marcus (1971) suggested that sex-of-parent by sex-of-child differences may depend on characteristics of the child. Using a similar procedure to Rothbart and Maccoby, Marcus obtained very different results. Parents reacted more nondirectively to behavior of same-sex, not opposite-sex children, especially when the children were independent. In addition, mothers were more responsive than fathers when children were dependent; mothers were also more likely to change their behavior toward children when children changed from dependent to independent behavior.

Summary. This brief review of the literature has demonstrated that fathers, in contrast to mothers, spend much less time with their children, engage in masculine sex-typed activities around the home, and spend little time in actual caregiving activities. Whereas fathers are perceived by their children as instrumental (controlling and aloof), mothers are seen as expressive (warm and nurturant). Fathers tend to be more concerned with sex-typing than mothers. Surprisingly, few clear-cut differences in specific behaviors engaged in by fathers and mothers with their children have emerged from observational studies. In fact, the similarities may be more striking than the differences. During preschool years and beyond, sex-of-parent differences may depend on the sex of the child and the nature of the child's behavior. Nevertheless, there is no evidence to suggest that fathers are second-class parents. Although they may express their involvement in slightly different styles with some children in some situations, fathers appear to be as sensitive and as concerned with the childrearing process as mothers.

Impact of Parental Sex Differences on Child Development

Are these differences between maternal and paternal styles of interaction responsible for the father's influence on the child's development? Do these differences (in quantity or quality of interaction) mediate the father's critical role? Many psychologists and lay people alike seem to have implicitly assumed that if fathers are important to children's development, and if fathers in general appear to interact differently with children than mothers, then these behavioral differences can account for fathers' contribution to children's development. Such reasoning has led some to suggest that these parental sex differences are necessary and parents should consciously attempt to perpetuate them. However, when explicitly stated, it becomes apparent that this line of reasoning is misleading. The differences in fathers' and mothers' styles

Fatherhood

of interaction may be irrelevant; the similarities (and though these are less frequently considered, they are numerous) may be more important than the differences in explaining the critical role of the father. Before we turn attention to the similarities and try to ascertain just what paternal functions are important in development, let us examine the origins of these sex differences in parental styles and their implications for father-child interactions.

Origins of Differences in Maternal and Paternal Roles

Differences in maternal and paternal styles of interaction may be ultimately traceable to differences in the biological contributions of mothers and fathers to childbearing (Lewis and Weinraub 1976). The mother's biological relationship to her child (through pregnancy, childbirth, and nursing) makes known to her, to all other individuals, and to the child, that she is "mother." This biological relationship, over the course of evolution, may have significantly influenced specific patterns of mother-child interaction. The mammalian mother, by definition, had to nurse her child. With feeding, other interactions naturally followed. Holding, looking at, and talking to the child, the mother satisfied not only the child's hunger needs but also the child's needs for tactile, kinesthetic, and intellectual stimulation. Early patterns of mother-child interaction, initially related to fulfillment of simple biological needs, were built into more complex patterns of interaction (Bowlby 1969). Even in today's technological society, predispositions toward specific patterns of mother-child interaction initially determined by biology persist. Thus, by one year of age, it is not surprising that children go to their mothers in times of hunger, fatigue, and fear (see Chapter 5).

Fathers, however, have presented a different case. Because the father's biological relationship to his child is not immediately obvious, the nature of the father's participation and extent of his involvement in childrearing has been less clearly defined over the course of evolution. Because for fathers and their children there are no predisposed patterns of interaction predicted by biological factors as there are for mothers, the extent and quality of the father-child interaction have been more heavily determined by cultural factors.

Differences in parental roles are inextricably entwined with differences in cultural sex roles. Over the years informational and technological advances have abolished the necessity of having biological mothers or other females nursing children, and today males are equally competent to perform all caregiving activities. Nevertheless, initial differences in the biological origins of parent-child relationships might have influenced the development of cultural sex-role stereotypes. Because of their close biological ties to children, mothers, then women in general, became associated with warmth, sensitivity, and nurturance. In contrast, partly because their contribution to childrearing was more indirect and partly because of overall biological differences in physical size and strength, fathers, and then men in general, became associated with action and power in the extrafamilial world and aloofness and insensitivity in the interpersonal world. Today's Western culture defines masculine attributes as independent and aggressive, assertive and authoritative; it defines feminine attributes as warm and nurturant, sensitive and expressive (Bem 1977; Broverman, Broverman, Clarkson, Rosenkrantz, and Vogel 1972). As these sex-role stereotypes became established, they in turn influenced the socialization of men and women, fathers and mothers. Because fathers, as *males*, have been socialized to be masculine, and because mothers, as *females*, have been socialized to be feminine, it is not surprising that differences between fathers and mothers in interacting with their children reflect these stereotyped characteristics of masculinity and femininity.

Regardless of their origins, modern day parental roles no longer need be influenced by biological differences between the sexes. With the exception of the initial pregnancy and delivery process, fathers appear equally competent—both biologically and psychologically—to fulfill the parenting role (Lewis and Weinraub 1976). The persistence of differences in paternal and maternal roles in modern Western societies may be attributed in large part to the persistence of sex-role stereotypes. Many of the differences between mothers and fathers described in preceding sections of this chapter—differences in quantity of interaction with infants and children, household division of labor, caregiving responsibilities, and styles of childrearing—may be explained largely as a result of differential socialization experiences stemming from differential sex-role expectations.

Significance of Parental Sex Differences

Difficulties of the Father's Role. That differences in father-child and mother-child relationships are related to sex-role stereotypes may give us a clue to the significance and, in particular, to the difficulties of the paternal role.

Different traits and abilities may be seen as required of the "ideal" parent, the traditionally sex-typed "masculine" man and the traditionally sex-typed "feminine" woman. To be an "ideal" parent implies being sensitive and responsive to the emotional, physical, and intellectual needs of others, taking pleasure in interacting with infants and children, setting an example of acceptable and desirable behavior, expressing warm and affectionate feelings, setting limits and being consistent and firm in making demands on children, and taking an ac-

Fatherhood

tive but nondirective role in allowing children freedom to explore the environment (Baumrind 1967; White 1972). To be "masculine" implies being independent and aloof, unemotional, insensitive to the needs and feelings of others, more interested and skilled in the affairs of work (business, sciences, athletics) than in children, powerful and self-confident, competitive rather than accepting. To be "feminine" implies being dependent and passive, emotional, sensitive to the feelings of others, able to express gentle and tender feelings, excitable even in minor crises, and unable to separate feelings from ideas. (For empirical support for these sex-role stereotypes, see Broverman et al. 1972.)

Since the characteristics required of the ideal parent are androgynous, rigidly sex-typed individuals of either sex may have difficulties adapting successfully to the parental role. However, the average woman can adapt to the parental role simply by adding some "masculine" characteristics without threatening her essential femininity (so long as she does not venture outside the home/family environment). For the average male, this may not be so easy. The characteristics of the "ideal" parent and the "masculine" man come into head-on conflict; it is therefore difficult to merge the two. This conflict between the role of the parent and the role of the male may make it especially challenging for the traditionally sex-typed man in today's society to accept, understand, and successfully fulfill the role of father.

Just as women in our society have few models of successful career women, so do men in our society have few models of successful, modern-day male parents. The paucity of male parenting models is especially disconcerting when we consider the sense of awe with which fathers in our society are viewed (Mobley 1975). The father's image is one of "god" or "superpower"—omniscient and omnipotent, as in "Father Knows Best." Only when fathers leave their family roles as decision makers and enter the realm of household tasks are they sometimes seen as bumbling.

Thus, these three factors—conflict between the ideal parent role and the traditional masculine role, lack of easily observable modern-day successful father models, and the overidealization of the image of "father"—conspire to make acceptance and fulfillment of the father role in our society a difficult task indeed.

Are Parental Differences Necessary? As long as sex-role stereotypes continue, they will affect differences in the roles of fathers and mothers. Until recently, if fathers were encouraged to take a more active role in the family, the role was still defined within narrowly conceived sex-role stereotypes. Men who were fathers had to fulfill the role of the benevolent but slightly aloof authority figure, all-powerful, all-knowing, assertive, athletic, and instrumental. Their role as "model of masculinity," particularly for their sons, was emphasized.

In addition, the masculine behavior of the traditional male might have been a necessary complement to the feminine behavior of the traditional female, thereby assuring the child exposure to a wide range of both "masculine" and "feminine" personality characteristics. However, as we move toward androgyny, what will become of paternal and maternal roles? Will the necessity for the desirability of two-parent families decline? As fathers, mothers, and even children become more androgynous and differences between the characteristics of mothers and fathers decrease, will either one of the two parents become more "dispensable"? The answer to this question depends, of course, on whether the differences between father-child and mother-child behaviors described earlier in this chapter are responsible for the critical impact of the role of the father in child development.

Recall the relationships between paternal behaviors and the development of sex roles, cognitive abilities, and achievement motivation reviewed earlier. You will note that three aspects of paternal behavior repeatedly emerged in relation to individual differences: paternal warmth, acceptance, and involvement. For the most part, the warmer, more accepting, and more involved the father is, the more optimal the child's development. These data prompt two observations. First, on the basis of these relationships there is no reason to assume that the differences observed between father-child and mother-child interactions are in any way responsible for the critical impact of the father on the child's development. The three aspects of the father-child relationship—warmth, acceptance, and involvement—which positively correlate with optimal development are those which are not more characteristic of fathers in comparison with mothers. In fact, fathers tend to score lower than mothers on these characteristics; fathers are generally perceived as less warm, less accepting, and less involved. Thus, it is hardly fair to argue on the basis of the evidence collected so far that *differences* between fathers' and mothers' interactions with their children can account for the importance of fathers' contributions.

A second observation suggested by these data can be phrased positively: The warmer, more accepting, and more involved the father is toward his child, the more positive his contribution may be. The characteristics of warmth, acceptance, and involvement may not be particular to either mothers or fathers; they may be three of the many characteristics necessary for optimal parenting behavior.* Thus, it is

---

* A note of caution is warranted. Despite the apparent validity of this observation, we cannot necessarily conclude that when fathers behave in an equally warm, accepting, and involved manner as mothers, they have optimal impact on their children. This conclusion is premature because of limitations within the data analyses demonstrating these relationships. Correlational analyses separately performed for mothers and fathers yield limited information. For example, fathers who score high on warmth are

possible that fathers and mothers may contribute to their children's optimal development by behaving not in *different* but in *similar* ways.

The expressive qualities of warmth, affection, and involvement may be some of the traditionally feminine stereotyped characteristics necessary for optimal parenting skills, while instrumental qualities such as self-confidence, mastery, consistency, and firm disciplinary techniques may be some of the traditionally masculine stereotyped characteristics necessary. As long as all behaviors are presented to the child, there may be no need to assign "feminine" characteristics to mothers and "masculine" characteristics to fathers; in fact, it appears highly preferable to have all these characteristics in the same person.

Viewed in this light, the future of the family in Western society is optimistic. Androgyny is increasingly being recognized as a mentally healthy state of affairs (Bem 1977; Marecek 1976). As individuals become more androgynous, they may become more successful and less conflicted parents. Fathers, in particular, will be free to behave in expressive as well as instrumental ways. Rather than threatening the nuclear family, androgyny may allow both men and women to develop their full parenting potential.

Fathers as "Second," Not "Second-Class" Parents

There is no longer any reason to doubt that fathers are significant contributors to child development. However, the mechanisms by which fathers affect child development are somewhat unclear. The father's influence appears to be mediated not by the differences in father-child as opposed to mother-child interaction styles, but by the similarities. Why, then, is the father's presence so important for the optimal development of the child? If the father's and the mother's behaviors toward the child can be characterized as more similar than different and, moreover, if the similarities, not the differences, in interaction styles appear to mediate the father's beneficial impact on the child, why does the father exert such an important influence on the child's development?

Essentially, fathers are and will be increasingly important contributors to children's development, not because they introduce styles of relating to children different from those of mothers, but because they act as second (or one of two) *co-equal* parents in children's social network. (The use of the word *second* in this context can apply to

---

not necessarily as warm as the "average mother." Moreover, if warmth is curvilinearly related to performance, making fathers more like mothers may not promote fathers' contributions to optimal development.

either mothers or fathers in a two-parent family, depending on the point of reference.) For some time, we have been aware of the fact that children need at least one individual in the role of "parent" for adequate social, emotional, and cognitive development (Bowlby 1951; Spitz 1945). Since in family settings where only one parent is available that parent is usually the mother, it is assumed that mothers or "mother-figures" are necessary for adequate child development. However, it seems likely that two individuals are even better able than one to meet a growing child's physical, emotional, and intellectual needs. In Western society, when families have a second parent, that individual is most often a father. It is in this second, though not necessarily "second-class," parental role that fathers are so important in influencing child development. Though second parents do not appear *necessary* for adequate child development (Biller 1970; Kopf 1970; Pedersen 1966), when they are present they exert significant effects. Fathers, as second co-equal parents, may have positive, negative, or neutral effects depending upon their parenting skills. Fathers who are effective parents—relatively warm, accepting, and involved—contribute in beneficial ways to child development; fathers who are not effective parents can interfere with the child's adequate development. Thus, although the father's presence per se may not be absolutely necessary, when fathers are present they can make substantial contributions to the childrearing process. In a variety of ways, directly and indirectly, families that include two competent parents, as opposed to only one, are in a better position to foster childrearing.

Direct Modes of Effect

Meeting Children's Needs. The most obvious and direct way in which fathers can contribute to children's development is by helping to fill children's physical, emotional, and intellectual needs. The parenting role is a big one. Children have many needs, all of which cannot always be met by one person. Two parents provide greater assurance that children's needs will be adequately met. Although this applies to emotional and intellectual needs, the role of the second parent in helping to meet child needs is most clearly seen in the area of financial support. Two parents are better able than one to economically support children. Two parents not only have larger incomes, they also have greater economic options. One can work outside the home while the other fulfills household functions or both can work outside the home, providing two incomes.

In addition, two parents can counterbalance or offset each other's negative traits. If one parent is too demanding and critical, the second parent can be more accepting and understanding. Likewise, if one parent has difficulty expressing emotion or affection, the second parent can compensate and help the child to understand the situation.

Finally, second parents offer insurance in case of temporary or long-term inability of either parent to fulfill childrearing obligations. If one parent is emotionally unable to lend emotional warmth, concern, and support to a child in need, the second parent may be called in to provide an extra supply. The importance of this extra-insurance function offered by second parents is again most clearly seen in the economic sphere. For many families, the specter of unemployment is less threatening because a second parent can be relied upon to help fill financial obligations. Children and parents without this extra measure of insurance may feel insecure and fearful about the future.

Relevant in this context are the findings regarding the effects of father absence on children's emotional adjustment. In general, there is very little relationship between children's emotional adjustment and any of the variables related to father absence, such as duration or age of onset. Instead, the effects of father absence appear to be mediated by maternal factors (Biller 1969, 1970; Kopf 1970; Pedersen 1966). The mother's perceptions of her ability to cope, her attitude toward the father, and her attitude toward the child seem to be critical determinants of the child's emotional adjustment to father absence.

Contrast Effects. Whenever two individuals perform similar tasks—such as parenting—contrasts in their behavior are certain to appear. This phenomenon is called *tension introduction* (Lewis and Weinraub 1976). Tension is introduced into a social network when more than one person fulfills a social function or interacts with the child in a particular context. Tension develops as the child learns to discriminate between the cues and responses of the different individuals. These contrasts between fathers' and mothers' parenting behaviors can have positive or negative effects on the child depending upon their degree. In most cases, contrasting effects may serve to enhance development. Having to relate to two similar but slightly different persons may force the child to be sensitive to social cues, to discriminate subtle differences between individuals, and to tolerate the frustration generated during the process of learning differential expectations about fathers' and mothers' behaviors. The presence of two adult authority figures with similar but different opinions and expectations regarding the child's behavior forces the child to learn to deal with differences of opinion and to consider more than one side of an argument or issue. In this way, the presence of two social objects can be expected to increase the child's analytic skills. In addition, the fact that these two social objects may have different opinions of the child's worth makes it more likely that if one person's opinion of the child is extreme and unjustified, the other parent's opinion may counteract the negative influences of the first parent's opinion. Thus, self-concept may be positively affected by the presence of two parents.

Of course, when the contrast is extreme, the effects of parental conflict can be negative. Irreconcilable and contradictory differences in behaviors of the two parents may be confusing to the child and lead to severe difficulties of adjustment. When parents' behaviors, views of the world, and attitudes toward the child are in extreme conflict, the child may not be able to construct a stable view of reality and a stable self-concept. In such cases, one parent may be preferable to two.

The Picture of Normalcy. Finally, the mere presence of a second parent, whether the mother or the father, but in most cases the father, is significant to the child—significant not because of the specific behaviors of the second parent, but because of what the parent's presence represents. Despite the increasing number of single-parent families, in the eyes of many children, parents, relatives, and communities, fathers and mothers are considered necessary components of the "total family." If no father is present, something is "wrong." Children often feel different from and left out of larger society when "everyone else" has two parents. Also, children often feel that they are missing something unless both parents are present. The importance of having two parents was recently expressed by ten-year-old Maurey Greenberg on the national television show, "Six American Families" (NBC 1977): "Why can't we all be together? It's much more funner than just one person." Possibly, as the media present us with more and more views of alternative family styles, admiration and longing for two-parent families—and embarrassment and feelings of absence in single-parent families—may diminish.

Indirect Modes

As members of the child's social network, second parents also exert indirect effects on the child. When two parents are present instead of only one, the parents can offer each other emotional support, the child's representational skills may be elaborated by references to the second parent, and the child's social network may be expanded by the transitive quality of relationships. In addition, children's views of adult-adult interactions may be significantly influenced by their exposure to the interaction between the two parents, and the contrasting sexes of the two parents may serve to highlight and exemplify the nature and importance of sex differences. Lewis and Weinraub (1976) discuss the significance of some of these indirect modes of influence.

Perhaps the most obvious way two parents can indirectly affect the child's development is through the provision of mutual emotional support and comfort. Two parents can enhance each other's ability to be sensitive and responsive to the child's needs. A parent whose needs for love, affection, and security are satisfied by another adult—the second parent—is better able to respond effectively to the child's needs. Several studies have demonstrated how the father may influence the mother-child relationship. The mother's perception of support from the father has been shown to be strongly associated with maternal sensitivity and responsivity to her infant (Feiring 1975). The father's presence during mother-child interaction has been related to the mother's increased display of interest and positive affect toward the infant (Parke and O'Leary 1976). In cases of father absence, when mothers are less likely to receive emotional support or comfort from a loved one, mothers are perceived by their children as less loving than in cases of two-parent families (Crain and Stamm 1965). Although more limited, there is also evidence of how the mother's relationship to the father affects the father-child relationship (Pedersen, Anderson, and Cain 1977). It is becoming increasingly recognized that the quality of the relationship between the two parents will affect each parent's ability to respond effectively to the child.

In summary, although the presence of a second parent does not appear to be critical for optimal child development, two-parent families are preferable to single-parent families in many ways. Two parents are better able than one to meet the full range of the child's physical, emotional, and intellectual needs. Differences between parenting behaviors may often complement each other. As long as the parents' behaviors are not conflicting, they may serve to enhance the child's social and cognitive development. For parents as well as children, two-parent families with a mother and a father are often preferable because they conform to current societal notions of what is normal and acceptable. Finally, by satisfying each other's emotional needs, two parents not only serve as models of adult-adult interactions, but also enable each other to be free to be more sensitive and responsive to the child's emotional needs.

Conclusion

There is no doubt that fathers are important contributors to child development. In particular, fathers significantly affect the development of sex roles, cognitive abilities, and achievement motivation. Although there are some clearly documented differences between father-child and mother-child relationships, there is as yet no evidence to suggest that these differences per se are responsible for the importance of the father's contribution. Rather, the similarities of father-child and mother-child relationships may be more significant than the differences in fostering optimal child development in a variety of areas. This is not to say that differences in the quality of mother-child and father-child relationships should not be further explored.

Certainly, such information may help fill in the details of the specific nature of the socialization process. However, we must be careful not to assume that differences between mother-child and father-child interactions are responsible for the father's contribution to child development and worthy of perpetuation until these differences in behavior are shown to be directly related to optimal child behavior. It is likely that the father's most important contribution to child development may be his role not as a uniquely masculine parent, but as an equally affectionate and involved second, co-equal parent. Because parenting is a difficult and demanding profession, two caregivers may be better able than one to meet the economic, social, and intellectual needs of children. Previous views of the father's role as less important and differing in quality may have caused fathers to feel conflict about and to withdraw from their parenting roles. By emphasizing the importance of two parents—both intimately involved in the child's development, both expressing attention, love, and affection toward the child—mothers and fathers may be better able to understand, accept, and adequately prepare for their parental roles.

I wish to thank David Hill for his critical reading of an earlier version of this chapter.

References

Aberle, D. F., and Naegele, K. D. "Middle-Class Fathers' Occupational Role and Attitude Toward Children." *American Journal of Orthopsychiatry* 22 (1952): 366-378.

Aldous, J. "The Search for Alternatives: Parental Behaviors and Children's Original Problem Solutions." *Journal of Marriage and the Family* 37 (1975): 711-722.

Angrilli, A. F. "The Psychosexual Identification of Pre-School Boys." *Journal of Genetic Psychology* 97 (1960): 327-340.

Armentrout, J. A., and Burger, G. K. "Children's Reports of Parental Childrearing Behavior at Five Grade Levels." *Developmental Psychology* 7 (1972): 44-48.

Bach, G. "Father Fantasies and Father Typing in Father-Separated Children." *Child Development* 17 (1946): 63-80.

Badaines, J. "Identification, Imitation, and Sex Role Preference in Father-Present and Father-Absent Black and Chicano Boys." *Journal of Psychology* 92 (1976): 15-24.

Ban, P., and Lewis, M. "Mothers and Fathers, Girls and Boys: Attachment Behavior in the One-Year-Old." *Merrill-Palmer Quarterly* 20 (1974): 195-204.

Barclay, A., and Cusumano, D. R. "Father Absence, Cross-Sex Identity and Field Dependent Behavior in Male Adolescents." *Child Development* 38 (1967): 243-250.

Baumrind, D. "Child Care Practices Anteceding Three Patterns of Preschool Behavior." *Genetic Psychology Monographs* 75 (1967): 345-388.

Baumrind, D. "Current Patterns of Parental Authority." *Developmental Psychology* 4 (1971): 1-102.

Bee, H. L.; Van Egeren, L. F.; Streissguth, A. P.; Nyman, B. A.; and Lackie, M. S. "Social Class Differences in Maternal Teaching Strategies and Speech Patterns." *Developmental Psychology* 1 (1969): 726-734.

Bem, S. "Probing the Promise of Androgyny." In *Psychology of Women: Future Directions of Research,* edited by J. Sherman and F. Denmark. New York: Psychological Dimensions, 1977.
Biller, H. B. "Father Absence and the Personality Development of the Male Child." *Developmental Psychology* 2 (1970): 181-201.
Biller, H. B. "Father Dominance and Sex-Role Development in Kindergarten Age Boys." *Developmental Psychology* 1 (1969): 87-94.
Biller, H. B. "A Note on Father Absence and Masculine Development in Lower Class Negro and White Boys." *Child Development* 39 (1968): 1003-1006.
Biller, H. B. "Paternal and Sex-Role Factors in Cognitive and Academic Functioning." In *Nebraska Symposium of Motivation,* edited by J. K. Cole and R. Dienstbier. Lincoln, Neb.: University of Nebraska Press, 1974.
Biller, H. B., and Borstelmann, L. J. "Masculine Development: An Integrative Review." *Merrill-Palmer Quarterly* 13 (1967): 253-294.
Bing, E. "Effect of Childrearing Practices on Development of Differential Cognitive Abilities." *Child Development* 34 (1963): 631-648.
Blanchard, R., and Biller, H. B. "Father Availability and Academic Performance among Third-Grade Boys." *Developmental Psychology* 4 (1971): 301-305.
Block, J. H. "Conceptions of Sex Role; Some Cross-Cultural and Longitudinal Perspectives." *American Psychologist* 28 (1973): 512-526.
Bowlby, J. *Attachment.* Attachment and Loss, vol. 1. New York: Basic Books, 1969.
Bowlby, J. "Maternal Care and Mental Health." Geneva: World Health Organization, 1951.
Bronfenbrenner, U. "Some Familial Antecedents of Responsibility and Leadership in Adolescents." In *Leadership and Interpersonal Behavior,* edited by L. Petrullo and B. M. Bass. New York: Holt, Rinehart and Winston, 1961.
Bronson, W. C. "Dimensions of Ego and Infantile Identification." *Journal of Personality* 27 (1959): 532-545.
Broverman, I. K.; Vogel, S. R.; Broverman, D.; Clarkson, F. E.; Rosenkrantz, P. S. "Sex Role Stereotypes: A Current Appraisal."*Journal of Social Issues 28 (1972): 59-79.*
Busse, T.V. "Child-Rearing Antecedents of Flexible Thinking." *Developmental Psychology* 1 (1969): 585-591.
Carlsmith, L. "Effects of Early Father Absence on Scholastic Aptitude." *Harvard Educational Review* 34 (1964): 3-21.
Clarke-Stewart, A. "The Father's Impact on Mother and Child." Paper presented at the Society for Research in Child Development meeting, New Orleans, March 1977.
Cohen, L. J., and Campos, J. J. "Father, Mother, and Stranger as Elicitors of Attachment Behaviors in Infancy." *Developmental Psychology* 10 (1974): 146-154.
Crain, A. J., and Stamm, C. S. "Intermittent Absence of Fathers and Children's Perception of Parents." *Journal of Marriage and the Family* 27 (1965): 344-347.
Crandall, V. J.; Dewey, R.; Katkovsky, W.; and Preston, A. "Parents' Attitudes and Behaviors and Grade-School Children's Academic Achievements." *Journal of Genetic Psychology* 104 (1964): 53-66.
Cross, H. J. "The Relation of Parental Training Conditions to Conceptual Level in Adolescent Boys." *Journal of Personality* 34 (1966): 348-365.
Douvan, E., and Adelson, J. *The Adolescent Experience.* New York: John Wiley & Sons, 1966.
Emmerich, W. "Young Children's Discriminations of Parent and Child Roles." *Child Development* 30 (1959): 403-419.
Epstein, A. S., and Radin, N. "Motivational Components Related to Father Behavior and Cognitive Functioning in Preschoolers." *Child Development* 46 (1975): 831-839.
Fagot, B. I. "Sex Differences in Toddler's Behaviors and Parental Reaction." *Developmental Psychology* 10 (1974): 554-558.

Feiring, C. "The Influence of the Child and Secondary Parent on Maternal Behavior: Toward a Social Systems View of Early Infant-Mother Attachment." Doctoral dissertation, University of Pittsburgh, 1975.

Feldman, S. S., and Ingham, M. E. "Attachment Behavior: A Validation Study in Two Age Groups." *Child Development* 46 (1975): 319-330.

Finch, H. M. "Young Children's Concepts of Parent Roles." *Journal of Home Economics* 47 (1955): 99-103.

Fitzgerald, M. P. "Six Differences in the Perception of the Parental Role for Middle and Working Class Adolescents." *Journal of Clinical Psychology* 22 (1966): 15-16.

Fling, S., and Manosevitz, M. "Sex-Typing in Nursery School Children's Play Interests." *Developmental Psychology* 7 (1972): 146-152.

Freeberg, N. E., and Payne, D. T. "Dimensions of Parental Practice Concerned with Cognitive Development in the Preschool Child." *Journal of Genetic Psychology* 111 (1967): 245-261.

Goodenough, E. W. "Interest in Persons as an Aspect of Sex Difference in the Early Years." *Genetic Psychology Monographs* 55 (1957): 287-323.

Hartley, R. E. "Children's Concepts of Male and Female Roles." *Merrill-Palmer Quarterly* 6 (1960): 83-91.

Heilbrun, A. B., Jr.; Harrell, S. N.; and Gillard, B. J. "Perceived Childrearing Attitudes of Fathers and Cognitive Control in Daughters." *Journal of Genetic Psychology* 111 (1967): 29-40.

Herzog, E.; and Sudia, C. "Children in Fatherless Families." In *Review of Child Development Research*, vol. 3, edited by B. M. Caldwell and H. N. Ricciuti. Chicago: University of Chicago Press, 1973.

Hetherington, E. M. "The Effects of Familial Variables on Sex Typing, on Parent-Child Similarity and on Imitation in Children." In *Minnesota Symposia on Child Psychology*, vol. 1, edited by J. P. Hill. Minneapolis: University of Minnesota Press, 1967.

Hetherington, E. M. "Effects of Paternal Absence on Sex-Typed Behaviors in Negro and White Preadolescent Males." *Journal of Personality and Social Psychology* 4 (1966): 87-91.

Hurley, J. "Parental Acceptance-Rejection and Children's Intelligence." *Merrill-Palmer Quarterly* 11 (1965): 19-31.

Johnson, M. M. "Sex-Role Learning in the Nuclear Family." *Child Development* 34 (1963): 319-333.

Kagan, J.; Hosken, B.; and Watson, S. "Child's Symbolic Conceptualization of Parents." *Child Development* 32 (1961): 625-636.

Kagan, J., and Lemkin, J. "The Child's Differential Perception of Parental Attributes." *Journal of Abnormal and Social Psychology* 61 (1960): 440-447.

Katkovsky, W.; Crandall, V. C.; and Good, S. "Parental Antecedents of Children's Beliefs in Internal-External Control of Reinforcement in Intellectual Achievement Situations." *Child Development* 38 (1967): 765-776.

Kohn, M. L., and Carroll, E. E. "Social Class and the Allocation of Parental Responsibilities." *Sociometry* 23 (1960): 372-392.

Kopf, K. E. "Family Variables and School Adjustment of Eighth Grade Father-Absent Boys." *Family Coordinator* 19 (1970): 145-150.

Kotelchuck, M. "The Nature of the Child's Tie to His Father." Doctoral dissertation, Harvard University, 1972.

Lamb, M. E. "Fathers: Forgotten Contributors to Child Development." *Human Development* 18 (1975): 245-266.

Lamb, M. E. "Interactions Between Eight-Month-Old Children and Their Fathers and Mothers." In *The Role of the Father in Child Development*, edited by M. E. Lamb. New York: John Wiley & Sons, 1976.

Lansky, L. M. "The Family Structure Also Affects the Model: Sex-Role Attitudes in Parents of Preschool Children." *Merrill-Palmer Quarterly* 13 (1967): 139-150.

Lewis, M., and Weinraub, M. "The Father's Role in the Child's Social Network." In *The Role of the Father in Child Development*, edited by M. E. Lamb. New York: John Wiley & Sons, 1976.

Lewis, M., and Weinraub, M. "Sex of Parent x Sex of Child: Socioemotional Development." In *Sex Differences in Behavior*, edited by R. Richert, R. Friedman, and R. Van de Wiele. New York: John Wiley & Sons, 1974.

Lynn, D. B. *The Father: His Role in Child Development*. Monterey, Calif.: Brooks/Cole, 1974.

Lynn, D. B., and Cross, A. DeP. "Parent Preference of Preschool Children." *Journal of Marriage and the Family* 36 (1974): 555-559.

Lynn, D. B., and Sawrey, W. L. "The Effects of Father-Absence on Norwegian Boys and Girls." *Journal of Abnormal and Social Psychology* 59 (1959): 258-262.

Maccoby, E. E., and Jacklin, C. N. *The Psychology of Sex Differences*. Stanford, Calif.: Stanford University Press, 1974.

Marcus, R. F. "The Child as Elicitor of Parental Sanctions for Independent and Dependent Behavior: A Simulation of Parent-Child Interaction." *Developmental Psychology* 11 (1975): 443-452.

Marecek, J. "Psychological Androgyny and Positive Mental Health: A Biosocial Perspective." Paper presented at the American Psychological Association meeting, Washington, D.C., September 1976.

Margolin, G., and Patterson, G. R. "Differential Consequences Provided by Mothers and Fathers for Their Sons and Daughters." *Developmental Psychology* 11 (1975): 537-538.

McCord, J.; McCord, W.; and Thurber, E. "Some Effects of Paternal Absence on Male Children." *Journal of Abnormal and Social Psychology* 62 (1962): 361-369.

Mobley, E. D. "Ego-Ideal Themes in Fatherhood." *Smith College Studies in Social Work* 45 (1975): 230-252.

Moulton, R. W.; Burnstein, E.; Liberty, P. G.; and Altucher, N. "Patterning of Parental Affection and Disciplinary Dominance as a Determinant of Guilt and Sex-Typing." *Journal of Personality and Social Psychology* 4 (1966): 356-363.

Mussen, P., and Distler, L. "Child Rearing Antecedents of Masculine Identification in Kindergarten Boys." *Child Development* 31 (1960): 89-100.

Mussen, P., and Distler, L. "Masculinity, Identification, and Father-Son Relationships." *Journal of Abnormal and Social Psychology* 59 (1959): 350-356.

Mussen, P., and Rutherford, E. "Parent-Child Relations and Parental Personality in Relation to Young Children's Sex-Role Preferences." *Child Development* 34 (1963): 589-607.

Oliver, L. W. "The Relationship of Parental Attitudes and Parent Identification to Career and Homemaking Orientation in College Women." *Journal of Vocational Behavior* 7, no. 1 (1975): 1-12.

Osofsky, J. D., and O'Connell, E. J. "Parent-Child Interaction: Daughters' Effects on Mothers' and Fathers' Behavior." *Developmental Psychology* 7 (1972): 157-168.

Parke, R. D., and O'Leary, S. "Father-Mother-Infant Interaction in the Newborn Period: Some Findings, Some Observations, and Some Unresolved Issues." In *The Developing Individual in a Changing World*, vol. II. Social and Environmental Issues, edited by K. Riegel and J. Meacham. The Hague: Mouton, 1976.

Parsons, T., and Bales, R. F. *Family, Socialization and Interaction Process*. Riverside, N.J.: Free Press, 1955.

Pedersen, F. A. "Relationship Between Father Absence and Emotional Disturbance in Male Military Dependents." *Merrill-Palmer Quarterly* 12 (1966): 321-333.

Pedersen, F. A.; Anderson, B. J.; and Cain, R. L. "An Approach to Understanding Linkages Between the Parent-Infant and Spouse Relationships." Paper presented at the Society for Research in Child Development meeting, New Orleans, March 1977.

Pedersen, F. A., and Robson, K. S. "Father Participation in Infancy." *American Journal of Orthopsychiatry* 39 (1969): 466-472.

Phelan, H. M. "The Incidence and Possible Significance of the Drawing of Female Figures by Sixth-Grade Boys in Response to the Draw-A-Person Test." *Psychiatric Quarterly* 38 (1964): 1-16.

Rebelsky, F., and Hanks, C. "Fathers' Verbal Interaction with Infants in the First Three Months of Life." *Child Development* 42 (1971): 63-68.

Ringness, T. A. "Identifying Figures, Their Achievement Values and Children's Values as Related to Actual and Predicted Achievement." *Journal of Educational Psychology* 61 (1970): 174-175.

Rothbart, M. K., and Maccoby, E. E. "Parents' Differential Reactions to Sons and Daughters." *Journal of Personality and Social Psychology* 4 (1966): 237-243.

Santrock, J. W. "Paternal Absence, Sex-Typing, and Identification." *Developmental Psychology* 2 (1970): 264-272.

Santrock, J. W. "Relation of Type and Onset of Father Absence to Cognitive Development." *Child Development* 43 (1972): 455-469.

Schaffer, H. R., and Emerson, P. E. "The Development of Social Attachments in Infancy." *Monographs of the Society for Research in Child Development* 29, no. 3 (1964): serial no. 94.

Sears, P. S. "Child-Rearing Factors Related to Playing of Sex-Typed Roles." *American Psychologist* 8 (1953): 431.

Sears, R. R.; Maccoby, E. E.; and Levin, H. *Patterns of Child Rearing.* New York: Row, Peterson, 1957.

Sears, R. R.; Pintler, M. H.; and Sears, P. S. "Effects of Father-Separation on Pre-School Children's Doll-Play Aggression." *Child Development* 17 (1946): 219-243.

Solomon, D. "The Generality of Children's Achievement-Related Behavior." *Journal of Genetic Psychology* 114 (1969): 109-125.

Spitz, R. A. "Hospitalism: An Inquiry into the Genesis of Psychiatric Conditions in Early Childhood." In *The Psychoanalytic Study of the Child,* edited by A. Freud et al. New York: International University Press, 1945.

Stehbens, J. A., and Carr, D. L. "Perceptions of Parental Attitudes by Students Varying in Intellectual Ability and Educational Efficiency." *Psychology in the Schools* 7 (1970): 67-73.

Stolz, L. M. "Old and New Directions in Child Development." *Merrill-Palmer Quarterly* 12 (1966): 221-232.

Tasch, R. J. "The Role of the Father in the Family." *Journal of Experimental Education* 20 (1952): 219-361.

Teahan, J. E. "Parental Attitudes and College Success." *Journal of Educational Psychology* 54 (1963): 104-109.

Thomes, M. M. "Children with Absent Fathers." *Journal of Marriage and the Family* 30 (1968): 89-96.

Thompson, S. K. "Gender Labels and Early Sex Role Development." *Child Development* 46 (1975): 339-347.

U.S. Department of Commerce. *Statistical Abstract.* Washington, D.C.: U.S. Government Printing Office, 1976.

Vener, A. M., and Snyder, C. A. "The Preschool Child's Awareness and Anticipation of Adult Sex Roles." *Sociometry* 29 (1966): 159-168.

Walstedt, J. J. "The Role of the Father in the Socialization of Altruism and Otherness in Women." *Dissertation Abstracts International* 35 (1974): 3003-3004.

Weinraub, M.; Brooks, J.; and Lewis, M. "The Social Network: A Reconsideration of the Concept of Attachment." *Human Development* 20 (1977): 31-47.

Fatherhood

Weinraub, M., and Frankel, J. "Sex Differences in Parent-Infant Interaction During Free Play, Departure and Separation." *Child Development* 48 (1978): in press.

Weinraub, M., and Leite, J. "Sex-Typed Toy Preference and Knowledge of Sex-Role Stereotypes in Two-Year-Old Children." Paper presented at the Eastern Psychological Association meeting, Boston, April 1977.

Werts, C. E. "Social Class and Initial Career Choice of College Freshmen." *Sociology of Education* 39 (1966): 74-85.

White, B. L. "Fundamental Early Environmental Influences on the Development of Competence." In *The Third Western Symposium on Learning: Cognitive Learning.* Bellingham, Wash.: Western Washington State College, 1972.

Willemsen, E.; Flaherty, D.; Heaton, C.; and Ritchey, G. "Attachment Behavior of One-Year-Olds as a Function of Mother vs. Father, Sex of Child, Session, and Toys." *Genetic Psychology Monographs* 90 (1976): 305-324.

Witkin, H. A.; Dyk, R. B.; Faterson, H. F.; Goodenough, D. R.; and Karp, S. A. *Psychological Differentiation.* New York: John Wiley & Sons, 1962.

James C. Young and Muriel E. Hamilton

7 Paternal Behavior: Implications for Childrearing Practice

Childrearing is an undertaking that is not easy. The responsibilities are tremendous. Parents are not only responsible for the physical well-being of their children, but they must care for their children's emotional and mental development as well. Parents are expected to give to society human beings who are able to interact with and function within the norms of this complex society. Parents are mediators for children's understanding of the world, and children's first perception of the world is their home environment. From there, the extent to which the parents provide meaningful experiences for young children largely determines the children's ability to discover meaning and value in their personal environments. Parents are models and teachers for a vast range of behaviors, values, and attitudes.

A clear understanding of parental behavior and how it can best support healthy development of young children is therefore crucial. One of the most urgent needs within the study of parenting is to look closely at the role of fathers in child development. Discussions of parenting have given very little attention to fathers and have basically limited that attention to father absence or dysfunction. Research is just beginning to focus on the positive and complex roles that most fathers play in the lives of their young children, or on the broad definitions of how these roles can be carried out.

With the goal of addressing the need for more comprehensive discussion of fathering roles and behavior, this chapter will focus on three general areas: a description of parental responsibilities and behaviors; the traditional role and function of the American father; and a redefinition of the father's role in childrearing.

Parental Responsibilities and Behaviors

Child development research (Baumrind 1971; Brophy 1970; Freeberg and Payne 1967; Radin 1971; Sears et al. 1957; Tulkin and Cohler 1973; Tulkin and Kagan 1972) has thoroughly documented the importance of a nurturant environment for producing a healthy child. Such an environment is characterized by consistently warm, caring, dependable, and emotionally healthy relationships with others. Parental behavior can be simply defined as an intimate relationship between two human beings, parent and child. This relationship is important to every person during early childhood and throughout life. How well a child's needs are met determines the quality of such a relationship. If the child's fundamental developmental needs are met first, subsequent interactions between parent and child will be more growth-enhancing.

While one or the other parent may be no more capable of fulfilling parental responsibilities, the great majority of research efforts have given attention only to the mother's influence. During the past decade, there has been a proliferation of studies examining the interaction between mother and child, influence of maternal behavior on cognitive development, mothers as teachers, mothers and children in the home environment, and influences of socioeconomic status on maternal teaching and nurturing styles. The importance of such studies is generally accepted based on several assumptions regarding human development. First, psychoanalytic theory emphasizes the importance of the early years of a child's life; the importance of the child's relationships, particularly with the mother, during these years; and how early experiences affect later personality development. Second, an investigation of historical trends in child research reveals an early interest in such variables as intelligence and physical growth. Positive growth and development in these areas has often been attributed in great measure to the quality of the interaction between parent and child. Third, the mental hygiene movement focuses its attention on prevention of mental illness; this has led to an interest in identifying causal antecedents in childhood of adult personality and adjustment.

Some research (Ainsworth 1963; Maccoby and Masters 1970; Schaefer et al. 1968) has suggested that the differences in children's development can be attributed to the amount and quality of direct physical care the mother provides. Other researchers have attempted to examine aspects of parenting that are less overt. Feelings and attitudes have been measured to determine whether or not they affect the parent-child relationship. Data from several studies (Caldwell and Hersher 1964; Davids 1968) reveal that maternal rejection significantly affects children's development. Research and demonstration programs designed to assist parents in developing new knowledge of child-rearing skills and methods of communicating with their children (Barbrack and Horton 1970; Gilmer 1970; Klaus and Gray 1968; Lambie et al. 1974; Levenstein 1971; Pickarts and Fargo 1971; and Schaefer 1972) have usually focused on the mother.

Traditional Role of the American Father

The term *parent* has frequently been used as though it were synonymous with the term *mother*. The omission of fathers from research about programs for parents is probably due to the fact that mothers are often the persons charged with the principal caregiving responsibilities. This omission may also be based on the following erroneous but commonly-accepted assumptions:

- Fathers are unimportant in the childrearing process, especially during children's early years.
- Mothers can report accurately what fathers think and feel.
- While mothers have a natural instinct for childrearing, fathers do not.
- Infants form strong psychological and physiological attachments to their mothers but not to their fathers.
- If a child must be raised by one parent, it should be the mother.
- Fathers serve only two basic functions in the family—providing financial support and serving as role models for sons.
- There are certain human activities which are exclusively "men's work" and certain human activities which are exclusively "women's work."

Let us examine some of the evidence that challenges these assumptions.

Billingsley (1968) described the father's essential family functions as being instrumental in character—serving to maintain the basic physical and social integrity of the family unit—for example, the provision of food, clothing, shelter, and health care. Pedersen (1969) suspected that the role of the father is to provide novelty of stimulation that augments the routines of the mother. While these responsibilities have been traditionally relegated to the father, the mother's function has been described as to respond to the expressive needs that maintain and enhance the socioemotional relationships and feelings among family members.

Historically, the family in the United States has been patriarchal; the family has been centered around the father as the main source of authority as well as the principal provider and protector. This patriarchal structure supports the tradition of a strong father to whom children must be submissive and obedient. Because "father knows best," he alone prescribed the activities which were in the best interest of each child. His interest in the child was limited to the child's accepting and attaining goals established exclusively by the father.

In addition to determining goals for their children, fathers have also been shown to exert a primary influence on the development of their children's sexual behavior. Patterns of sexual behavior are greatly influenced by the differential treatment of boys and girls by their fathers (Biller 1969; Lynn 1974; Rothbart and Maccoby 1966). Male children are more likely to be physically punished, whereas female children are verbally admonished for misbehavior. Fathers will roughhouse with boys but treat girls in a dainty fashion.

The way children are treated tends strongly to influence sexual behavior throughout the developmental process, even as early as the latter part of the first year of life. For example, a boy's perception of himself as a male, and thus more similar to his father than his mother, is an impetus for the boy to imitate his father. Kagan (1958) stressed the significance of the child's perceived similarity to the parent of the same sex, both as a motive to imitate and as a reinforcement—the more the child imitates that parent, the more the child's self-perception is similar to that parent.

An important factor in the development of a masculine orientation is the availability of an involved father, or another significant older male, as a discriminable male. If the boy is to develop a positive masculine self-concept, he must receive consistent nurturance and positive feedback. Parental nurturance facilitates the development of a boy's masculine orientation, and a high level of father's availability seems to be important for positive growth in this area.

A daughter's feminine development is influenced by how her father differentiates his masculine role from her feminine role and what type of behavior he considers appropriate for her. Sears, Rau, and Alpert (1965), found a high and significant correlation between girls' femininity and their fathers' expectations of their participation in feminine activities. Heilbrun (1965) concluded that daughters who perceived themselves as feminine were likely to view their fathers as demonstrating strong masculine characteristics of paternal behavior.

Evidence from investigations by Tasch (1952, 1955) also demonstrated that paternal behaviors varied by sex of the child. Fathers viewed their daughters as more delicate and sensitive than their sons. These fathers used physical punishment more frequently with their sons than with their daughters. They also tended to define all household tasks based upon sex-role appropriateness. Parsons (1964) argued that fathers actively encouraged and reinforced children's sex-typing, often through the assignment of household chores. Fathers preferred to label outdoor jobs such as emptying the garbage and taking out trash as things boys do, whereas girls did the indoor duties like making beds, dusting, and helping with cooking. Whether such differential treatment by fathers is optimal for the individual child is questionable, but it appears that fathers do have a significant impact on children's personality and development.

Thus interaction with a competent and involved father provides both daughters and sons with basic experiences which they tend to generalize to other relationships with peers, male or female. We can safely assume from this research that children who have positive relationships with their fathers are more likely to be able to obtain satisfaction in their personal and professional adult relationships with both men and women.

In spite of the demonstrated importance of the father role in setting goals and influencing the development of attitudes in the area of sexual identification with his children, the literature stops far short of giving fathers the attention they deserve with regard to all aspects of early childhood development. A review of selected college-level textbooks in areas of child development, child care, early childhood education, and psychology clearly shows that fathers have received practically no attention compared to mothers. A cursory examination of the indexes of most of these books reveals that the terms *father, fathering,* or *paternal* are either lacking entirely or limited to subheadings such as control of family (disciplinarian), aggression, absence of, sex-typing, or occupation and intellectual development. (Texts reviewed include Mussen 1960, 1970; Papalia and Olds 1975; Munsinger 1971; Mussen, Conger, and Kagan 1974; Smart and Smart 1977; Lavatelli and Stendler 1972; Stone and Church 1968; McCandless and Evans 1973; McCandless 1967; Hurlock 1950; Ames 1970; Comer and Poussaint 1975; Yarrow, Rubenstein, and Pedersen 1975; Rebelsky and Dorman 1970.)

Similarly, the increasingly popular "how-to-parent" books tend either to take fathers for granted or assign them to extremely limited roles in meeting the needs of young children today. The popularity of these parental guidebooks (Dodson 1970, 1974; Green 1976; Gordon 1970; Ilg and Ames 1972) strongly suggests that parents sincerely want to improve upon their knowledge of how best to care for and teach their children. However, judging from their content, fathers remain the forgotten parent.

This overview of the literature regarding parenting and the roles and functions of fathers is far from exhaustive. Nevertheless, a consistent trend is evident: Fathers are described as having very limited contact with their children, especially during children's first few years. Fathers' roles are narrowly defined, and therefore their importance in providing a healthy environment for child development is often minimized, except in one or two isolated functions revolving around sex-role orientation. The discussion presented below will suggest a more active role for fathers—a redefinition of fathering which can better facilitate a wholesome developmental process for young children.

Redefining the Father Role in Childrearing

There is growing concern among child development specialists, teachers, and parents about the father's role in childrearing. As noted, fathers have too often been overlooked and undervalued in considering parenting responsibilities and contributions. Let us look briefly at some of the trends in modern America. It is common knowledge that the status of women has been going through a quiet but steady revolution for the past thirty years. Changed social values have enabled women to select parenting as simply one of many career alternatives. Economic pressures have also forced millions of women to work full-time outside the home, regardless of whether or not there are young children in the family. As extended families have become fewer, child care centers or homes have been used by more families to help care for and train children. But professional child care is expensive and not always available when needed. Therefore, in many families, both mother and father are now sharing the child care and housekeeping tasks, just as they share in the financial support of the family.

In addition to having new work roles and responsibilities, American women are reevaluating traditional assumptions about the importance of childrearing as a life goal. Many mothers now take the position that raising children is just one of several activities to which they wish to devote their lives. Increasing numbers of fathers are therefore faced with the decision of either assisting their wives in dividing time between children and career or thwarting their wives' ambitions by leaving them with the entire burden of child care. More and more fathers are choosing to share more equally in family responsibilities.

While in many families the father has assumed a more active role because of the mother's work schedule and career goals, it is our contention that there are a number of other reasons for increasing and broadening the definition of father roles. Mead (1976) suggested convincingly that children benefit from having two adults in their immediate family environment. By exposure to more than one adult role model, children are more able to accept the fact that all adults are not the same, that more than one kind of adult personality can be acceptable, and that living in the complex world of the twentieth century requires the capacity to deal with many different types of human beings. Mead also asserts that children who are raised in a two-adult household benefit from hearing adult conversations on a regular basis, an important experience for the development of verbal and cognitive skills beyond the baby talk level. Other sociologists feel that two parents might not even be sufficient to meet children's needs and that perhaps the extended family model, with several adults assuming parenting roles for each child, is in fact better than the small nuclear families most children now experience. This is a basic belief in a commune or a kibbutz community. (See Chapter 10.)

Significant benefits accrue to children who learn about the similarities and the differences in male and female adults from firsthand, consistent experience. Sex-role modeling was discussed in some detail above; we need only to reiterate that having both a male and a female adult around helps children—both girls and boys—to visualize and prepare for their own futures as adults.

A further reason for redefining the father's role focuses on fathers themselves. The traditional role of the father is limited to the instrumental family tasks of protection and financial support, taking care of the heavy discipline problems, and teaching sons how to act "masculine." Such a role cheats fathers of being fully human and of offering a wider range of behaviors, emotions, and skills to their children. Men are beginning to realize the negative implications of this often self-imposed stereotype of a money machine having no emotions and lacking the slightest knowledge about babies, other than that needed to create them. As women become more independent financially and take on more of the instrumental tasks required to sustain the family, men may find themselves in the very precarious situation of being totally unnecessary for their family's survival—unless they begin to redefine and expand the functions they are to assume.

Let us first separate some basic myths about fathers from the realities.

Myth #1: Men do not have a natural inclination toward parenting or nurturing behavior. *Reality:* Parenting skills, like most other skills, are basically learned behaviors, not biological endowments. Social customs have taught women and girls to care for the young; social customs could also teach, encourage, and reward men and boys for the same types of skills and behavior.

Myth #2: Infants (both male and female) show no interest in their fathers. *Reality:* Recent research by Lamb (1975) and others casts serious doubts on our earlier assumptions. When the father takes an active role during the first few months of the infant's life, a strong bond seems to develop between them, just as it does between infant and mother. An infant may be more concerned with basic needs of nourishment, comfort, sleep, and a predictable, positive environment than with the sex of the person who meets these needs.

Myth #3: There is a single and universal description of a "successful father." He is financially secure, emotionally tough, and has a natural strength and inclination to control his environment through rational thought and behavior. *Reality:* As women and men honestly raise questions about traditional sex-role definitions and expectations, both are acknowledging much broader characteristics and options for being a successful woman or a successful man. There is no single definition for masculinity or femininity; neither is there a single or universal definition for a good father or a good mother.

Myth #4: Fathers do not want to be bothered with the daily routines of childrearing. *Reality:* Although many fathers have accepted a narrow definition of their role and feel that their time should be spent on non-child-related tasks, many *are* eager to participate in direct interaction with their children at all levels. Many more fathers would feel this way if they were encouraged to realize their capabilities as parents.

Against this rationale for redefining the role of fathers in present and future families, let us look at some concrete strategies for accomplishing this change. We must remember that patterns of social behavior do not change easily or rapidly; most people do what they do out of habit, not because of rational considerations. Parents behave toward their children by and large in the same way their parents behaved toward them. However, we hope that changes in our society will enable us to break old habits and find new and positive ways of coping with modern childrearing.

Our goal is simple: to create family-living environments that allow both men and women to demonstrate their full potential as human beings and that offer children the maximum exposure to the loving support and the skills which they need for optimal emotional and intellectual development.

To achieve this redefinition of fatherhood, it is appropriate to outline a few basic ground rules for both parents. First, in order to move toward a new set of roles, a father must choose whether he will assume an active (or a passive) role with his children. The decision cannot be made lightly; being an active father will take a great deal of time, energy, and emotional stamina. The second ground rule is that the mother must cooperate by sharing the children and helping the father develop new skills and understandings of the children. The mother must also be willing to offer moral support as the father attempts to develop behaviors which may have few other social supports. The third rule requires that both parents agree to cooperate rather than compete for the attention and affection of their children. Both the discipline and fun, the dirty diapers and the hugs, must be shared on an equal basis.

Positive interactions can begin literally at birth. The father should become a familiar, nonthreatening person in the infant's everyday environment by taking care of some of the diapering, feeding, playing, bathing, and talking to the infant. During the toddler and preschool years, fathers can play a vital role in children's discovery of concepts, language, emotions, self-identity, sexuality—the whole learning process of what the world is all about. This can be done by planning shared activities and conversations, by being sensitive to children's developmental stages, and by demonstrating positive emotions and affection to children. When children enter school and begin to focus more on peer relationships, fathers can help bridge the gap between family and outside world by participating in the school process through teacher conferences, school visits, talking about school at home, and accepting children's peer friendships.

These suggested activities during the various stages of child development have focused on families where father, mother, and children are all living together, yet more and more families are not all living under the same roof. What is a positive, active role for fathers in situations of divorce or long-term separation? Again, at the risk of sounding simplistic, the role should be as similar as possible to that of fathers in intact families. In the small but growing number of cases where the father has primary custody of the children after a divorce, he will obviously play an active childrearing role. However, in most cases, the father does not live with his children and is severely (and often unfairly) limited in the amount and type of contact he can maintain with the children. This limited contact has no reasonable basis; fathers should be actively encouraged to maintain as much contact as possible with their children, with the commitment by both parents that marital problems will not be confused with the rights and responsibilities of parenthood. (See Chapter 8.)

As already stated, none of the fathering activities outlined here as part of our redefinition is revolutionary. Numerous questions remain unanswered. What *is* certain is that family life in America is experiencing changes that will require new definitions, new styles of parenting, and new role responsibilities and privileges for both men and women. We are not suggesting that differences between men and women will disappear or that fathers and mothers will play exactly the same roles in any family. What we are suggesting is that mothers and fathers can and should determine how best to divide up the tasks necessary for raising healthy children and achieving a comfortable family environment. This division of tasks should not be based on stereotypes or myths about what a man is and what a woman is, but on human values which accept both instrumental and socioemotional roles for mothers and fathers. It is our belief this will enable fathers, mothers, and especially children to have a much fuller world of expectations and much more freedom of personality and life goals than ever before.

References

Ainsworth, M. D. S. "The Development of Infant-Mother Interaction among the Ganda." In *Determinants of Infant Behavior,* vol. II, edited by B. M. Foss. New York: John Wiley & Sons, 1963.

Ames, B. L. *Child Care and Development.* Philadelphia: J. B. Lippincott, 1970.

Barbrack, C. R., and Horton, D. M. "Educational Intervention in the Home and Paraprofessional Career Development: A First Generation Mother Study." Urbana, Ill.: ERIC Microfilms, 1970. (ERIC Document Reproduction Service No. ED 045 190.)

Baumrind, D. "Some Thoughts about Child Rearing." In *Influences on Human Development*, edited by U. Bronfenbrenner. Hinsdale, Ill.: Dryden Press, 1972.

Biller, H. B. "Father Dominance and Sex-Role Development in Kindergarten-Age Boys." *Developmental Psychology* 1, no. 2 (1969): 87-94.

Billingsley, A. *Black Families in White America*. Englewood Cliffs, N.J.: Prentice-Hall, 1968.

Brophy, J. E. "Mothers as Teachers of Their Own Preschool Children: The Influence of Socioeconomic Status and Task Structure on Teaching Specificity." *Child Development* 40 (1970): 79-94.

Caldwell, B. M., and Hersher, L. "Mother-Infant Interaction During the First Year of Life." *Merrill-Palmer Quarterly* 10 (1964): 119-128.

Comer, J. P., and Poussaint, A. F. *Black Child Care*. New York: Simon and Schuster, 1975.

Davids, A. "A Research Design for Studying Maternal Emotionality Before Childbirth and After Social Interaction with the Child." *Merrill-Palmer Quarterly* 14 (1968): 345-354.

Dodson, F. *How to Father*. Los Angeles: Nash, 1974.

Dodson, F. *How to Parent*. Los Angeles: Nash, 1970.

Freeberg, N. E., and Payne, D. T. "Parental Influence on Cognitive Development in Early Childhood: A Review." *Child Development* 38 (1967): 65-87.

Gilmer, B. R. *Intervention with Mothers of Young Children: A Study of Intrafamily Effects*. Urbana, Ill.: ERIC Microfilms, 1970.

Ginott, H. G. *Between Parent and Child*. New York: Macmillan, 1965.

Gordon, T. *Parent Effectiveness Training*. New York: Wyden, 1970.

Green, M. *Fathering*. New York: McGraw-Hill, 1976.

Heilbrun, A. B. "The Measurement of Identification." *Child Development* 35 (1965): 111-128.

Hurlock, E. B. *Child Development*, 2nd ed. New York: McGraw-Hill, 1950.

Ilg, F. L., and Ames, L. B. *Child Behavior from Birth to Ten*. New York: Barnes and Noble, 1955.

Kagan, J. "The Concept of Identification." *Psychological Review* 65 (1958): 295-305.

Kamii, C. K., and Radin, N. C. "Class Differences in the Socialization Practices of Negro Mothers." *Journal of Marriage and Family* 29 (1967): 302-310.

Klaus, R. A., and Gray, S. W. "The Early Training Project for Disadvantaged Children: A Report after Five Years." *Monographs of the Society for Research in Child Development* 33, (1968): no. 4, serial no. 120.

Lamb, M. E. "Fathers: Contributions to Child Development." *Human Development* 18 (1975): 245-266.

Lambie, D. Z.; Bond, J. T.; and Weikart, D. P. *Home Teaching with Mothers and Infants*. Ypsilanti, Mich.: High/Scope Educational Research Foundation, 1974.

Lavatelli, C. S., and Stendler, F. *Readings in Child Behavior and Development*. New York: Harcourt Brace Jovanovich, 1972.

Levenstein, P. "Learning Through (and from) Mothers." *Childhood Education* 48 (1971): 130-134.

Lynn, D. B. *The Father: His Role in Child Development*. Monterey, Calif.: Brooks/Cole, 1974.

Maccoby, E. E., and Masters, J. C. "Attachment and Dependency." In *Carmichael's Manual of Child Psychology*, vol. 2, edited by P. H. Mussen. New York: John Wiley & Sons, 1970.

Maier, H. W. *Three Theories of Child Development*. New York: Harper & Row, 1969.

McCandless, B. R. *Children: Behavior and Development*. New York: Holt, Rinehart and Winston, 1967.

McCandless, B. R., and Evans, E. D. *Children and Youth: Psychosocial Development*. Hinsdale, Ill.: Dryden Press, 1973.
Mead, M. "Every Home Needs Two Adults." *Redbook*, May 1976, p. 38.
Munsinger, H. *Fundamentals of Child Development*. New York: Holt, Rinehart, and Winston, 1971.
Mussen, P.H., ed. *Carmichael's Manual of Child Psychology*, vols. 1 and 2. New York: John Wiley & Sons, 1970.
Mussen, P.H. *Handbook of Research in Methods in Child Development*. New York: John Wiley & Sons, 1960.
Mussen, P.H.; Conger, J.J.; and Kagan, J. *Child Development and Personality*. New York: Harper & Row, 1974.
Papalia, D.E., and Olds, S. W. *A Child's World: Infancy Through Adolescence*. New York: McGraw-Hill, 1975.
Parsons, T. *The Social Structure and Personality*. New York: Free Press, 1964.
Pedersen, F.A., and Robson, K.S. "Fathers' Participation in Infancy." *American Journal of Orthopsychiatry* 39 (1969): 466-472.
Pickarts, E., and Fargo, J. *Parent Education*. New York: Appleton-Century-Crofts, 1971.
Radin, N. "Maternal Warmth, Achievement Motivation, and Cognitive Functioning in Lower-Class Preschool Children." *Child Development* 42 (1971): 1560-1565.
Rebelsky, F., and Dorman, L., eds. *Child Development and Behavior*. New York: Alfred A. Knopf, 1970.
Rothbart, M.K., and Maccoby, E.E. "Parents' Differential Reactions to Sons and Daughters." *Journal of Personality and Social Psychology* 4 (1966): 237-243.
Schaefer, E.S. "Parents as Educators: Evidence from Cross-Sectional, Longitudinal, and Intervention Research." In *The Young Child: Reviews of Research*, vol. 2, edited by W.W. Hartup. Washington, D.C.: National Association for the Education of Young Children, 1972.
Schaefer, E.S.; Furfey, P.H.; and Hart, T.S. "Infant Education Research Projects, Washington, D.C." In *Preschool Program in Compensatory Education*, no. 1. Washington, D.C.: U.S. Government Printing Office, 1968.
Sears, R.R.; Maccoby, E.E.; and Levin, H. *Patterns of Child Rearing*. New York: Row, Peterson, 1957.
Sears, R.R.; Rau, L.; and Alpert, R. *Identification and Child Rearing*. Palo Alto, Calif.: Stanford University Press, 1965.
Smart, M.S., and Smart, R.C. *Children: Development and Relations*. 3rd ed. New York: Macmillan, 1977.
Spock, B. *Baby and Child Care*. New York: Pocket Books, 1970.
Stone, L.J., and Church, J. *Childhood and Adolescence*. 2nd ed. New York: Random House, 1968.
Streissguth, A.P., and Bee, H.L. "Mother-Child Interactions and Cognitive Development." In *The Young Child: Reviews of Research*, vol. 2, edited by W.W. Hartup. Washington, D.C.: National Association for the Education of Young Children, 1972.
Tasch, R.J. "Interpersonal Perceptions of Fathers and Mothers." *Journal of Genetic Psychology* 87 (1955): 59-65.
Tasch, R.J. "The Role of the Father in the Family." *Journal of Experimental Education* 20 (1952): 319-361.
Tulkin, S.R., and Cohler, B.J. "Childrearing Attitudes and Mother-Child Interaction in the First Year of Life." *Merrill-Palmer Quarterly* 19 (1973): 95-106.
Tulkin, S.R., and Kagan, J. "Mother-Child Interaction in the First Year of Life." *Influences on Human Development*, edited by U. Bronfenbrenner. Hinsdale, Ill.: Dryden Press, 1972.
Yarrow, L.J.; Rubenstein, J.L.; and Pedersen, F.A. *Infant and Environment: Early Cognitive and Motivational Development*. Washington, D.C.: Hemisphere, 1975.

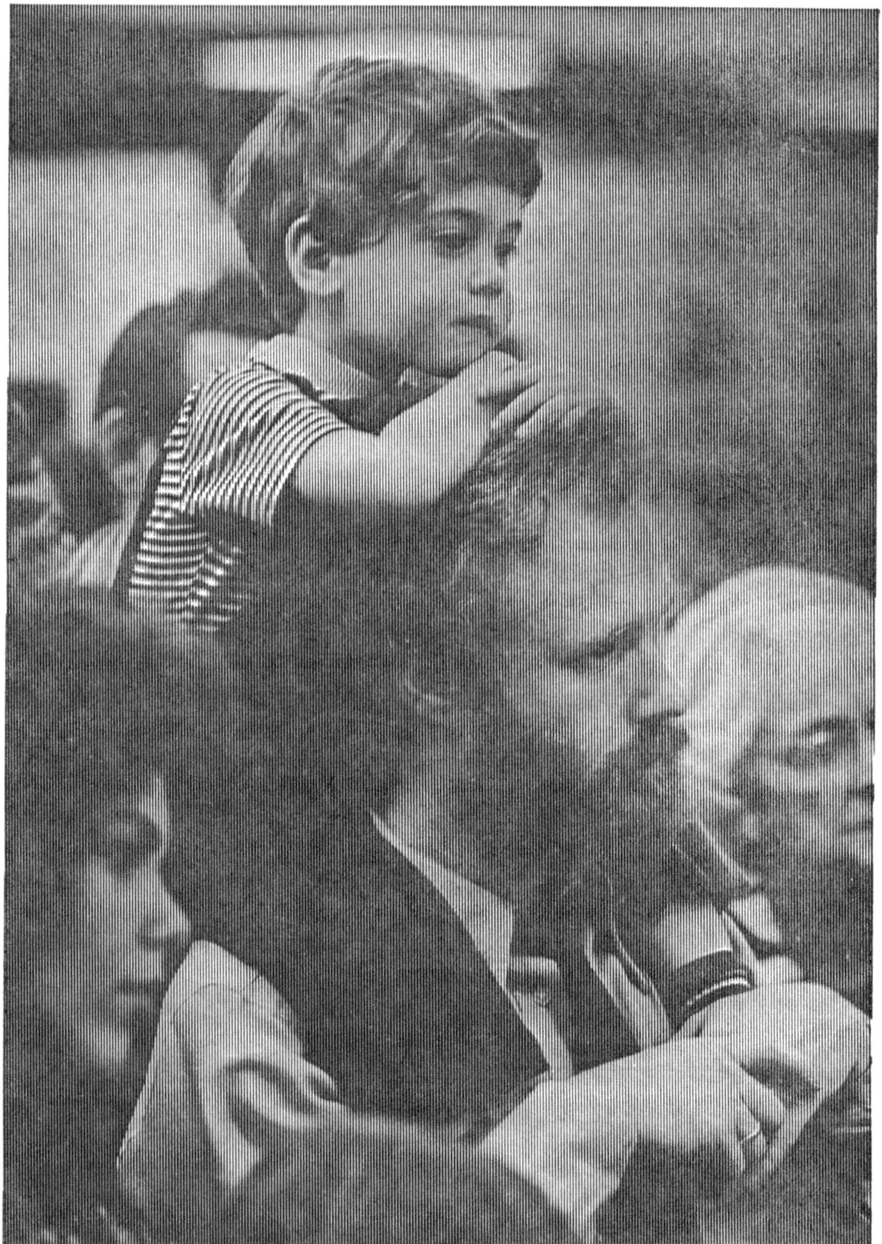

III

The Influence of Family Characteristics and Structure

The quality of the parent-child relationship and its consequences for children's development is influenced by both family structure and the family's relationship to its environment (i.e., its connectedness to that environment). There are widely-held assumptions in this country about the effects of family structure (e.g., single-parent, extended, divorced, communal) on children's development. World War II was followed by increased concern about the effects of father absence on children's development, particularly boys' sex-role development. Interest in the effects of different family structures on children's development has greatly expanded, due largely to the increased variation found in family composition. Questions are being investigated such as: Do such families construct differing support systems and social networks that facilitate the family's childrearing function? Examination of the family's relationship to social, economic, and political institutions and the consequences of these relationships for children's development are being pursued. The effects of poverty have been extensively researched in the past twenty years. Fortunately researchers have become concerned about documenting how governmental policy and programs, as a whole, support or constrain family life and childrearing. Kenniston's book, *All Our Children: The American Family Under Pressure* (1977), and *Toward a National Policy for Children and Families* (1976), a report of the Advisory Committee on Child Development of the National Academy of Sciences, are examples.

The chapters in this section, however, highlight the importance of both of these issues: the relationship between family structure and children's development, and the importance of social networks (e.g., the kin-help system) for family functioning.

Divorce results in a dramatic, precipitous change in family structure with significant emotional, social, and cognitive sequelae both for parents and children. Hetherington, Cox, and Cox's research provides compelling data about the effects of divorce on the family system. Disintegration in the family's functioning and its interrelationships occurs, followed by an apparent period of recovery and stabilization. However, individuals within this system appear to be differentially influenced at various points during the total two-year post-divorce period studied.

McAdoo's discussion of the structure of minority families and the socialization of children therein also provides much needed insights. Differences in values and socialization priorities are highlighted. McAdoo makes a strong case for the importance of kin-help and other support systems for optimal family functioning. Such social networks, based on and fostering reciprocity, appear to be most characteristic of minority families. This may be accounted for by the greater need of minority families for a cushion against an often hostile and alienating environment.

Eiduson and Weisner's interim report of their longitudinal study provides us with rich descriptive information about the differences among nuclear, single-parent, social contract, and communal families. This massive and multidisciplinary study illustrates and reinforces the importance of careful documentation of target variables: parents' values, their attitudes toward and aspirations for children, the physical setting of the home, the people who inhabit the home, parents' construction and use of social supports, and their childrearing practices.

E. Mavis Hetherington, Martha Cox, and Roger Cox

8 The Aftermath of Divorce

The incidence of divorce has increased dramatically over the past decade. If the divorce rate stabilized at its 1974 level, it is estimated that over 40 percent of new marriages would ultimately end in divorce. In addition, although the birthrate in the United States is declining, the number of divorces involving children is rising. While the rate of remarriage has also risen, it has not kept pace with the divorce rate, especially in families where children are involved. Thus, during the past ten years there has been an increase in the proportion of divorced persons, particularly divorced parents, relative to partners in intact marriages (Bronfenbrenner 1975).

In divorces in which children are involved, the mother usually gains custody of the child, except in unusual circumstances. Although the proportion of children living with their divorced fathers is increasing, in the latest yearly population survey by the Census Bureau only 8.4 percent of children of divorced parents were reported as residing with their fathers (Current Population Report Series P-20, 1976). Thus, the most frequently found family condition in the immediate postdivorce situation is that the child lives in a home with the mother and has intermittent or no contact with the father. It may be because of these circumstances that social scientists studying divorce have focused on the impact of divorce on mothers and children, rather than on the entire family system, including the fathers. Even in studies with these restricted perspectives, the approach has been largely descriptive. The characteristics of divorced mothers and their children are described and compared to those of mothers and children in intact homes (Biller 1974; Herzog and Sudia 1973; Hetherington and Deur 1971; Lynn 1974). Attempts to study changes in family interaction and functioning after divorce are rare.

Divorce can be viewed as a critical event that affects the entire family system and the functioning and interactions of members within that system. To get a true picture of the impact of divorce, its effects on the divorced parents and on the children must be examined.

©1978, E. Mavis Hetherington, Martha Cox, and Roger Cox

The findings reported here are part of a two-year longitudinal study of the impact of divorce on family functioning and children's development. The first goal of the larger study was to examine family responses to the crisis of divorce and then examine patterns of family reorganization over the two-year period following divorce. It was assumed that the family system would go through a period of disorganization immediately after the divorce, followed by recovery, reorganization, and eventual attainment of a new pattern of equilibrium. The second goal was to examine the characteristics of family members which contributed to variations in family processes. The third goal was to examine the effects of variations in family interactions and structure on children's development.

In this chapter, we will focus on changes and stresses experienced by family members, and factors related to alterations in parent-child interactions in the two years following divorce.

Method

Subjects

The original sample was composed of 72 White, middle-class children (36 boys, 36 girls) and their divorced parents from homes in which custody had been granted to the mother, and the same number of children and parents from intact homes. The mean ages of the divorced mothers and fathers and the mothers and fathers from intact homes were 27.2, 29.6, 27.4, and 30.1 respectively. All parents were high school graduates and the large majority of parents had some college education or advanced training beyond high school. Divorced parents were identified and contacted through court records and lawyers. Only families with a child attending nursery school (who served as the target child) were included in the study. The intact families were selected on the basis of having a child of the same sex, age, and birth order in the same nursery school as the child from a divorced family. In addition, an attempt was made to match parents on age, education, and length of marriage. Only first- and second-born children were included in the study.

The final sample consisted of 24 families in each of four groups (intact families with girls, intact families with boys, divorced families with girls, divorced families with boys)—a total of 96 families for which complete data were available. Sample attrition was largely due to remarriage in the divorced families (19 men, 10 women); separation or divorce in the intact sample (5 families); relocation of a family or parent; and lack of cooperation by schools, which made important measures of the children unavailable. Also, 8 families no longer wished to participate in the study. Because one of the interests of the investigation was to determine how mothers and children functioned in father-absent homes and how their functioning might be related to deviant or nondeviant behavior in children, families with stepparents were excluded from this study but remained in a stepparent study. In the analyses presented here, 6 families were randomly dropped from groups to maintain equal sizes of groups.

When a reduction in sample size from 144 families to 96 families occurs, bias in the sample immediately becomes a concern. On demographic characteristics such as age, religion, education, income, occupation, family size, and maternal employment, there were no differences between those subjects who dropped out or were excluded from the sample and those who remained. When a family was no longer included in the study, a comparative analysis was done of its interaction patterns and those of the continuing families. Some differences in these groups will be noted subsequently. In general, there were few differences in parent-child interactions in families who did or did not remain in the study. However, there were some differences in the characteristics of parents who remarried and how they viewed themselves and their lives.

Procedure

The study used a multimethod, multimeasure approach to the investigation of family interaction. The measures used included interviews with, and structured diary records of, the parents, observations of the parents and child interacting in the laboratory and home, behavior checklists of child behavior, parent rating of child behavior, and a battery of personality scales administered to the parents. In addition, observations of the child were conducted in the nursery school. Peer nomination, teacher ratings of the child's behavior, and measures of the child's sex-role typing, cognitive performance, and social development also were obtained. The parents and children were administered these measures two months, one year, and two years after divorce.

Parent Interviews. Parents were interviewed separately on a structured parent interview schedule designed to assess discipline practices and the parent-child relationship; support systems outside the family household system; social, emotional, and heterosexual relationships; quality of the relationship with the spouse; economic stress; family disorganization; satisfaction and happiness; and attitudes toward themselves. The interviews were tape-recorded. Each of the categories listed in Table 1 was rated on scales by two judges. In some cases the category involved the rating of only a single 5- or 7-point scale. In others it represented a composite score of several ratings on a group of subscales. Interjudge reliabilities ranged from .69 to .95, with a mean of .82. The interviews were derived and modified from those of Baumrind (1967, 1971), Martin and Hetherington (1971), Sears, Rau, and Alpert (1965), and others.

Table 1. Categories for Rating Parent Interviews

Control of child	Economic stress
Maturity demands of child	Family disorganization
Communication with child	Problems in running household
Nurturance of child	Relationship with spouse
Permissiveness-restrictiveness with child	Emotional support in personal matters
Negative sanctions with child	Immediate support system
Positive sanctions with child	Social life and activities
Reinforcement of child for sex-typed behaviors	Contact with adults
	Intimate relations
Paternal availability	Sexuality
Maternal availability	Number of dates
Paternal face-to-face interaction with child	Happiness and satisfaction
Maternal face-to-face interaction with child	Competence as a parent
	Competence as a male/female
Quality of spouse's relationship with child	Self-esteem
Agreement in treatment of child	Satisfaction with employment
	Conflict preceding divorce
Emotional support in childrearing from spouse	Tension in divorce

Parent Personality Inventories. The parent personality measures included the Personal Adjustment Scale of the Adjective Checklist (Gough and Heilburn 1965), the Socialization Scale of the California Personality Inventory (Gough 1969), Rotter's I-E Scale (Rotter 1966), and the Spielberger's State-Trait Anxiety Scale (Spielberger, Gorsuch, and Lushene 1970).

Structured Diary Record. Each parent was asked to complete a structured diary record for three days (one weekday, Saturday, and Sunday). Fathers were asked to include at least one day when they were

The Aftermath of Divorce 153

with their children. The diary record form was divided into half-hour units and contained a checklist of activities, situations, people, and five 7-point bipolar mood rating scales. The dimensions on the mood rating scales included: (1) anxious—relaxed; (2) hostile, angry—friendly, loving; (3) unhappy, depressed—happy; (4) helpless—competent, in control; and (5) unloved, rejected—loved.

Each 30-minute unit was subdivided into three 10-minute units. If very different events had occurred in a 30-minute period, the subject was encouraged to record these separately and sequentially. For example, if a father had a fight with his boss and a phone call from his girl friend in the same half hour, these were recorded sequentially in separate columns. Parents were instructed to check off what they were doing, where they were located, who they were with, and how they were feeling on the mood scales in each 30-minute unit from the time they rose in the morning until they went to sleep at night. The record sheet also left space for any additional comments parents cared to make.

Although parents were encouraged to record at the end of each 30-minute period, because of the situation in which they found themselves, this was sometimes impossible. Any retrospective recording was noted, and the time the entry was made was also recorded. In the first session, a series of standardized scales dealing with affect, stress, and guilt had been included in the battery of parent measures; however, since the diary mood rating scales were found to be better predictors of behavior than these more time-consuming tests, the standardized scales were subsequently dropped from the study.

Parent-Child Laboratory Interaction. Parents were observed separately interacting with their children in the laboratory in half-hour free play situations and half-hour structured situations involving puzzles, block building, bead stringing, and sorting tasks. The interaction sessions with each parent were scheduled on different days, separated by a period of about a month. One-half of the children interacted with the mother first, and one-half with the father first. All sessions were video-taped to permit multiple coding of behavior. Behavior was coded in the categories presented in Table 2. The coding procedure was similar to that used by Patterson, Ray, Shaw, and Cobb (1969); the observation period was divided into 30-second intervals, and an average of approximately five behavior sequences of interactions between the subject and other family members was coded in the 30-second interval. To improve reliability, a tone sounded every six seconds during the recording interval. Two raters rated all sessions; interjudge agreement on individual responses averaged 83 percent.

Table 2. Parent-Child Laboratory Interaction Coding

Parent behavior	Child behavior
Command (positive)	Opposition
Command (negative)	Aversive opposition
Question (positive)	Compliance
Question (negative)	Dependency
Nonverbal intrusion	Negative demands (whining, complaining, angry tone)
Ignores	
Affiliate (interact)	Aggression (tantrums, destructiveness)
Positive sanctions	Requests
Negative sanctions	Affiliate
Reasoning and explanation	Self-manipulation
Encourages	Sustained play
Dependency	Ignores
Indulgence	Cries
Opposition	
Compliance	
Encourages independence	

Checklist of Child Behavior. Although at least three hours of observations of the parent and child interacting in the home situation were collected at three different times, this was not a sufficient time period to obtain an adequate sample of the child's behavior in which we were interested and which occurred relatively infrequently. Parents were given a behavior checklist and a recording form divided into half-hour units, and were asked to record whether a given child behavior had occurred in a particular half-hour period. Three hours of recording were available for fathers, but twenty-four hours were available for mothers. Given behaviors included both acts regarded by parents as noxious, such as yelling, crying, whining, destructiveness, and noncompliance, and those regarded as desirable, such as helping, sharing, cooperative activities, compliance, sustained play, or independent activities.

Parent Rating Scales of Child Behavior. A parent rating scale of child behavior was constructed and standardized on a group of 100 mothers and fathers. Items used in previous observation questionnaires and rating scales, or items which seemed relevant to the interests of this study, were included in an initial pool of 96 items. Parents were asked to rate their children on these items using a 5-point scale, with 1 being never occurs, occurs less often than in most children, and 5 being frequently occurs, occurs more often than in most children. Items which correlated with each other, seemed conceptually related, or had been found to load on the same factor in previous studies, were clustered in seven scales containing a total of 49 items. Only items which correlated with the total score in the scales were retained. Items were phrased to describe very specific behavior, as many of these items were also used on the Checklist of Child Behavior previously described. The seven scales were aggression, inhibition, distractibility, task orientation, prosocial behavior, habit disturbance, and self-control. Divorced parents were asked to rate each item on the basis of the child's current behavior.

Data Analysis

Repeated measure manovas* involving test session (two months, one year, two years), sex of child, sex of parent, and family composition (divorced versus intact) were performed for each measure, interview, and laboratory interaction task. Repeated measure manovas were also performed on the mood ratings and the amount of time spent in various activities reported in the structured diary records, on the checklist, and in the rating scales. A repeated measure manova excluding the sex of child variable was performed for the parents' personality measures. Correlational analyses of all variables within and across subgroups also were performed. In addition, multiple regression and cross-lagged panel correlations and structural equations were calculated for selected parent and child variables in an attempt to identify functional and causal relationships contributing to changes in the behavior of family members across time.

Results

The results of the study will not be presented separately for each procedure used. Instead, the combined findings of the different procedures will be used to discuss alterations in lifestyle, stresses, and coping by family members and family relations, and how these factors changed in the two years following divorce.

Change, Stress, and Coping in Divorce

How does the life of a single parent differ from that of married parents? In changing to a new single lifestyle, what kinds of stresses and satisfactions are experienced by members of a divorced couple? How

---
* multiple analysis of variance

might these be related to parent-child relations? The main areas in which change and stress were experienced were: (1) those related to practical problems of living; (2) those associated with emotional distress and changes in self-concept and identity; and (3) those related to interpersonal problems in maintaining a social life, developing intimate relationships, and interacting with the ex-spouse and child.

Practical Problems. The main practical problems of living encountered by divorced parents were those related to household maintenance and economic and occupational difficulties. Many divorced men, particularly those from marriages in which conventional sex roles had been maintained and the wife had not been employed, initially experienced considerable difficulty in maintaining a household routine and reported distress associated with what one termed "a chaotic lifestyle."

One of the sets of interview scales was family disorganization, which dealt with the degree of structure in proscribed household roles, problems in coping with routine household tasks, and the regulating and scheduling of events. On this scale and in the structured diaries, the households of the divorced mothers and fathers were more disorganized than those of intact families, although this disorganization was most marked in the first year after divorce and decreased significantly by the second year. Members of separated households were more likely to eat pickup meals at irregular times. Divorced mothers and their children were less likely to eat dinner together. Bedtimes were more erratic, the children were read to less often at bedtime, and the children were more likely to arrive at school late. Divorced men were less likely to eat at home than married men. They slept less and had more erratic sleep patterns, and had more difficulty with shopping, cooking, laundry, and cleaning. Some relief from stress associated with housework occurred with six of the fathers when female friends or an employed cleaning woman participated in household tasks.

Eleven of the 48 divorced fathers reported little difficulty in household maintenance and said they enjoyed having full responsibility for ordering their lives. Most of these men had participated actively in household tasks and child care during their marriages and, following divorce, were more likely to assist their ex-wives in maintaining their homes than fathers who previously had difficulty in coping with such tasks.

Greater economic stress in divorced couples as opposed to married couples was apparent in our sample. Although the average income of the divorced families was equal to that of the intact families, the economic problems associated with maintaining two households led to more financial concerns and limitations in purchasing practices for divorced couples. Divorced fathers were more likely than married fathers to increase their workload in an attempt to raise incomes. This created some duress in the first year after divorce when many fathers reported feeling immobilized by emotional problems and unable to work effectively. In addition, financial conflicts were one of the main sources of disagreement between divorced couples.

It has been suggested by Herzog and Sudia (1973) that many of the deleterious effects of a father's absence on children could be eliminated if economic stability was provided for the mother with no husband at home. However, in our study the number of significant correlations between income and reported feelings of economic stress, parents' reported or observed interactions with children, and children's behavior in nursery school, was not above chance. This was true whether we used the total income for divorced husbands and wives or the separate income for each of the households of the divorced spouses in the analyses. It may be that in our middle-class sample, with an average combined maternal and paternal income of about $22,000, the range was not great enough to detect the effects of economic stress.

Changes in Self-Concepts and Emotional Adjustment of Parents. Interview findings, diary mood ratings, and parents' personality tests showed many differences between the self-concepts and emotional adjustments of parents in divorced and intact families. Many of these differences diminished over the two-year period after divorce, with a marked drop occurring between one year and two years. In the first year following divorce, divorced mothers and fathers felt more anxious, depressed, angry, rejected, and incompetent. The effects were more sustained for divorced mothers—particularly for divorced mothers of boys, who at the end of two years were still feeling less competent, more anxious, more angry, and more externally controlled, as measured by the I-E Scale, than married mothers or divorced mothers of girls. The diary record indicated that these negative feelings were most likely to occur in episodes involving interactions with sons. This finding should be noted, for a position to be advanced later is that the mother-son relationship is particularly problematic in divorced families.

Divorced parents also scored lower on the socialization scale of the California Personality Inventory and Personality Scale of the Adjective Checklist throughout the three sets of measures. Does this mean that divorced people are less well-adjusted than married couples, or that an adverse response to the stresses associated with a conflictual marriage and divorce endure over the two-year postdivorce period? This question could not be answered from our data. The five couples in the larger intact sample who subsequently separated or divorced scored lower on these scales than the nondivorcing couples, and scored as more external on the I-E Scale only in the period immediately preceding the divorce, which suggests that these scales may be affected by the conflict associated with an unsatisfactory marriage and divorce.

Perhaps because he left the home and suffered the trauma of separation from his children, the divorced father seemed to undergo greater initial changes in self-concept than the mother, although effects were longer lasting in the mother. The continued presence of children and a familiar home setting gave mothers a sense of continuity that fathers lacked. Mothers complained more often of feeling physically unattractive, of having lost the identity and status associated with being married women, of a general feeling of helplessness. Fathers complained of not knowing who they were, of being rootless, of having no structure and no home in their lives. The separation induced great feelings of loss, previously unrecognized dependency needs, guilt, anxiety, and depression.

Changes in self-concept and identity problems were greatest in parents who were older or had been married longest. Two months after divorce, about one-third of the fathers and one-fourth of the mothers reported an ebullient sense of freedom which alternated with apprehension and depression; by one year the elation had been largely replaced by depression, anxiety, or apathy. These negative feelings markedly decreased by two years.

A pervasive concern of the fathers was the sense of loss of their children. For most this feeling declined with time, but for many it remained a continual concern. Eight fathers who initially were highly involved, attached, and affectionate parents reported that they could not endure the pain of seeing their children only intermittently. By two years after the divorce, they coped with this stress by seeing their children infrequently, although they continued to experience a great sense of loss and depression. However, it should not be thought that all divorced fathers felt less satisfied with their fathering roles following divorce. Ten of the fathers reported that their relationships with their children had improved and that they were enjoying their interchanges more. Most of these fathers came from marriages in which there had been a high degree of husband-wife conflict.

One of the most marked changes in divorced parents in the first year following divorce was a decline in feelings of competence. They felt they had failed as parents and spouses, and they expressed doubts about their ability to adjust well in any future marriages. They reported that they functioned less well in social situations and were less competent in heterosexual relationships. Nine of the divorced fathers reported an increased rate of sexual dysfunction. In addition to these feelings specifically related to marriage, 36 of the divorced fathers reported that they felt they were coping less well at work.

The flurry of social activity and self-improvement which occurred during the first year following divorce, particularly in divorced fathers, seemed to be an attempt to resolve some of the problems of identity and loss of self-esteem experienced by divorced parents.

One year after the divorce, the father was in a frenzy of activity. Although at this time contacts with old friends had declined, dating and casual social encounters at bars, clubs, cocktail parties, and other social gatherings had increased. In this period many of the divorced men and women were also involved in programs of self-improvement. Twenty-eight of the divorced fathers, in contrast to 14 married mothers, were engaged in activities such as night school courses in photography, languages, potting, jewelry-making, modern dance, and creative writing; structured physical fitness programs; and tennis, golf, or sailing lessons. However, by two years following the divorce, both the social life of divorced fathers and self-improvement programs for both divorced parents had declined. It should be noted that although these activities kept the parents busy and were associated with more positive emotional ratings, the most important factor in changing the self-concept two years after divorce was the establishment of a satisfying, intimate, heterosexual relationship. Only one father became involved in a homosexual relationship. He happened to have low ratings of self-esteem and happiness, but it is obvious that on the basis of this finding no conclusion can be drawn about the relative satisfaction of homosexual or heterosexual relationships.

Interpersonal Problems, Social Life, and Intimate Relationships. Stresses are experienced by most divorced couples in social life and in establishing meaningful, intimate interpersonal relationships. Almost all the divorced adults in this study complained that socializing in our culture is organized around couples and that being a single adult, particularly a single woman with children, limits recreational opportunities. Both the interview findings and the diary records kept by parents indicated that social life was more restricted for the divorced couples in the two years following divorce, and that this effect initially was most marked for women. Divorced parents reported that two months following divorce married friends were supportive, and diary records indicated that considerable time was spent with them. However, these contacts rapidly declined. The dissociation from married friends was greater for women than for men, who were more often included in social activities and sometimes participated in joint family outings on visitation days. Shared interests and concerns led to more frequent contact with other divorced, separated, or single persons. Divorced mothers reported having significantly less contact with adults than did married parents and often commented on their sense of being locked into a child's world. Several described themselves as prisoners and used terms like being "walled in" or "trapped." This was less true of working than nonworking mothers. Many nonworking mothers complained that most of their social contacts had been made through their husbands' professional associates and that with divorce these associations had terminated. In contrast, the employed mothers had contact with their co-workers, and these relations often extended into after-hour social events. Although the employed women complained of the difficulty of finishing household chores and of their concern about getting adequate care for their children, most felt the gratifications associated with employment outweighed the problems. Social life for our total sample of divorced women increased over the two-year period; however, it always remained lower than the social life for married women.

Divorced men had a restricted social life two months after divorce, followed by a surge of activity at one year, and a decline in activity to the wives' level by two years. In contrast to divorced women who felt trapped, divorced men complained of feeling shut out, rootless, and at loose ends, and of a need to engage in social activities even if they often were not pleasurable. Divorced men and women who had not remarried in the two years following divorce repeatedly spoke of their intense feelings of loneliness.

Heterosexual relations played a particularly important role in the happiness and attitudes toward self of both married and divorced adults. Happiness, self-esteem, and feelings of competence in heterosexual behavior increased steadily over the two-year period for divorced males and females, but such feelings were not as high even in the second year as those for married couples. It should be noted, however, that the subjects who later remarried, and were shifted from this study to a stepparent study, scored as high on happiness, although lower on self-esteem and feelings of competence, as parents in intact families. Frequency of sexual intercourse was lower for divorced parents than married couples at two months, higher at one year for males, and about the same at two years. Divorced males particularly seemed to show a peak of sexual activity and a pattern of dating a variety of women in the first year following divorce. However, the stereotyped image of the happy, swinging single life was not altogether accurate. One of our sets of interview ratings attempted to measure intimacy in relationships. Intimacy referred to love in the sense of valuing the welfare of the other as much as one's own, a deep concern and willingness to make sacrifices for the other, and a strong attachment and desire to be near the other person. It should be understood that this use of the term *intimacy* is not synonymous with sexual intimacy although, of course, the two frequently occur together. Intimacy in relationships showed strong positive correlations with happiness, self-esteem, and feelings of competence in heterosexual relations for both divorced and married men and women. Table 3 shows that if subjects in the divorced sample, but not the married sample, were divided into those above and below the median in terms of intimacy in relationships, happiness correlated negatively with frequency of intercourse in the low-intimacy group and positively in the high-intimacy group. The same pattern held for self-esteem. This was true for both divorced males and females. The only nonsignificant correlation was for low-intimacy males immediately following divorce. Many males, but few females, were pleased at the increased opportunity for sexual experiences with a variety of partners immediately following divorce. However, by the end of the first year both divorced men and women were expressing a desire for intimacy and a lack of satisfaction in casual sexual encounters. Women expressed particularly intense feelings about frequent casual sexual encounters, often talking of feelings of desperation, overwhelming depression, and low self-esteem following such exchanges. A pervasive desire for intimacy, which was not satisfied by casual encounters, characterized most of our divorced parents, and the formation of an intimate relationship seemed to be a powerful factor in the development of happiness and satisfaction.

Table 3. Correlations Between Frequency of Sexual Intercourse and Happiness in High- and Low-Intimacy Divorced Groups

	High intimacy		Low intimacy	
	Male (N = 24)	Female (N = 24)	Male (N = 24)	Female (N = 24)
Two months	+.40*	+.43*	−.09(n.s.)	−.42*
One year	+.40**	+.47**	−.41*	−.46*
Two years	+.54**	+.52**	−.48**	−.57**

* $p < .05$
** $p < .01$

Relationships Between Divorced Partners. At two months following divorce, relations with the ex-spouse and children remained the most salient and preoccupying concern for divorced parents. Most (66 percent) of the exchanges between divorced couples in this period involved conflicts. The most common areas of conflict were finances and support, visitation and childrearing, and intimate relations with others. The relationships between all but four of the divorced couples were characterized by acrimony, anger, feelings of desertion, resentment, and memories of painful conflicts, all tempered by considerable ambivalence. Attachments persisted, and in some cases increased, following the escape from daily confrontations. Six of the 48 couples had sexual intercourse with each other in the two months after divorce. Thirty-four mothers and 29 fathers reported that, in case of a crisis, the ex-spouse would be the first person they would call. Eight of the fathers continued to help the mother with some home maintenance and 4 baby-sat when she went out on dates. With time, both conflict and attachment decreased, although anger and resentment were sustained longer by mothers than by fathers. The establishment of new intimate relationships and remarriage were particularly powerful factors in attenuating the intensity of the divorced couple's relationship.

At one year after divorce—which seemed to be the most stressful period for both parents—29 fathers and 35 mothers reported that they thought the divorce might have been a mistake, that they should have tried harder to resolve their conflicts, and that the alternative lifestyles available to them were not satisfying. By the end of the second year, only 9 fathers and 12 mothers felt this way.

In our larger sample, which included parents who remarried, remarriage by the spouse was accompanied by a reactivation of feelings of depression, helplessness, anger, and anxiety—particularly in mothers. Many reported that their feelings of panic and loss were similar to those experienced at the time of the original separation and divorce. Anger by the mother was almost an invariable concomitant of the ex-husband's remarriage, even if she was the first to remarry. Sometimes this anger took the form of reopening conflicts about finances or visitation; sometimes it was directed at the children and their split loyalties; often it focused on resentment and feelings of competition with the new wife. While 5 of the 10 men whose ex-wives remarried reported approval of the new husband, only 4 of the 19 women whose ex-husbands remarried approved of the new wife. The new wives seemed to exacerbate these feelings by entering into particularly hostile competitive relationships with the ex-wives in which criticism of the children and the ex-wives' childrearing often were used as the combative focus.

Parent-Child Relations

Thus far we have been focusing mainly on changes in the divorced partners in the two years after divorce and have seen that divorced couples encountered and coped with many stresses. We will now look at differences in family functioning and parent-child interactions as measured in both interviews and direct observations in the laboratory situation.

The interaction patterns between divorced parents and children differed significantly from those of intact families on many variables studied in the interview and on many of the parallel measures in the structured interaction situation. On these measures the differences were greatest during the first year; a process of reequilibration seemed to be taking place by the end of the second year, particularly in mother-child relationships. However, even at the end of the second year, parent-child relations in divorced and intact families still differed on many dimensions. Although there were still many stresses in the parent-child interactions of divorced parents after two years, it is noteworthy that almost one-fourth of the fathers and one-half of the mothers reported that their relationships with their children had improved over those during the marriage when parental conflict and tensions had detrimental effects.

Some of the findings for fathers must be interpreted in view of the fact that divorced fathers became increasingly less available to their children and ex-spouses over the course of the two years. Although at two months divorced fathers were having almost as many face-to-face interactions with their children as fathers in intact homes—who were often highly unavailable to their children (Blanchard and Biller 1971)—these interactions declined rapidly. At two months, about one-fourth of the divorced parents reported that fathers, in their eagerness to maximize visitation rights and maintain contact with their children, were having even more face-to-face contact with their children than they had before the divorce. This contact was motivated by a variety of factors. Sometimes it was based on the father's deep attachment to the child or continuing attachment to the wife; sometimes it was based on feelings of duty or attempts to assuage guilt; often it was an attempt to maintain a sense of continuity in the father's life. Unfortunately, it was often at least partly motivated by a desire to annoy, compete with, or retaliate against the spouse. By two years after the divorce, 19 divorced fathers saw their children once a week or more, 14 fathers saw them every two weeks, 7 every three weeks, and 8 once a month or less.

Results of the diary record, interview findings, and laboratory observations relating to parent-child interactions will be presented in a simplified fashion and, when possible, presented together. The patterns of parent-child interaction showed considerable congruence across these measures.

Divorced parents made fewer maturity demands, communicated less well, tended to be less affectionate, and showed marked inconsistency in discipline and control of their children in comparison to married parents. Poor parenting was most apparent when divorced parents, particularly divorced mothers, interacted with their sons. Divorced parents communicated less, were less consistent, and used more negative sanctions with sons than with daughters. Additionally, in the laboratory situation divorced mothers exhibited fewer positive behaviors (such as positive sanctions and affiliations) and more negative behaviors (such as negative commands, negative sanctions, and opposition to children's requests) with sons than with daughters. Sons of divorced parents seemed to have a difficult time, and this may partly explain why—as we shall see shortly—the adverse effects of divorce are more severe and enduring for boys than for girls.

Fortunately, parents learned to adapt to problem situations, and by two years after divorce the parenting practices of divorced mothers had improved. Poor parenting seemed most marked, particularly for divorced mothers, one year after divorce, which appeared to be a peak of stress in parent-child relations. Two years after divorce mothers were demanding more autonomous, mature behavior of their children, communicated better, and used more explanations and reasoning. They were more nurturant and consistent, and were better able to control their children than before. A similar pattern occurred for divorced fathers in maturity demands, communication, and consistency, but they became less nurturant and more detached from their children with time; in the laboratory and home observations, divorced fathers ignored their children more and showed less affection.

The interviews and observations showed that the lack of control divorced parents had over their children was associated with very different patterns of relating to children by mothers and fathers. The divorced mother tried to control her child by being more restrictive and giving more commands which the child ignored or resisted. The divorced father wanted his contacts with his child to be as happy as possible. He began by being extremely permissive and indulgent with his child and becoming increasingly restrictive over the two-year period, although he was never as restrictive as fathers in intact homes. The divorced mother used more negative sanctions than the divorced father or than parents in intact families. However, by the second year the divorced mother's use of negative sanctions declined as the divorced father's increased. In a parallel fashion, the divorced mother's use of positive sanctions increased after the first year as the divorced father's decreased. The "every day is Christmas" behavior of the divorced father declined with time. The divorced mother decreased her futile attempts at authoritarian control and became more effective in dealing with her child over the two-year period.

The lack of control divorced parents had over their children, particularly one year after divorce, was apparent in both home and laboratory observations. The observed frequency of children's compliance with parents' regulations, commands, or requests could be regarded as a measure of either parental control or resistant child behavior. A clearer understanding of functional relationships in parent-child interaction may be obtained by examining the effectiveness of various types of parental responses in leading to compliance by children and parents' responses to children following compliance or noncompliance. It can be seen in Table 4 that boys are less compliant than girls and that fathers are more effective than mothers in obtaining compliance from

Table 4. Compliance with Positive and Negative Parental Commands and Parental Reasoning and Explanation

Percentage of compliance with positive parental commands

	Intact				Divorced			
	Girl		Boy		Girl		Boy	
	Father	Mother	Father	Mother	Father	Mother	Father	Mother
Two months	60.2	54.6	51.3	42.6	51.3	40.6	39.9	29.3
One year	63.4	56.7	54.9	44.8	43.9	31.8	32.6	21.5
Two years	64.5	59.3	57.7	45.3	52.1	44.2	43.7	37.1

Percentage of compliance with negative parental commands

	Intact				Divorced			
	Girl		Boy		Girl		Boy	
	Father	Mother	Father	Mother	Father	Mother	Father	Mother
Two months	55.7	49.3	47.5	36.4	47.0	34.8	35.6	23.4
One year	59.2	51.5	50.3	38.8	39.1	27.2	28.3	17.2
Two years	60.5	54.6	53.6	39.0	49.9	39.7	39.7	31.8

Percentage of compliance with parental reasoning and explanation

	Intact				Divorced			
	Girl		Boy		Girl		Boy	
	Father	Mother	Father	Mother	Father	Mother	Father	Mother
Two months	49.1	43.3	41.0	31.1	41.3	29.2	29.6	18.4
One year	55.4	48.0	46.2	34.5	26.3	23.1	24.5	14.1
Two years	62.3	58.1	58.1	47.6	50.3	42.5	41.4	36.9

children in both divorced and intact families. This may be at least partly based on the fact that mothers gave over twice as many commands as fathers, and divorced mothers gave significantly more commands than divorced fathers or parents in intact families.

The curvilinear effect—with the least effectiveness of any type of parental behavior at one year and a marked increase in control of the child by two years—is again apparent, although divorced mothers and fathers never gained as much control as their married counterparts. Because developmental psychologists have traditionally regarded reasoning and explanation as the font of good discipline from which all virtues flow, the results relating to types of parental demands were unexpected. Negative commands were less effective than positive commands and, somewhat surprisingly, in the two-month and one-year groups, reasoning and explanation were less effective than either positive or negative commands. By the last test session the effectiveness of reasoning and explanation significantly increased over the previous sessions. Two things were noteworthy about the pattern of change in reasoning.

First, it should be remembered that the average age of the subjects was two years older at the final session. The mean age of children at the two-month session was 3.92 years; at the one-year session, 4.79 years; and at the final session, 5.81 years. It may be that as children became more cognitively and linguistically mature reasoning and explanation were more effective because children could better understand and had longer attention spans. It may also be that internalization and role-taking were increasing and explanations involving appeals to the rights and feelings of others became more effective. Some support for the position that younger children may not fully comprehend or attend to explanations is found in a point biserial correlational post hoc analysis between the number of words in explanations and children's compliance or noncompliance. After reviewing videotapes of the laboratory situation to see what happened in cases with high use of reasoning and low compliance, we observed that parents often used long-winded, conceptually complicated explanations and the children seemed to become rapidly inattentive, distracted, and bored. Then the children either continued their previous activity or ignored the parents. The average point biserial correlation between noncompliance and number of words across the group was -.58 at two months, -.44 at one year, and -.13 at two years. "Short and sweet" would seem to be an effective maxim for instructing young children. The same type of analysis was performed on the home observations, which had been audiotaped but not videotaped, and the same pattern of results was obtained. Long explanations were associated with noncompliance in younger children.

Second, two years following divorce reasoning was superior to negative parental commands in obtaining compliance from boys (with the exception of sons interacting with their divorced fathers) but not from girls. Why should reasoning be relatively more effective in gaining compliance from boys? Martin (1974) in his recent review of research on parent-child interactions suggests that coercive parental responses are more likely to be related to oversocialization and inhibition in girls, and to aggression in boys. It may be that the greater aggressiveness frequently observed in preschool boys and the greater assertiveness in the culturally proscribed male role necessitate the use of reasoning and explanation to develop the cognitive mediators necessary for self-control in boys. Some support for this idea was found in the greater number of, significantly larger, and more consistent correlations for boys than for girls between the communication scale of the parent interview, frequency of observed parental reasoning and explanation, and parents' ratings of children's prosocial behavior, self-control, and aggression. A similar pattern of correlations was obtained between these parental measures and the frequency of negative and positive behavior on the behavior checklist. In contrast, high use of negative commands was positively related to aggression in boys, but not in girls. Although reasoning and explanation are not clearly superior to other commands in gaining short-term compliance, these methods are more effective in the long-term development of self-control, inhibition of aggression, and prosocial behavior in boys.

We can extend our analysis of compliance one step further and examine how parents respond to compliance or noncompliance by children. Developmental psychologists and behavior modifiers have emphasized the role of contingent reinforcement in effective parenting. Parental responses to compliance are presented in Table 5, and parental responses to noncompliance are presented in Table 6; the most frequently occurring responses are included in these tables. Only the most significant effects will be noted.

Table 5. Parents' Consequent Behaviors Toward Compliance

Percentage of positive sanctions (affiliate, encourage)

	Intact				Divorced			
	Girl		Boy		Girl		Boy	
	Father	Mother	Father	Mother	Father	Mother	Father	Mother
Two months	39.0	51.1	34.6	49.8	46.6	37.0	44.2	31.8
One year	42.6	49.7	37.2	45.6	47.4	32.5	42.4	28.8
Two years	44.4	49.4	39.8	48.1	36.8	41.6	34.7	37.3

Percentage of ignoring or no response

	Intact				Divorced			
	Girl		Boy		Girl		Boy	
	Father	Mother	Father	Mother	Father	Mother	Father	Mother
Two months	21.4	15.8	18.7	16.3	19.2	28.9	17.6	27.9
One year	23.9	16.2	20.9	17.8	20.4	30.0	17.1	30.3
Two years	22.6	14.9	19.5	16.4	30.2	19.8	25.1	20.0

Percentage of positive commands

	Intact				Divorced			
	Girl		Boy		Girl		Boy	
	Father	Mother	Father	Mother	Father	Mother	Father	Mother
Two months	11.6	16.2	15.1	20.3	6.2	18.8	10.0	20.4
One year	12.3	15.3	14.9	18.6	6.6	20.7	8.3	21.1
Two years	10.9	14.7	15.5	19.9	8.3	17.0	13.5	20.0

Percentage of negative commands or negative sanctions

	Intact				Divorced			
	Girl		Boy		Girl		Boy	
	Father	Mother	Father	Mother	Father	Mother	Father	Mother
Two months	8.6	4.3	10.5	7.6	2.4	8.2	5.0	13.4
One year	6.7	5.1	9.7	6.6	4.2	10.3	8.1	14.9
Two years	6.9	4.8	9.9	6.9	7.6	5.6	9.3	10.5

First, it can be seen that children received positive reinforcement in less than one-half of the times they complied—not a very lavish reinforcement schedule for good behavior. Second, boys who complied received less positive reinforcement; more commands, both positive and negative; and more negative sanctions (such as, "You didn't do that very fast" or "You'd better shape up if you know what's good for you") than girls. Boys were not as appropriately reinforced for compliance as girls. This seemed to be the case particularly for divorced mothers and sons across all ages, although divorced mothers became significantly more appropriate in responding to compliance by children from one year to two years after divorce. In contrast, divorced fathers became less reinforcing and attentive to children's positive behaviors in this period.

Table 6. Parents' Consequent Behaviors Toward Noncompliance

Percentage of positive commands

	Intact				Divorced			
	Girl		Boy		Girl		Boy	
	Father	Mother	Father	Mother	Father	Mother	Father	Mother
Two months	26.3	27.9	24.2	29.3	23.6	20.6	22.0	23.9
One year	24.8	23.6	25.7	27.5	20.5	16.9	20.0	15.3
Two years	25.1	26.8	26.0	27.9	19.1	23.0	18.0	20.6

Percentage of reasoning, explanation, and encouraging positive questions

	Intact				Divorced			
	Girl		Boy		Girl		Boy	
	Father	Mother	Father	Mother	Father	Mother	Father	Mother
Two months	20.1	25.6	17.9	22.7	18.9	20.1	15.0	16.5
One year	22.7	25.3	20.1	23.2	18.1	16.3	16.9	11.9
Two years	26.8	30.4	24.3	28.5	14.0	27.4	13.2	22.7

Percentage of negative commands, negative sanctions, and negative questions

	Intact				Divorced			
	Girl		Boy		Girl		Boy	
	Father	Mother	Father	Mother	Father	Mother	Father	Mother
Two months	18.5	14.0	20.0	18.3	9.0	24.0	12.0	26.2
One year	20.4	15.7	22.5	17.0	9.9	26.8	13.1	28.1
Two years	22.2	17.5	26.8	17.5	19.8	20.2	22.2	21.7

Percentage of ignoring or no response

	Intact				Divorced			
	Girl		Boy		Girl		Boy	
	Father	Mother	Father	Mother	Father	Mother	Father	Mother
Two months	5.3	8.1	4.1	9.9	13.5	15.8	14.3	16.0
One year	4.8	6.7	3.9	7.3	16.7	17.9	18.1	19.3
Two years	4.0	4.9	3.0	5.8	18.1	11.6	21.6	10.2

Percentage of physical intrusion

	Intact				Divorced			
	Girl		Boy		Girl		Boy	
	Father	Mother	Father	Mother	Father	Mother	Father	Mother
Two months	10.8	6.9	9.5	5.8	11.2	8.3	9.3	8.0
One year	8.6	5.7	8.7	5.4	9.1	8.2	8.4	7.5
Two years	7.2	5.8	6.9	5.0	8.1	6.0	7.3	5.9

The Aftermath of Divorce

How did parents respond when children failed to obey their commands? In most cases, they gave another command, sometimes using negative sanctions. Parents in intact families, especially mothers, were also likely to deal with noncompliance by reasoning with children. Sometimes parents, notably fathers, intruded physically by moving the children or surrounding objects. There was much less ignoring of noncompliance than of compliance, especially by fathers in intact families. If parental ignoring responses are examined, it is clear that one way divorced parents coped with noncompliance was by pretending it did not happen. The chains of noncompliance by children, followed by ignoring, were of longer duration in divorced families than in intact families, especially in the interactions of divorced mothers and their sons.

Divorced mothers dramatically increased their use of reasoning and explanation in response to noncompliance in the second year after divorce, while divorced fathers became less communicative and more negative in their responses.

After reviewing the interview and observational findings one might be prone to state that disruptions in children's behavior after divorce are attributable to emotional disturbance in the divorced parents and poor parenting, especially by mothers of boys. However, before we point a condemning finger at these parents, especially the divorced mothers who face the day-to-day problems of childrearing, let us look at the children involved. The findings on the behavior checklist, recording the occurrence of children's positive and negative behaviors in the home in 30-minute units, showed not only that children of divorced parents exhibited more negative behavior than children of intact families, but also that these behaviors were most marked in boys and had largely disappeared in girls two years after divorce. Such behaviors were also significantly declining in boys. Children exhibited more negative behavior with their mothers than with their fathers; this was especially true with sons of divorced parents.

These checklist results were corroborated by the home and laboratory observations, and by parent ratings of children's behavior. Divorced mothers may have given their children a difficult time, but mothers, especially divorced mothers, got rough treatment from their children. As previously remarked, children were more likely to exhibit oppositional behavior to mothers and comply with fathers. The children made negative complaining demands of the mother more frequently. Boys were more oppositional and aggressive; girls were more whining, complaining, and compliant. Children of divorced parents showed an increase in dependency over time, and exhibited less sustained play than children of intact families. The divorced mother was harassed by her children, especially her sons. In comparison with fathers and with mothers in intact families, children of the divorced mother did not obey, affiliate, or attend to her in the first year after divorce. They nagged and whined, made more dependency demands, and were more likely to ignore her. Aggression of sons of divorced mothers peaked at one year, then dropped significantly, but was still higher at two years than aggression of sons in intact families. Some divorced mothers described their relationships with their children one year after divorce as "declared war," "a struggle for survival," "the old water torture," or "getting bitten to death by ducks." One year following divorce seemed to be the period of maximum negative behaviors for children, as it was for the divorced parents themselves. Great improvement occurred by two years, although negative behaviors were more sustained in boys than in girls. The second year appeared to be a period of marked recovery and constructive adaptation for divorced mothers and children.

Who is doing what to whom? It has been proposed—most recently by Patterson in a paper entitled "Mothers: The Unacknowledged Victims" (1976)—that the maternal role is not a very rewarding or satisfying one. Patterson demonstrates that the maternal role, particularly with mothers of problem children, demands high rates of responding with very low levels of positive reinforcement for the mothers. He assumes that mothers and their aggressive children get involved in a vicious circle of coercion. The mother's lack of management skills accelerates the child's aversive behavior of which the mother is the main instigator and for which she is the main target. This is reciprocated by increased coercion in the mother's parenting behavior, and feelings of helplessness, depression, anger, and self-doubt. In his study, Patterson shows that decreases in the noxious behaviors of aggressive children through treatment procedures aimed at improving parenting skills are associated with decreases of maternal scores on a number of clinical scales on the Minnesota Multiphasic Personality Inventory (MMPI), with a decrease in anxiety on the Taylor Manifest Anxiety Scale, and with improvement on several other measures of maternal adjustment.

Patterson's model may be particularly applicable to divorced mothers and their children in our study. High synchronous correlations between reported and observed poor parenting in divorced mothers and between reported and observed negative behavior in children occurred at each time period. The greater use of poor maternal parenting practices and higher frequency of undesirable behaviors in children from divorced families, even in the first sessions with mothers and sons, suggests that the coercive cycle was already underway when we first encountered our families two months after divorce. Stresses and conflicts preceding or accompanying divorce might have initiated the cycle. High rates and durations of negative exchanges between divorced mothers and their sons were apparent throughout the study. Sequence analyses of the home and laboratory observations showed that divorced mothers of boys were not only more likely than other parents to trigger noxious behavior, but also that they were less able to control or terminate this behavior once it occurred.

We attempted to use cross-lagged panel correlations between selected parent and child measures at the three time periods to identify causal effects in these interactions. Panel correlations were problematic with our study, which involved a relatively small sample size. Kenney (1975), in his review of cross-lagged panel correlations, stated that it is difficult to obtain significant results with Ns under 75. In our study, if we analyzed divorced and intact families separately, but pooled boys and girls, we had only 48 families in a group. Because the family dynamics differed somewhat in families with boys and girls, especially for divorced families, it seemed conceptually unsound to combine sexes, but then we were left with a meager 24 families per group. In spite of these difficulties, we did obtain some findings of interest on the panel correlations.

There were many significant synchronous correlations between parent and child behavior. Poor parenting practices and coercive behavior in parents correlated with undesirable and coercive behavior in children; this was particularly true for divorced mothers and their sons. This suggests that the coercive cycle was already underway. Causal direction for poor parenting practices and noxious child behavior could not be identified consistently by the panel correlations. However, the observational measures and child checklist measures—but not the interview and rating measures—indicated that poor parenting by divorced mothers at two months after divorce caused problem behaviors in children at one year. These effects were similar but not significant between one year and two years.

A striking finding was that divorced mothers' self-esteem, feelings of parental competence as measured by the interview, state anxiety as measured by the Spielberger State-Trait Anxiety Scale, and mood ratings of competence, depression, and anxiety on the structured diary record not only showed significant synchronous correlation with ratings of children's aggression and checklist frequency of noxious behaviors, but also yielded significant cross-lagged panel correlations, suggesting that the behavior of the children—particularly of the sons—was causing the emotional responses of the mother. The findings were similar but less consistent for mothers in intact families. Mothers from divorced and intact families showed more state and trait anxiety, feelings of external control and incompetence, and depression than fathers. This suggests that the feminine maternal role is not as gratifying as the masculine paternal role, regardless of whether the family is intact or divorced. The more marked findings in divorced mothers seemed in accord with Patterson's view that mothers of problem children are trapped in a coercive cycle that leads to debilitating attitudes toward themselves, adverse emotional responses, and feelings of helplessness.

In Patterson's study and others comparing parents of problem and nonproblem children, fathers were found to be much less affected by problem children than were mothers. Fathers, particularly divorced fathers, spent less time with their children than did mothers, thereby escaping some of the stresses imposed by coercive children and obtaining more gratification in activities outside the family. Fathers seemed less likely to get involved in a coercive vicious cycle because children exhibited less deviant behavior in their presence; furthermore, fathers were more able to control deviant behavior by children once it occurred, as was shown in fathers' ratings of children's behavior, frequencies of behavior on the checklist, and observations in the home and laboratory.

The cross-lagged panel correlations showed a larger proportion of effects going in the direction of fathers causing children's behavior rather than in children causing fathers' behaviors, relative to the number found in mother-child interactions. Children's behavior showed few effects on the state anxiety, mood ratings, or self-esteem of fathers, especially divorced fathers. In addition, in intact families, negative child behaviors at the one- and two-year periods seemed to be partially caused by poor control, low nurturance, and high use of negative sanctions by fathers at the earlier periods.

The 48 divorced fathers involved in this study probably showed more concern about their children and interacted with them more than most divorced fathers. The fact that they were available for study and willing to participate may reflect a more sustained and greater degree of paternal involvement than is customarily found. However, despite this possible bias, the impact of divorced fathers on children declined with time, and was significantly less than that of fathers in intact families. At two months following divorce, the number of significant correlations between paternal characteristics and behavior and child characteristics was about the same as in intact families. However, two years after divorce the divorced fathers clearly had less influence with their children while divorced mothers had more influence. Divorced mothers became increasingly salient relative to divorced fathers in the social, cognitive, and personality development of their children. This decrease was less marked for divorced fathers who maintained a high rate of contact with their children.

It would seem that in the period leading to and following divorce, parents go through many role changes and encounter many problems, and that they would benefit from support in coping with these problems.

In both divorced and intact families, effectiveness in dealing with the child was related to support from the spouse in childrearing and agreement with the spouse in disciplining the child. When support and agreement occurred between divorced couples, the disruption in family functioning appeared to be less extreme, and the restabilizing of family functioning occurred earlier—by the end of the first year.

When divorced parents agreed about childrearing, had positive attitudes toward each other, and were low in conflict, and when the divorced father was emotionally mature—as measured by the Socialization Scale of the California Personality Inventory (Gough 1969) and the Personal Adjustment Scale of the Adjective Checklist (Gough and Heilbrun 1965)—frequent contact between father and child was associated with positive mother-child interactions and positive adjustment of the child. Where there were disagreements and inconsistencies in attitudes toward the child and conflict between the divorced parents, or when the father was poorly adjusted, frequent visitation by the father was associated with poor mother-child functioning and disruptions in the child's behavior. Emotional maturity in the mother was also found to be related to her adequacy in coping with stresses in her new single life and her relations with the child.

Other support systems, such as parents, siblings, close friends (especially other divorced friends or intimate male friends), or a competent housekeeper, also were related to the mother's effectiveness in interacting with the child in divorced, but not in intact, families. However, none of these support systems was as salient as a continued, positive, mutually-supportive relationship between the divorced couple and continued involvement of the father with the child. For the divorced father, intimate female friends, married friends, and relatives offered the next greatest support in his relationship with the child.

Among our 48 divorced couples, only 6 mothers and 4 fathers sought professional counseling or therapy; the main motivating factor seemed to be having friends who had been in therapy and recommended it. However, in our larger sample of 72 divorced couples, we identified 11 mothers and 6 fathers on whom we had records for one year following entry into therapy. Both the divorced mother and the child demonstrated improved adjustment only in the subgroup of 5 mothers involved in programs to improve parenting skills which made available 24-hour telephone contact with the parent trainer. This was obviously not a large enough group from which to draw firm conclusions about the efficacy of therapy as a support system, but it does suggest that focusing on effective parenting may alleviate some of the problems encountered by the divorced mother and child.

Discussion and Summary

In this study, divorced mothers and fathers encountered marked stresses in practical problems of living, self-concept and emotional adjustment, and interpersonal relations following divorce. Low self-esteem, loneliness, depression, and feelings of helplessness were characteristic of the divorced couple. Although the establishment of new intimate relations helped mitigate these effects, divorced parents were still less satisfied with their lives two years after divorce than parents in intact families.

Disruptions occurred in parent-child relations in many divorced families. Divorced parents infantilized their children and communicated less well with them than parents in intact families. In addition, they tended to be more inconsistent and less affectionate, and to have less control over their children's behavior. Children in divorced families were more dependent, disobedient, aggressive, whining, demanding, and unaffectionate than children in intact families. These effects were most marked in mother-son interactions. A peak of stress in parent-child interactions appeared one year after divorce, and marked improvement, particularly in mother-child relations, occurred thereafter.

Personal and emotional adjustment also deteriorated in the year following divorce. This seemed to be a period in which members of divorced families were testing a variety of coping mechanisms—many of them unsuccessful—in dealing with changes and stresses in their new life situations. However, by the second year after divorce a process of restabilization and adjustment was apparent.

In our current culture, the myth of romantic love and marriage is being replaced by the myth of the romance of divorce. The literature on divorce is replete with titles such as *Creative Divorce, Divorce: Chance of a New Lifetime,* and *Divorce: Gateway to Self Realization.* Many couples initiating divorces are prepared for reduced stress and conflict, the joys of greater interpersonal freedoms, and the delights of self-discovery and self-actualization associated with liberation. Few are prepared for the traumas and stresses they will encounter in attaining these goals after divorce, even if the goals are ultimately reached.

Because this was a longitudinal study, it presented an opportunity to examine how family members responded to and coped with the divorce experience. In the families we studied, there was none in which at least one family member did not report distress or exhibit disrupted behavior, particularly during the first year after divorce. We did not encounter a victimless divorce. Most of the members of divorced families ultimately were able to cope with many of their problems, but the course of adjustment was often unexpectedly painful.

Because this study lasted only two years, it is impossible to state whether the restabilizing process in the divorced family was largely completed at two years, or whether readjustment would continue over a longer period until such adjustment ultimately would resemble more closely that of intact families.

It should be remembered that the results reported in a study like this represent averages and that there are wide variations in coping and parenting within intact and divorced families. There are many inadequate parents and children with problems in intact families. Our study and previous research show that a conflict-ridden intact family is more deleterious to family members than a stable home situation in which parents are divorced. Divorce is often a positive solution to destructive family functioning, and the best statistical prognostications suggest that the rate of divorce is likely to increase. Because this is the case, it is important that parents and children be realistically prepared for the problems associated with divorce that they may encounter. More research and applied programs oriented toward the identification and application of constructive parenting and coping after divorce should be initiated. Divorce is one of the most serious crises in contemporary American life. It is a major social responsibility to develop support systems for the divorced family in coping with changes associated with divorce and in finding means of modifying or eliminating the deleterious aftereffects of divorce.

References

Baumrind, D. "Child Care Practices Anteceding Three Patterns of Preschool Behavior." *Genetic Psychology Monographs* 75 (1967): 43-88.

Baumrind, D. "Current Patterns of Parental Authority." *Developmental Psychology Monographs* 4 (1971): 1-102.

Biller, H. B. *Paternal Deprivation*. Lexington, Mass.: Lexington Books, 1974.

Blanchard, R. W., and Biller, H. B. "Father Availability and Academic Performance among Third Grade Boys." *Developmental Psychology* 4 (1971): 301-305.

Bronfenbrenner, U. "The Changing American Family." Paper presented at the Society for Research in Child Development meeting, Denver, April 1975.

Gough, H. G. *Manual for California Personality Inventory*. Palo Alto, Calif.: Consulting Psychologists Press, 1969.

Gough, H. G., and Heilbrun, A. B., Jr. *The Adjective Checklist*. Palo Alto, Calif: Consulting Psychologists Press, 1965.

Herzog, E., and Sudia, C. E. "Children in Fatherless Families." In *Review of Child Development Research*, edited by B. M. Caldwell and H. N. Ricciuti. Chicago: University of Chicago Press, 1973.

Hetherington, E. M., and Deur, J. "The Effects of Father Absence on Child Development." *Young Children* 26, no. 4 (March 1971): 233-248.

Kenney, D. A. "A Quasi-Experimental Approach to Assessing Treatment Effects in the Monequivalent Control Group Design." *Psychological Bulletin* 82, no. 3 (1975): 345-362.

Lynn, D. B. *The Father: His Role in Child Development.* Belmont, Calif.: Wadsworth, 1974.

Martin, B. "Parent-Child Relations." In *Review of Child Development Research,* edited by B. M. Caldwell and H. N. Ricciuti. Chicago: University of Chicago Press, 1973.

Martin B., and Hetherington, E. M. "Family Interaction in Withdrawn, Aggressive and Normal Children." Unpublished manuscript, 1971.

Patterson, G. "Mothers: The Unacknowledged Victims." Paper presented at the Society for Research in Child Development meeting, Oakland, Calif., April 1976.

Patterson, G. R.; Ray, R. S.; Shaw, D. A.; and Cobb, J. A. *A Manual for Coding of Family Interaction.* rev. ed. NAPS Document #01234, 1969.

Rotter, J. B. "Generalized Expectancies for Internal Versus External Control of Reinforcement." *Psychological Monographs* 80, no. 1 (1966): whole no. 609.

Sears, R. R.; Rau, L.; and Alpert, R. *Identification and Child Rearing.* Stanford, Calif.: Stanford Press, 1965.

Spielberger, C. D.; Gorsuch R. L.; and Lushene, R. *State-Trait Anxiety Inventory.* Palo Alto, Calif.: Consulting Psychologists Press, 1970.

Harriette Pipes McAdoo

9 Minority Families

Minority families in the United States are composed of individuals who are classified as belonging to a group other than the majority White population. Minority family life and patterns differ from the so-called "modal" family in varying degrees, but basic family functions are identical in all groups. All reproduce themselves, nurture their young, and socialize them to become members of their own group and the wider society. While the family functions are the same, stresses differ based upon the perceptions of that minority group by the wider group, its socioeconomic status, its unique cultural values, and the avenues that are open to it for social mobility.

A knowledge of the unique orientations of these families could avoid potential conflicts and discontinuities in educational programs designed and provided for minority children. Cultural differences that, if disregarded, may have a marked impact on the success or failure of a particular program will be discussed in this chapter.

Socializing Children in Minority Families

Parenting is the process by which the family socializes children into the gender, cultural, and economic roles that the parents and/or society deem appropriate. Parenting is more difficult and frustrating for groups than for majority families. The lowered expectations for achievement of minority children held in many educational institutions will thwart all but the most intense motivation to achieve. Economic discrimination will undermine the functioning of such a family unit, and inferior medical services will lead to decreased efficiency and a lower quality of life.

Parents must guide children through a series of conflicting developmental tasks. Children must inculcate the dominant views of society and at the same time move to actualize their own potential. This double thrust is conflicting because these societal views prevent minority children from reaching their potential (McAdoo 1974). The Native American family may stress pride in its ancestors, yet the media and school may present these ancestors in a derogatory manner. Another parent may see education as the only hope of lifting the family out of poverty, yet the child may face a teacher who automatically classifies the child's potential on the basis of skin color or family background. Such a child will face obstacles in attempting to bring reality to the family's dreams, and eventually the child may become a focus of the discontinuities between school and family.

Minority families face all of the same stresses experienced by other families, with the added burden of discrimination, which has forced many minority family units to rely solely upon themselves for the support needed to parent their children competently, rather than to call upon community agencies. This reliance upon themselves, and upon nonkin who function as kin, is found in many forms: extended family structure, close interaction between domestic units, and the kin-help system. Many ethnic groups, such as the Chinese Americans, have developed extensive community organizations that provide support to parents and their children, often without contacting outside agencies. People who are facing crises are more likely to turn to a person of similar background who will be able to translate their situation quickly and to offer help. There are cultural differences between groups so that an educator or counselor from one group may not understand the nuances of meaning that certain events hold for another group, and thus may not provide the needed assistance.

Growth in Ethnic Heritage Consciousness

In American society the push toward the "melting pot" in which all were to become one group did not succeed except to perpetrate one prevalent view: Any differences were usually viewed as pathological and inferior. Ethnic differences were considered an element common to lower-income and/or recent immigrants. Upward mobility was assumed to require a discarding of ethnic differences as the family members attempted to assimilate into the mainstream.

The mid-1960s brought the society to a harsh realization that we were not moving toward "one society." Moreover, we had talked of equality of groups while practicing an inequality that had increased rather than decreased inequalities. The civil rights movement and an increase in Black consciousness set the model that all other ethnic groups were to follow. A reaffirmation of pride in their ancestral group, an increase in demand for equality of treatment, and a stress on the value of diversity have been brought forth by Afro-Americans, Spanish-speaking Americans, Native Americans, and Asian-Americans.

Those movements were quickly followed by a similar increase in demands of support for White ethnic groups. These European descendant groups racially were part of the American mainstream, but in certain areas they had continued their strong cultural involvement through religious organizations, social groups, and celebration of special holidays. The reaffirmation of heritage occurred for them on one level, but practical economic fears occurred on another. Many of these participants were of working-class status and might have seen the activities of the subjugated ethnic minorities as a direct threat to their jobs, neighborhoods, and security. The melting pot had been turned over totally.

The White ethnic revival flowed into a strong ethnicity movement in which assimilation-oriented middle-class members of ethnic and minority religious groups were reactivated. Some Jewish, Islamic, and other distinct religious cultural groups resought ties with their culture that had been partially rejected in the previous generation. The ethnic pluralism movement intensified, concentrating on White groups, often to the exclusion of the darker-hued subjugated groups. Only now are members in the pluralist movement reaching out for non-White groups in an attempt to form coalitions.

One important element of our American value system is the continuing lack of support for cultural diversity. The consciousness of group members has been raised and reinforced, but the prevailing policies, and hence programs, are not supportive of diversity; instead they aim at reaching a cultural consensus. Support of diversity has not become part of the training of professionals who will implement future programs, nor has support for the integrity of the family been implemented in the various educational, social, or medical service-providing institutions.

Unique Characteristics of Selected Cultural Groups

To understand an ethnic group and to be able to provide support for its values, one must be aware of its unique qualities and the variations of lifestyles, values, and structures found within that subgroup.

One must be cautious in presenting descriptions of any group, for more variations will be found within a group than will ever be found between groups. Individual adaptations to life stresses and developmental stages produce infinite variety, while certain cultural beliefs and socialization practices produce similarities within an ethnic group. The variability of practices and beliefs found within any one group are so great that overlaps are found between any two groups. As a whole the differences between groups are not fundamental, but are important to group members because they serve as important cultural boundary markers of self-identity for group members.

The clustering of working-class ethnics into ethnic areas is due partially to the migration of individuals into places where kin or those of like culture already live. The kin-help system is most obvious in this migration process. Families often offered total support to others until they were able to learn the new environment and possibly a new language, and until they had begun to become self-supporting. This clustering maximized security in a difficult and often hostile world (Schneider and Smith 1973). In spite of extensive contact and a fair degree of assimilation, differences between groups have persisted in expressions, foods, taste, lifestyles, choice of religious observations, music, and values within the family, pointing to the soul-satisfying role that cultural heritage plays in maintenance of positive self-identity and mental health.

The only customs that continue are those that escape the conforming crush of the law—customs such as foods, religion, music, and dance. These then become the essence of cultural difference, the only remnants of cultures that were once quite different. Price (1976) has stated that in the basic pattern of cultural retention, sociocultural groups become transformed into ethnic subcultures. Outright destruction of a culture seldom occurs even when, as in slavery, every attempt is made to prevent continuation of cultural identity. The transformation begins during participation in the American economic system, whether in slavery, sweat shops, or agriculture. Internal adjustments are made to these tasks, and to the laws applied by missionaries, owners, or government officials. These adjustments produce social changes. Then elements of the previous culture and the new culture are intertwined to produce what is often a totally unique subculture (McAdoo 1977). Assimilation of the language occurs throughout this process.

Several elements are common to all subcultures:

- There are involvements and frequent interactions in close kin-help patterns.

- Extended family patterns are important and often include friends who become fictive kin.

- Poverty is widespread because of isolation from economic and social supports of the broader community.

- Conflict occurs between the family and the wider society when the child ventures into the society and faces conflicting values.

- Subculture members are viewed by the wider society in a stereotypical manner that does not allow deviations.

- There is a lack of respect for cultural uniqueness.

Broad summaries of values and characteristics of selected ethnic groups are presented below to provide background for the design of effective educational programs and social policies. The ethnic groups are presented roughly in the order in which their presence became evident on this continent. Readers desiring further details are referred to the references.

Native American Families

Native Americans were present on this continent before all other groups; they have no allegiance to former homes.

The one element that is most important in examining the Native American child is that of diversity. It is impossible to present one common description. Native Americans have cultural and linguistic diversity and are as racially differentiated as are the inhabitants of all the countries of Europe (Price 1976). Because this variety is difficult to comprehend, the response has been an attempt to simplify Native Americans into one stereotype.

In addition to language, religious, and cultural differences, Native American marriage and family patterns were adapted to the geographic and economic demands of their early environment. Like the African ancestors of American Blacks, earlier Native Americans practiced almost all of the known major forms of marriage in the world. Some groups in the northwest practiced polygamy; others in the northeast were monogamous. Agriculture groups in the East and Southwest were matrilocal, while others were patrilocal with men predominantly producing food. In contrast, the early European settlers practiced only one form of marriage and could not understand the varieties encountered; they sought to make "good Christians out of the savages" who obviously did not know how to live with the European way being judged as the only valid way. Laws that emphasized only European family models were passed, ruthlessly destroying cultural practices that had existed for thousands of years (Eggan 1966).

Native Americans subsequently were subjected to slaughterings, massive removal to less desirable and unproductive lands, and confiscation of ancestral lands that were an essential element of their religious practices. State and federal governments enforced compliance with laws on education, marriage, and the settlement of disputes. Native Americans were systematically isolated from American society because of resettlement on reservations. Paternalistic governmental policies, which have continued for the most part to the present time, stripped them of any control of their family or tribal life.

Native Americans have differed in their adaptations to the dominant society through migration and urbanization. The ethnic values allowed to survive have continued to shape the socialization of Native American children, and some similarities do seem to exist in most groups. A sense of tribalism and the pride in their heritage is foremost. Tribal values continue to be stressed and are taught to children by their elders. There is a respect for the elderly and the wisdom that comes from experience. Families tend to be less child-oriented and usually follow the child's natural rhythm in toilet training and food habits. Children are encouraged to become self-reliant early. Parents often stress humility—a trait not understood by teachers who expect competitive classroom behavior. Discipline is a tribal concern, and children are shamed into behaving (Price 1976; Sample 1976). Urbanization in some groups has tended to cause a breaking away of the younger from the older. Again caution must be taken; these summaries do not describe *all* Native Americans.

The rise in the ethnic consciousness of Native Americans has gradually allowed the tribe to become more active in their governance and in the education of their children. A rebirth of interest in cultural history, crafts, dance, and foods indicates an increase of interest in their own ethnicity. This has led to the creation of a general Native American movement that will provide the framework of increased progress in the control of individual and family life experiences of Native Americans.

Afro-American Families

Blacks came from a variety of cultural groups, both on the African continent and in America. The slavery experience led to two highly different types of family structures and values. Africans in the plantation system thus had different experiences, different family structures, and family interaction patterns than families who were placed on a smaller farm in the North or in the South. Under the farm system, brutality did occur, but the domestic unit was protected to some extent. Because of the economic unit of kin, these slave families tended to be patricentral (Jones 1965).

The slave experience on which most literature is based and from which most stereotypes of the Black family evolved, is the plantation system. The plantation system, which Haley's (1976) Kunta Kinte experienced, was an impersonal economic organization in which the master was the head of all family units, and the strongest bond was often between mother and child. However, the economic system required a surplus of males; therefore, an adequate supply of male models was available for the children in the family units. In one examination of the plantation-based units, Gutman (1976) tested Moynihan's hypothesis of Black family pathology (1965). Gutman felt that if a disorganized family was the modal form perpetuated as the result of slavery, then the structural form should be even more common during and immediately after slavery. He examined records of birth, death, marriage, slave transferral, and the United States census and found that data to support Moynihan's hypothesis were not available. Indications of strong family units were found dating from the middle of the slave period into the early part of this century.

From these two slavery patterns, coupled with the diversity provided by the different cultural and religious groups from Africa, evolved a unique family form which was neither African nor mainstream. The continuity of African culture was hampered by slavery and continuing discrimination, but elements remained that have evolved as part of Afro-American family values and lifestyle. Spanish, Asian, and White ethnics brought to America a total cultural support system that helped maintain cultural patterns and family integrity, such as church, clubs, and native-land identity groups. For Africans, these cultural supports were deliberately destroyed and replaced with alien forms of social control and religion that were designed to ensure dominance of the White owners. Afro-Americans, therefore, have had to go back and consciously research and re-create cultural links with their ancestral home—a stress faced by no other ethnic group (Haley 1976).

There is a great deal of diversity in the experiences, lifestyles, and values within the Black community. Members of this community all have the common experience of prejudice, legally reinforced racism, and economic isolation. These negative commonalities, coupled with unique physical characteristics, have led to the reinforcement of cultural similarities of an ethnic group that has been strongly resistant to total assimilation into the majority society.

It is difficult to obtain an objective picture of the Black American family because of the many negative stereotypes that have been perpetuated for centuries. Contrary to stereotype, the data show that the majority of Black families in all economic levels have both parents present, both of whom tend to work outside the home because of the economic discrimination faced by the head of the household (Hill 1971). Migration to northern urban centers has caused additional strains. This economic isolation has placed such great stress on Blacks that a higher proportion of families are being raised by mothers than in other groups.

Long-established cultural patterns and high level of maternal employment have led to families with a shared decision-making process in which both parents are active in childrearing and in making decisions within the home (Mack 1974; McAdoo 1977). This is a family model toward which middle-class White families are now moving. The family functions as a source of refuge from the harshness of the outside world. Extensive kin-help patterns exist, and community and nonkin support groups—often church-based—are active in augmenting the family's needs. As with other minority groups, the Black family has often found a lack of positive reinforcement from outside educational services or legal institutions. The home and church are often the emotional center of Black life, with members openly showing affection for each other. The conflict between generations is not as prevalent as in Spanish or Chinese ethnic groups. Parents and children are born and move into comparable environments, and even when upward mobility occurs, family contacts are maintained.

Chinese-American Families

The early Chinese did not intend to stay in America but came to earn money to support the family members at home. This sustained family contact and orientation served as a barrier to withstand the persecution and racism directed at them. Chinese-American males were welcomed as laborers in the 1800s, but with the economic decline of the 1880s, their presence in the West began to be resented. The completion of the cross-continental railroads, the decline of the mining economy, and competition with White ethnic workers for the limited number of jobs caused great division within communities (Huang 1976), and restrictions were placed on immigration. The Chinese were victims of extensive racism, ridicule, and legal restrictions that bonded them together (Rice 1977).

Chinese-American children generally grew up in a closely knit family and were highly involved in the kin interaction. They were an integral part of the adult world, which fostered an early assimilation of socially-approved patterns of behavior. Social control and ethnic solidarity within the community was very strong. There was strict control of aggressive behavior, sibling rivalry was not tolerated, and gentleness was considered the most appropriate behavior. Nonaggression was coupled with a restraint of external expression of affection between family members. Children would not fight back and were often intimidated in school by their peers (Huang 1976; Sollenberger 1968).

In the Chinese-American family, educational achievement has been traditionally stressed. Great sacrifices are often made by families for their children's education. Coleman (1966) found that aspirations for advanced education were higher among Chinese Americans than any other minority or majority group. Strong community and parental pressure to achieve has led to unusually high levels of education and to the greater economic security that comes from professional occupations. The survey also revealed that Chinese-American children had a higher sense of control over their environment than any other ethnic group; these children felt that hard work and effort would eventually pay off in greater mobility and security.

Great respect for the elderly is the key to the Chinese-American culture, and continuity between generations is prized in traditional families. In the past, the elderly retired to China to enjoy a glorious old age. Today fewer of them can return to China, and the cultural pattern of support of the elderly by kin and community has begun to disintegrate. The Americanization of younger members of the family has tended to break down the respect and system of care for these older family members (Huang 1976).

Now the gap between generations is often as serious as between other immigrants and their American-born children. The children often turn to their peers for models of blending the older traditions with those of the new (Mead 1970). Parents are often ambivalent in the focus they should place on the assimilation and retention of cultural differences (Chan 1977). In school, Chinese-American children face the strains of all bicultural students. Only recently have there been programs designed to reflect accurately the diversity of Chinese-American children.

Since 1965, with the lifting of immigration quotas, the new wave of immigrants, mainly from Hong Kong, has created a cultural discontinuity within the Chinese community. The difference in language, childhood experiences, educational achievement, and, therefore, economic level, between the newer arrivals and those here for several generations has led to an alienation of the younger arrivals. One result has been an increase in youth gangs in urban Chinatowns (Huang 1976; Rice 1977).

A growing awareness of the conflicts brought about by the latest wave of immigrants, a heightened level of awareness of pride in their ethnic identity, and a willingness to speak up for their rights has led the Chinese Americans to a beginning of political activism similar to other ethnic groups.

Spanish-Speaking American Families

Spanish-speaking American families compose the second largest ethnic group in America, which includes Chicanos, Spanish-Americans, Hispanos, Mexicanis, Californios, Latin Americans, and Puerto Ricans (Chapman 1976). The diversity found in other groups is clearly apparent here.

Like Native Americans, the Chicanos in the Southwest were defeated at war by Whites and have experienced severe programs of Americanization. They both still lay claim to territories stolen from them (de la Garza, Kruszewski, and Arcimega 1971). Puerto Ricans are more recent immigrants into the urban northeast.

Spanish-speaking minorities are isolated from wider society by religion, language, culture, and class. They have experienced severe oppression and have also been the victims of stereotypes detrimental to their individual and group development. Many migrant workers are still subjected to cruel working and living environments. Spanish Americans are often pictured as recent urban migrants who are unable to cope. In reality, 80 percent of the Spanish Americans live in urban settings, and because they were the founders of cities in the Southwest, their urban residence is often of longstanding (Hirsch 1970).

The Spanish-American family traditionally is one of clearly defined parental roles characterized by male dominance with the mother as primary caregiver. There is a subordination of younger to older, with apparent power in the family resting in the oldest male member. However, the actual routine decisions within the family may be made by the eldest female family member. Families are often larger than those of other ethnic groups, and the needs of the family are viewed as superseding those of the individual (Alvirez and Bean 1976; de Berlin 1976). The extended family structure and interaction patterns are seen as the idealized model. The elderly are respected, and the godparent may hold an important place in the family (Archuleta 1976). This family also serves as a refuge from the hostile outside environment.

The traditional family form is now being influenced by urbanization and social mobility. The higher fertility and lack of employment opportunities for the male head has placed the family under great stress. There is a growing generational conflict between the desire for cultural retention by the elder and rejection by the younger. Spanish Americans face the conflict and lack of support from the educational system common to all bilingual families. Attempts are often made by teachers to anglicize their names, and instruction is rarely offered in Spanish. Economic needs of the family and a desire to prove their loyalty and manhood have resulted in a heavy involvement of Mexican-American youth in the armed services; Mexican Americans had the highest death rate in Vietnam of any group (Guzman 1976). The elimination of young men from the community has had multiple negative effects, including an increased number of families headed by women (Aquilar 1973).

Chicano children often have high aspirations for education that are strongly reinforced by parents (Wright et al. 1971), who see this as the only way out of poverty. However, they frequently cannot provide the incentives and financial support needed for continued education.

The Role of Education for Minorities

One element common to all these minority groups is their great faith in education as a pathway into wider American society. Chinese Americans have actualized this dream more than any other group but at a cost of de-emphasizing their cultural heritage. Blacks have achieved mobility for some groups, but the masses still receive inferior education. Spanish-speaking Americans have had severe problems in achieving higher education for their children. Native Americans have been most severely deprived, with education frequently requiring that the child be taken away from the family and taught within an alien system.

Minority family members have had to accept the reality that support for their aspirations for high achievement seldom is found in the public school. Black and Native American children have been subjected to legally-sanctioned segregation and inferior schools. Chicano children face hostility from large agribusiness owners, who fear that education might make the children unwilling to work for low wages.

In spite of the documented evidence on ethnicity, socioeconomic status, and achievement, myths still persist in professional and lay literature on the genetic deficiency and the culture of poverty of minorities that account for lowered achievement. Two myths that have been assimilated into the mainstream of society have had profound impact: (1) the belief in the inherent cognitive inferiority of minorities, and (2) the belief that early educational programs have no impact on later cognitive development of minority children. These beliefs are so firmly imbued into the society that research findings consistent with this view (Herrnstein 1973; Jensen 1972; Moynihan 1965; Shockley 1965) are widely acclaimed, in spite of their faulty or nonexistent data bases and sharp criticisms made against these views. Meanwhile, data that refute these myths are neither picked up by the media nor translated into current folk beliefs.

These myths ignore the "norm of reaction" concept that the same genotype can give rise to a wide array of phenotypes, depending upon the environment in which it develops (Hirsch 1970). As an example, Chase (1977) reported an example of the dispersion of IQ scores of all racial groups in 1969 in Los Angeles, in which the highest of all groups was a Black group in an upper middle-class Black school, while the lowest was also a Black group in a poverty area school. The highest socioeconomic status group had parents who had been born into poverty but escaped via college education with help from the GI Bill of Rights. These children, therefore, had been born into an optimum setting in which they were able to gain the most from their inherited abilities.

Their children's higher educational achievement is often seen by parents as a prerequisite or almost the only route of mobility open to the minority individual. Wider society's lack of appreciation of the diversity of nonmajority groups has been shown in the perpetuation of myths about the minority groups. It is important to document factors that are supportive of the family's functioning because of evidence that school achievement and scores on IQ tests are directly related, not to ethnicity, but to the sociocultural economic factors of parental occupation and education (Chase 1977; Coleman 1966; Mercer 1972). In other words, the quickest way to increase achievement of a group is to provide resources that would raise the standard of living of that group's members.

Of all the studies on factors related to the child's mental development, the infant and maternal death rate of the socioeconomic group and weight of the infant at birth is the most accurate clinical indicator of the child's future high or low IQ and classroom achievement (Chase 1977; Department of Health, Education and Welfare 1969). Therefore, the child's natural ability level will be increased or decreased according to the physical health of the child and income of the parents. In addition, Chase (1977), Coleman (1966), Mercer (1972), and Mayeske (1971) have presented carefully designed large-scale studies and detailed reviews that have revealed elements connected with achievement: the environmental press, economic level of the family, and preventive health services for children. Data on school achievement have consistently shown that when socioeconomic factors are equalized, there are no differences in measured intelligence between ethnic/racial groups.

Gordon (1970) is one of the few researchers who have continued to monitor the achievement patterns of minority children enrolled in Head Start and who have compared them with control groups not receiving this extra help. Follow-up data have shown general long-term differences between the two groups. Differences in achievement and placement in classes for the retarded are significant, with the Head Start children performing consistently better than the control group. Mothers whose children attended these programs tended to further their own education, had higher aspirations for their children's educational achievement, and had stronger feelings of efficacy toward schools (Shipman 1977). Meanwhile, unfortunately, funds for these preschool programs have been systematically reduced across the country.

These recent findings are not consistent with the prevailing societal beliefs in the myths of racial ability differentiation and the lack of impact of early education programs. Therefore, these results are not disseminated to the educational and social service professionals in training or to policymakers who are designing and implementing programs for minority families. The lack of early education programs and the belief in myths of lowered ability have resulted in the warehousing of these children in school buildings until they are released, unskilled, to become nonproductive adults, perpetuating the low achievement cycle. Such educational programs provided to a group stressed with poverty will have only limited impact when compared to that achieved by raising the general economic security of the family. Therefore, to improve the academic achievement of a group, it is necessary also to improve its economic status.

Structures and Values in Minority Families

Identity with a distinct culture and the understanding of cultural roots is essential to strengthening a minority individual's identity. While different groups vary considerably in how they are structured, how affection is expressed, and how roles are defined within the family, family response is deeply rooted in all ethnic groups. These responses are unconsciously passed from one generation to another to reinforce acceptable behaviors (Giordano and Levine 1977). The desire for a happy family life is central to all peoples.

The study of family structure is often clouded with folkways and generalizations. Some historians believed the extended family structure was destroyed by industrialization (Parsons 1949; Wirth 1938), while others agreed that the extended family never existed in our country and that the nuclear form has always predominated (Gordon 1970; Sussman 1974). Regardless of the historical structure, the extended family form is seldom found in present societies.

The most frequently found contemporary family structure is neither extended nor isolated nuclear, but rather either a modified extended or neolocal nuclear form. The modified extended form is essentially a unit of parent(s) and children and another relative also living with them. The father would still be the titular head of the family, even if his elder parent were living with him. A neolocal form occurs when separate households are established by relatives who relate closely with each other through frequent visits, exchanges of goods and services, and close relations among the children (Litwak 1960; Leichter and Mitchell 1967; Sussman 1974). Newer models are evolving as the family undergoes changes internally and from the wider effects of societal changes.

While there have been conflicting views on the structure of the White family, there have been even greater controversies and misconceptions of minority family structures. A continuing criticism of most research using minority subjects, presented by Billingsley (1968) on Blacks and Hirsch (1970) in reference to Chicanos, is that such research has concentrated predominantly on the most oppressed families who, by definition, face many stresses. These data are then generalized to all minority families and thus perpetuate and reinforce the biased view. Another tendency is to ignore the majority of stable ethnic families and the processes by which they are economically mobile. The last trend is the tendency to view the family, rather than outside racism and economic discrimination, as the causal factor of each success or failure.

Hill (1971) has stressed that we must stop confusing the *structure* of a family with its *capacity* functionally to meet its members' developmental needs. Two parents may not really be intact, and a single-parent home may not always be broken. Although the majority of all families have both parents in the home, different minority groups have, through economic necessity, developed a variety of structures.

Billingsley (1968), Ladner (1972), Heiss (1971), and Stack (1975) have all stated in their studies that the urban poor minority mothers who are rearing children without fathers often exist within an extended family context of kin and fictive kin. This offsets some of the detrimental strains such families may experience. The structural forms that have evolved are seen as the best to emerge from the alternatives that were possible (Gutman 1976).

Kin-Help Systems

While the nuclear family has continued to be the "ideal" family form, many observers are becoming aware of the stresses and isolation faced by the nuclear family. Systems are now being formed across the country to help parents through life stages by providing support found in earlier, more rural communities and contemporary ethnic families. The goal of being a totally self-sufficient unit is becoming more difficult for all American families (Bronfenbrenner 1975).

When relatives are unavailable, members of ethnic groups often will turn to a friend and become involved in an extensive help exchange that closely resembles the extended family. These "fictive" or "play" kin often are given titles of identification such as aunt, uncle, cousin, or sister, that tend to bring them into the family circle.

The term *extended family* as used with present-day minority families refers to patterns of help, visitation, and social interactions that have developed over the years to support families. Heiss (1971) found that even in lower-status groups, most families can call on several relatives for help. He also found that living in a multigenerational home does not produce decreased satisfaction or self-esteem. The involvement of families in extended familism tends to increase the farther the family is from the American mainstream. The discrimination and racism experienced by some ethnic groups has continued to reinforce the necessity of family members to seek support from each other.

Sussman and Burchinal (1962) reached the following conclusions in their study on family help patterns: Help takes many forms; it is widely spread; the direction of flow is varied; all SES groups participated; financial aid was common, often disguised as special gifts. Billingsley (1968) viewed the family help system, based on networks of intimate mutual aid, as one of the sources of "screens of opportunity" within Black families that facilitated mobility. Stack (1975) found an extensive and intensive kin-help system in her anthropological study of low-income Black families. The help system expanded to include nonrelatives, who supported domestic functions, but was focused on an extended cluster of kinspeople related through children, marriage, and friendship. Stack found that ties between women often constituted the core of the network. A variety of family structures were found, and members were selected from a single network that had continuity over time. Similar kin-help systems are found in Spanish-speaking, Chinese, and Native American families.

The kin-help system—so essential in minority groups for support in coping with a hostile or impoverished environment—may also call for reciprocal responses that tend to perpetuate the network. Stack (1975) found, in an anthropological study of midwestern Black low-income families, that when a couple's income exceeded the welfare benefits of other kin, the more fortunate individuals attempted to alter the diversity of obligations in order to capitalize on their economic gains. Stack reiterated (1977) that the mobile families did not cut themselves completely off from their kin. They participated by willingly making loans to other family members who were less fortunate, not expecting to be repaid. The unequalness of their situation in relation to the "loans" tended to stifle the unending requests for money. However, they did continue to participate in shared child care and to help out their less mobile kin. This model is often seen in minority families as they attempt to move into an economically secure lifestyle while also wanting to maintain close family interactions.

Another model of becoming mobile has been for more prosperous members to cut themselves off from the family because of the nonsupportive draining aspect of the kin-help network (McQueen 1971). A similar theme was found in Stack's (1975) study where the extensive kin-help system provided substance, but strong family reciprocal obligations often resulted that prevented stable marriages and could hinder the mobility of younger family members.

Familism in Mexican-American families was found to be a hindrance to mobility because it cultivates attachments to people and places (Grebler, Moore, and Guzman 1970). Mobility often requires an abandonment of ethnic lifestyle, no matter how strong the retention of formal allegiance to a general ethnic identity. Some minority members select the route of isolation, assimilation, and a nuclear domestic unit as the only possible way of coping with economic insecurity.

On the other hand, many individuals have identified with the family and have made great sacrifices so that another sibling or child could receive the educational opportunities they never had. McAdoo (1977) found many middle-class Blacks who continued their involvement in the kin network after their upward mobility, and who desired to remain an integral part of the family, many of whose members were working class. These families frequently gave financial help and emotional support to their kin. Only the passage of time will show which model the different ethnic groups will find to be supportive of their mobility.

Implications for Parent Education of Minority Families

Educators have often failed in the past to meet young children's needs because programs are not tuned in to the diversity found in the American population. Social service programs have often destroyed the natural support systems of ethnic families rather than augmenting them. Respect for minority cultures will be the first move in the right direction. Gaining knowledge about the group is needed, followed by a sensitivity to the concerns of the target group.

An example of an apparently small concern or issue that has profound significance to the minority person is the term of self-identification preferred by a group. Family members may be alienated easily, for the term of self-identification is important to the development of pride for minorities. Often newer terms of self-identification are adopted first by the youth or more militant members, causing different terms to coexist in the same community. Older persons may still be using earlier terms, and care must be taken to use appropriate terms so as not to alienate different members of a target group.

Replacement of the term *Indian*, mistakenly used by Europeans who thought they were in India, by the term *Native American,* is one indication of the increase in consciousness. The majority of Mexican Americans have today adopted the term *Chicano,* and Afro-Americans have adopted the term *Black*. The labels used for Afro-American descendants illustrate clearly how language is imparted in the cultural delineation and growth toward self-identity. The changes from "colored," to "Negro," to "Black" clearly speak of this cultural change.

Teachers should be discouraged from anglicizing children's names; they should allow the child's home language to be used at times within the classroom, and bilingual curriculum should be incorporated with majority-oriented material. Minority culture and history should be made a part of the everyday curriculum and not saved for special events.

All children from minority or majority groups need adults outside of the family who respect and care for them. Minority parents are often so distracted by outside discrimination and economic insecurities that it is difficult to have the energy to meet fully all of the developmental needs of their children. Professionals or paraprofessionals must become sensitive to these children's unique stresses in order to support the family.

Needs differ; therefore, approaches also must differ. Differences must not be interpreted by the nonethnic professional as deficiencies. The parent educator will need to examine the myths that surround minority children, develop a sensitivity to their needs, and foster parent participation in their educational program in order to maximize the children's potential.

References

Alvirez, D., and Bean, F. "The Mexican-American Family." *Ethnic Families in America, Patterns and Variations*. New York: Elsevier, 1976.
Aquilar, L. "Unequal Opportunity and the Chicano." *Civil Rights Digest* 5 (Spring 1973).
Archuleta, N. "The Chicano Child." *With Pride to Progress, The Minority Child*. New York: Parents' Magazine Films, 1976.
Billingsley, A. *Black Families in White America*. Englewood Cliffs, N.J.: Prentice-Hall, 1968.
Bronfenbrenner, U. "The Ecology of Human Development: A Research Perspective Master Lecture." Paper presented at the American Psychological Association Annual Meeting, Chicago, August 1975.
Chan, I. Personal communication, May 11, 1977. Boston Public School System.
Chapman, L. Quoted by Alvirez, D., and Bean, F. in "The Mexican-American Family." *Ethnic Families in America, Patterns and Variations*. New York: Elsevier, 1976.
Chase, A. *The Legacy of Malthus: the Social Costs of the New Scientific Racism*. New York: Alfred A. Knopf, 1977.
Coleman, J., et al. "Pupil Achievement and Motivation." *Equality of Educational Opportunity*. Washington, D.C.: U.S. Government Printing Office, 1966.
de Berlin, A. "The Puerto Rican Child." *With Pride to Progress, The Minority Child*. New York: Parents' Magazine Films, 1976.
de la Garza, R. O.; Kruszewski, Z.; and Arcimega, T., eds. *Chicano and Native Americans, the Territorial Minorities*. Englewood Cliffs, N.J.: Prentice-Hall, 1971.
Department of Health, Education, and Welfare. *Vital Statistics of the United States, 1969*, Public Health Service Annual Report.
Eggan, F. *The American Indian: Perspectives for the Study of Social Change*. Chicago: Aldine, 1966.
Giordano, J., and Levine, I. "Carter's Family Policy: The Pluralist's Challenge." *Journal of Current Social Issues*, Winter 1977, pp. 48-52.
Gordon, T. "Self-Concept and Sex Identity in Black Pre-Adolescent Boys." Unpublished manuscript, University of Michigan, 1970.
Grebler, L.; Moore, J. W.; and Guzman, R. C. *The Mexican-American People*. New York: Free Press, 1970.
Gutman, H. S. *The Black Family in Slavery and Freedom: 1750-1925*. New York: Pantheon, 1976.
Guzman, R. "Mexican-American Casualties in Vietnam." In *Three Perspectives on Ethnicity, Blacks, Chinese and Native Americans*, edited by C. Cortis, A. Ginsburg, A. Green, and J. Joseph. New York: Capricorn Books, 1976.
Haley, A. *Roots*. New York: Doubleday, 1976.

Heiss, J. *The Case of the Black Family: A Sociological Inquiry*. New York: Columbia University Press, 1971.
Herrnstein, R. "The Perils of Expounding Meritocracy." *Science,* July 6, 1973.
Hill, R. *Strengths of Black Families*. Washington, D.C.: National Urban League, 1971.
Hirsch, J. "Behavior-Genetic Analysis and Its Biosocial Consequences." *Seminars in Psychiatry* 11, no. 1 (1970): 97.
Huang, L. "The Chinese American Family." In *Ethnic Families in America: Patterns and Variations,* edited by Mindel and Haberstein. New York: Elsevier, 1976.
Jensen, A. *Genetics and Education*. New York: Harper and Row, 1972.
Jones, B. F. "A Cultural Middle Passage: Slave Marriage and Family in the Antebellum South." Doctoral dissertation, University of North Carolina at Chapel Hill, 1965.
Ladner, J. *The Death of White Sociology*. New York: Vintage, 1972.
Leichter, H. J., and Mitchell, W. E. *Kinship and Casework*. Russell Sage: 1967.
Litwak, E. "Geographic Mobility and Family Cohesion." *American Sociological Review* 25 (1960): 385-94.
Mack, D. "The Power Relationship in Black Families and White Families." *Journal of Personality and Social Psychology* 30 (1974): 409-413.
Mayeske, G. *On the Explanation of Racial-Ethnic Group Differences in Achievement Test Scores*. Washington, D.C.: Department of Health, Education, and Welfare, Office of Education, 1971.
McAdoo, H. "The Socialization of Black Children: Priorities for Research." *Social Research and the Black Community: Selected Issues and Priorities,* edited by L. Gary. Washington, D.C.: Howard University, Institute for Urban Affluence and Research, 1974.
McAdoo, H. "Family Factors Related to Parenting for Mobility in Black Families." Paper presented at a conference on *Toward the Competent Parent,* Georgia State University, February 1977.
McAdoo, H. "Family Therapy in the Black Community." *American Journal of Orthopsychiatry.* 47, no. 1 (January 1977): 75-79.
McAdoo, H. "The Father's Role in Mobility within Black Families." Paper presented at the National Conference on Black Families, University of Louisiana, March 1977.
McQueen, A. "Incipient Social Mobility among Poor Black Urban Families." Paper presented at Howard University Research Seminar, Spring, 1971.
Mead, M. *Culture and Commitment: A Study of the Generation Gap*. Garden City, N.Y.: Doubleday Natural History Press, 1970.
Mercer, J. *Labeling the Mentally Retarded*. Berkeley: University of California Press, 1972.
Moynihan, D. *The Negro Family: The Case for National Action*. Washington, D.C.: U.S. Government Printing Office, 1965.
Parsons, T. "The Social Structure of the Family." In *The Family: Its Function and Destiny*. New York: Harper & Row, 1949.
Price, J. A. "North American Indian Families." *Ethnic Families in America: Patterns and Variations,* edited by Mindel and Haberstein. New York: Elsevier, 1976.
Rice, B. "The New Gangs of Chinatown." *Psychology Today,* May 1977, pp. 60-69.
Sample, W. "The Indian Child." *With Pride to Progress, The Minority Child*. New York: Parents' Magazine Films, 1976.
Schneider, D., and Smith, R. *Class Differences and Sex Roles in American Kinship and Family Structure*. Englewood Cliffs, N.J.: Prentice-Hall, 1973.
Shipman, V. "Stability and Change in Family Status, Situation, and Process Variables and Their Relationship to Children's Cognitive Performance." Princeton, N.J.: Educational Testing Service, 1977.

Shockley, W. Reviewed in Chase, A. *The Legacy of Malthus: The Social Costs of the New Scientific Racism*. New York: Alfred Knopf, 1977.

Sollenberger, R. "Chinese-American Child-Rearing Practices and Juvenile Delinquency." *Journal of Social Psychology* 74 (1968): 13-23.

Stack, C. B. *All Our Kin*. New York: Harper & Row, 1975.

Stack, C. B. Personal communication, 1977.

Sussman, M. *Sourcebook in Marriage and the Family,* Boston: Houghton Mifflin, 1974.

Sussman, M., and Burchinal, L. "Kin Family Network: Unheralded Structure in Current Conceptualizations of Family Functioning." *Marriage and Family Living* 24 (August 1962): 231-240.

Winch, R.; Green, S.; and Blunberg, R. "Ethnicity and Extended Familism in an Upper Middle-Class Suburb. *American Sociological Review* 32 (1967): 265-272.

Wirth, L. "Urbanism as a Way of Life." *American Journal of Sociology* 44 (1938): 1-24.

Wright, D.; Salinas, E.; and Jurlesky, W. "Opportunities for Social Mobility for Mexican-American Youth." In *Chicano and Native Americans, the Territorial Minorities,* edited by R. O. de la Garza, Z. Kruszewski, and T. Arcimega. Englewood Cliffs, N.J.: Prentice-Hall, 1971.

Bernice T. Eiduson and Thomas S. Weisner

10 Alternative Family Styles: Effects on Young Children

As alternative lifestyles have become part of American culture, interesting attempts to shape social attitudes, competencies, and behaviors of children in new ways have emerged. Children are being raised in single-parent families, living groups, social contract marriages, and other nontraditional family styles. These family forms emerged in the late 1960s and early 1970s in increasing numbers as young Americans, and young people throughout the Western world looked for ways of living that expressed a humanistic orientation, their desires for closeness and intimacy, and a feeling of being one with the environment—attitudes they thought could no longer be embodied in the traditional nuclear family. In their alternative philosophies they sought to replace the competitive strivings, disaffection, and alienation among individuals in mainstream society by a more emotionally meaningful, warm, empathic family relationship. The family forms under study in our interdisciplinary longitudinal project reflect some of the units that were viable after the heyday of the counterculture. These now seem to have stabilized, and, while not as numerous as the traditional nuclear two-parent unit, seem to be presaging changes in childrearing values and attitudes and, perhaps, in infant and child behaviors that are already diffusing into the nuclear mainstream family.

In pilot work which served to identify and document parent values and behaviors in some of these nontraditional families, we learned of some socialization practices likely to have important implications for social development (Eiduson, Cohen, and Alexander 1973). In living groups, for example, a number of parenting persons, in addition to the biological parent(s), were often available and used during the early years. In some instances, six months after birth children were placed in a 24-hour nursery with special adults designated as caregivers and where relationships with parents were more infrequent. At times, such caregiving arrangements were purposefully developed to engender in the child a generalized attitude of trust toward others; at other times, they were parental expedients. These examples illustrate some of the interesting naturalistic experiments in caregiving that can influence infants and young children, and the capacity of various family milieus to meet children's needs. What is the effect of multiple caregivers on early parent-child attachments? Are extensive relationships developed at the expense of intensive attachments? What would be the effect on the social competencies of the child who is being raised essentially in two cultures—one, that of the immediate family, and the other, a mainstream culture often antithetical to the parents' beliefs and practices? What is the impact of changed attitudes toward traditional indexes of a child's academic achievement? How would nontraditional parents define their roles as parents? Would they abrogate the parental authority function in line with their antiestablishment stance? Or would they find some way to reinterpret their roles as authorities regarding the small child?

Interdisciplinary Longitudinal Study

In order to examine a number of such issues relevant to our understanding of the family's role as socializing agent for the child, we engaged more than 200 California children and their families as research participants in an interdisciplinary longitudinal study. The sample comprised 50 children in each of three variants of the traditional two-parent family (social-contract families, single-mother households, and living groups or communities) and 50 children born into the traditionally married two-parent nuclear family, who served as a comparison group. In accordance with the demographic characteristics of counterculture groups which had given impetus to the contemporary development of alternative family styles, our populations were Caucasian and primarily of middle-class or stable working-class backgrounds.

General Strategy of the Study

Data collection began with in-depth interviews with parents. Socialization processes in children's families were studied through interviews, questionnaires, and naturalistic observations of children and parents during home visits. In addition, data about the social and physical milieu of the home, collected through a variety of field techniques, provided an ecological focus. These studies have been continued at close intervals during the first three years and will be continued until the children complete first grade. This schedule of assessments permits followup of families to the point at which children interact with mainstream society, so we can examine the impact of family socialization processes on children's school adjustment. Developmental studies of the child have paralleled studies of families—pediatric and neurological examinations were conducted at birth, home observations were initiated at six months, and intelligence testing was initiated at eight months. Standardized and semistandardized instruments and experimental situations designed to assess cognitive and socioemotional development are periodically administered in the home or alternately in project offices.

The child, rather than the family or living group, is the cohort participant in the study. The child is followed, whatever the changes in family lifestyles; thus, changes in family status and/or residence become study data.

In deciding which of the many extant contemporary American variations in family structure to study, we limited selection to those that had been shown to be most viable and that provided some range of conceptual interest, such as number of parents available to the child or extent to which lifestyles varied from two-parent nuclear families. Within the three family variants chosen, we tried to include a range of family types so that child development issues of interest—such as multiple caregiving, fathering behaviors, role modeling along sex egalitarian lines—could be addressed with as much generality as possible. This methodological position was supported by findings in our pilot work that showed no "typical" or representative commune, social-contract marriage, single-mother household, or even traditionally married couple in a nuclear unit. The alternative groups were identified through a combination of referrals from professional agencies and resources and the indigenous networks in which these populations moved. Referral resources included Lamaze teachers, birth centers, and women's organizations. In addition, notices addressed to prospective parents were posted at universities, natural food stores, communal co-op centers, and other appropriate places. The traditionally married group was obtained by randomly sampling the obstetricians in the California American Medical Association Directory and asking each doctor to nominate one pregnant woman who met our criteria for all participants. The woman was then encouraged to contact the project. Selected women in all groups were pregnant, preferably with their first child.

Incentives for participating were of two kinds: (1) parents were paid $5.00 per procedure to cover expenses involved; (2) $80.00 per year for each child was given to any provider of pediatric services selected by the parent. The service provider shared with the project codifiable information concerning the nature of illness, reason for contact, diagnosis, and recommended treatment.

Demographic Characteristics of the Population

The 208* mothers in the study had a mean age of 25.4 ± 3.8 years, with a range of 18 to 33 years. The fathers' average was 27.9 ± 4.9 years, with a range of 19 to 49 years. The greatest concentration of participants (well over one-half of the mothers and fathers) were born in the Pacific states. At the time they entered the study, 50 percent of the families lived in Los Angeles and its environs, with the remainder fairly evenly divided among San Diego, San Francisco, and the northern California area. Eighty-three percent of the families resided in urban settings, with the remainder in semirural settings.

Both parents had an average of slightly more than three siblings. Mothers were most often second-oldest children, while one-half of the fathers were eldest children. Data about the socioeconomic status (SES) of mothers' families (Hollingshead-Redlich classification using criteria of fathers' education and occupation) showed that 16 percent were from upper-class families, 18 percent upper-middle-class, 31 percent middle-class, 27 percent lower-middle-class, and 7 percent lower-class.** Fathers' families showed a similar SES distribution: 16 percent upper-class, 12 percent upper-middle-class, 33 percent middle-class, 32 percent lower-middle-class, and 8 percent lower-class. The SES of parents at the time of entry in the study was, of course, very different, because the nontraditional families, by and large, had become downwardly mobile, while the traditional families were more on a par with their previous backgrounds.

To understand the parents' motivations for entering into the various types of families, we examined a large number of demographic and social background variables, such as place of birth, birth order, years of education completed, present perception of past relationships with parents and siblings, and history of previous drug use. In general, our data supported findings by other investigators which showed that young people who had opted for variations from the nuclear family were, in the main, not different from their peers in similar social classes (Keniston 1968).

We found relatively few background variables and attitudes which seemed to differentiate the traditional and nontraditional lifestyle groups; however, the ones that were significant added to our understanding of the motivations of those seeking an alternative family. The alternative-family parents had moved from one residence to another as

---

* The total N occasionally varies from the aimed-for population N of 200 because a few extra cases in hard-to-reach groups are being carried in case substitutions have to be made because of attrition.

** Percentages have been rounded for easy reading in this and following sections. Thus, totals of figures cited may not always equal 100%.

children much more frequently than the traditional-family parents. Also, their parents had remarried significantly more often. As would be expected from the literature on young adults attracted to the counterculture movement in the late 1960s, the alternative group interrupted their education more frequently than the traditional group; nevertheless, differences in years of education completed were not significant.

There was a significantly greater tendency for the alternative group to view their early childhoods as unhappy; by contrast, the traditional group more frequently perceived this period as happy. Traditional mothers tended to maintain a better relationship with their own mothers throughout childhood and adolescence than mothers who chose alternative lifestyles. Interview data from fathers showed the same trend in relationship with their mothers. Mothers who were currently living in groups and in social-contract marriages appeared to have had the most difficulty with their own parents. Among the alternative groups, the single mother seemed to have maintained the best relationship with her parents in the growing-up years.

Values and Perspectives of the Families

The data presented suggest a few commonalities in early background features that differentiate those persons who entered alternative families from those who chose two-parent nuclear units. Studies of ideologies and value systems in the third trimester of pregnancy suggest that there were notable differences between the groups in attitudes toward conventionally valued achievement and success; attitudes toward reliance on rationality and intellect, problem solving, goal-setting, and planning for the future; and attitudes toward established educational and medical institutions. The traditionally married sample was significantly and powerfully different as a group from the nontraditional participants. Yet, within each of the four lifestyles, there was a range of perspectives and values among the participants.

Social-Contract Marriages. Living together in a social contract rather than a legal marriage involves an ideological commitment that the relationship should be viable only as long as it is emotionally meaningful. Having a marriage license is perceived as encouraging a relaxation of the dedication to working at the relationship.

Kornfein, Weisner, and Martin (1977) have distinguished two groups of families within this category: those strongly committed by personal and social philosophy, and those who ideally would like to marry but are confined to this status because of legal, economic, or other pragmatic considerations. Kornfein et al. found that the latter group behaved in many ways that approach the more traditional married relationship;

for example, they were more likely to present themselves as married, wear wedding rings, and give the baby the father's surname. By contrast, those couples who were more ideologically committed to the principle underlying social-contract marriage stressed interpersonal relationships and sensuality, and spent more of their time together.

By the women's third trimester of pregnancy, one-third of our sample of social-contract couples had been with their present partners for three years or longer, and one-half had been together from one to three years. Slightly more than half of these couples had planned the pregnancy; in over one-fourth of the cases, this was the second child. Over one-third of the social-contract partners had been previously married—a larger percentage than in any other participant group. One-half as many social-contract fathers had some graduate education as fathers in a legal, traditional marriage. Social-contract families earned $3,000 to $20,000, with a mean between $7,000 and $8,000; by contrast, traditionally married families earned $6,000 to $30,000, with a mean between $12,000 and $14,000.

Many of the women in social-contract relationships reported that they were in sympathy with the women's movement. As a consequence, these parents had sexually egalitarian caregiving roles, expectations, and aspirations for their children; it was in this group that the largest percentage of parents stated that they would not emphasize sex-role differences.

Single Mothers. Although there have always been unwed mothers, the availability of birth control and legal abortion has made childbearing a voluntary condition and single parenthood a pioneering venture. In our population, single mothers were women who opted to keep their babies, although they arrived at single parenthood through a number of circumstances and motivations.

Kornfein, Weisner, and Martin (1977) identified in the family lifestyle group of single mothers three subgroups: nestbuilders, post hoc adaptors, and unwed mothers.

• Nestbuilders were those who saw single motherhood as a desirable role and part of the "total female experience." These women were a few years older (28 to 32 years) than the total population, and were usually identified with the women's movement. Some sought out men whom they perceived as good biological fathers and with whom they had only minimal psychological involvement. These women had good educations and good jobs, and had provided for insurance needs. They were often ingenious in searching out and creating the support systems they needed to provide companionship and social activities, and even to exchange information about their children. Most were back at work six months after birth and used household workers or day care homes to provide child care.

- Post hoc adaptors were those women who did not seek to be single mothers; in a few cases, the pregnancy was carried to term with the notion that marriage would follow. These women tended to be younger and less well-educated than the first group. Although some had stable working records, many had not yet established themselves in a particular occupation, and many relied on Aid to Families with Dependent Children for financial support. Some of the mothers returned to their own families once the baby was born. More frequently, women separated emotionally from their families sought out other women in similar circumstances. Some also lived with men who at least temporarily took on a fathering role toward the child.

- Unwed mothers were the third subgroup of single mothers. They resembled the familiar model of single motherhood of their parents' generation. These women tended to be the youngest of the single mothers; they seemed barely out of their own nests, still in the habit of turning to their parents for support. The maternal grandmother often related to the new baby as the youngest member of her own family, with the dependent young mother ambivalent about her own and her baby's status in the home.

Living Groups. Living groups which create a group alternative to the isolated nuclear family are not new in this country (Eiduson, Cohen, and Alexander 1973). The range of lifestyles displayed by the current living group movement is perhaps even greater than the well-known historical models, making definition of this alternative lifestyle problematic. Groups vary today in types of membership, organization, and subsistence patterns. Communities are often formed around common interests, crafts, or goals. They begin with people who find one another, like one another, and share similar value systems.

In our population, the living group mothers included 65 percent who were legally married to mates also in the group, 20 percent in social-contract arrangements, and 15 percent who were single mothers when they joined the study. Most often, the mother retained full primary caregiving responsibility for the child. However, some groups appointed or hired "chief" caregivers. In other groups, members (either all group members, all parents, or all who were willing) took turns in some sort of schedule, with a written log of each child's behavior handed from caregiver to caregiver. Some groups had only a general agreement that whatever adult happened to be present would assume responsibility for supervision.

Many of today's living group arrangements seem to be domestic groups eager to share the emotional and social advantages identified with the former extended family. Personal compatibility, a search for mutual assistance, and, sometimes, disillusionment and alienation from traditional values bring these people together; there may be no shared ideology, leader, or joint ownership of formal resources. Group living has sometimes been sought to facilitate career opportunities because of the capacity to simplify household maintenance, child care, and accessibility of social contacts. Other communities are attempts to live close to the land and out of the mainstream urban America in search for a more humane, creative, and satisfying form of family life.

Creedal living groups are distinguished from domestic living groups by a system of values and beliefs that all members share as a condition for membership. Western and Eastern religious beliefs, and personal philosophies of strong commune group leaders all provide ideological frameworks for different creedal groups. These groups also have clearer boundaries for group membership and more hierarchical forms of organization. Sixty percent of our sample of living groups were creedal, and 40 percent domestic.

Several other modern living groups are dedicated to revising the typical sexual bonding in the family unit to include more people. Our sample included three triadic "marriages" and one group "marriage" consisting of eight adults. The ties were sexual, emotional, and financial, paralleling conventional legal marriage. All adults were viewed as each child's mothers and fathers.

Traditional Legal Marriages. For most of this group, the two-parent nuclear family, legally attested and tied into an established framework of kin and neighbor relationships, is still the ideal family model. The wife is expected to maintain the domestic sphere while the husband is designated as the material provider, but, interestingly, the largest proportion of part-time and full-time working women were found in this group. These women, as a group, have received more formal education, more often have had careers prior to childbirth, and are most comfortable with the dual roles of the educated American woman. More than one-half of the legally married sample had been with their mates five years or more, and 90 percent had been together for three years or more. This is longer than the typical social-contract arrangements, and, of course, much longer than the typical relationship between single mothers and their men. The traditionally married group was also far less likely to have been divorced; for 90 percent this was the first marriage. The husband was almost always employed, and family income was at the national urban average—higher than in any other family lifestyle.

Early Socialization Patterns

In this section we will present some portions of the extensive data we have accumulated on the socialization patterns of the child during the first year of life. We will start with parental behaviors, care patterns, aspirations, and expectations for the forthcoming child. Birth data are summarized briefly and the developmental status of the children at birth is presented. Some of the five- and six-month data provide a picture of the trend of our findings at this point in the baby's life. Paternal caregiving behaviors are singled out for some special mention because of the contemporary interest in that topic.

Anticipatory Socialization Behavior

Drug Use. It was quite clear that pregnancy had a considerable impact on behaviors perceived as important to the well-being of the child; for example, there were changes in drug use patterns and concern for nutrition. When studied during the last trimester all groups reported a dramatic decrease from previous drug use (see Table). The drug intake of the alternative lifestyle group had been reduced prior to or during pregnancy to a far greater extent than that of the traditionally married group because of their greater incidence of use during earlier years; the traditionally married group almost totally abstained from drug use during pregnancy. The trend to less drug use during pregnancy was also found among fathers; the reduction was not as dramatic, but there seemed to be an attempt to support mothers' reduction in intake or to show lack of interest in drug use in the absence of mothers' participation.

Mother's Prior Drug Use by Mother's Current Drug Use*

		Current Use						
		No Use	Marijuana Only	Experimental Use	Social Use	Career Use	Addicted	Total
Prior Use	No Use	46	2	0	0	0	0	48
	Marijuana Only	20	9	0	0	0	0	29
	Experimental Use	27	32	1	0	0	0	60
	Social Use	12	9	1	0	0	0	22
	Career Use	14	12	2	9	3	0	40
	Addicted	2	3	0	0	0	2	7
	Total	121	67	4	9	3	2	206**

McNemar $\chi^2 = 137.73$; df $= 15$; p $= .01$.
* Usage codes were based on self-reporting of drug use.

** The total N occasionally varies from the aimed-for population N of 200 because a few extra cases in hard-to-reach groups are being carried in case substitutions have to be made because of attrition.

Data are similar for food intake. In general, all mothers were concerned about appropriate nutrition to ensure the health of the child. Accordingly, they reduced their tendency to be involved in unusual diets. No significant differences in nutrition during pregnancy were discovered between alternative and traditionally married groups, or between the various alternative groups.

These findings reflect a theme which recurs throughout the first-year data: The new baby altered a variety of prior practices that had conformed to the parents' ideologies; the appearance of a new baby shaped all parents' behaviors often in very similar ways.

Use of Prenatal Care Services. Organized medical services were used by nearly all mothers regardless of lifestyle and attitudes toward established institutions. While the majority of both groups planned to use hospital facilities, there was a significant difference between the traditional and alternative groups in their plans for home or hospital delivery. The alternative groups more often planned to have the delivery in their home with significant people in their lives attending the birth. Prenatal care was practically universal for both groups, and 98 percent were involved in some sort of preparation for childbirth. In general, attitudes toward established institutions such as the medical care system were modified to some extent by even the staunchest antiestablishment participants in the study when it came to serving their child's anticipated needs. However, who the service providers were was a matter of greater concern: Families went to clinics or to physicians known to be sympathetic to home births or nonconventional families, for example.

Attitudes Toward Pregnancy. Attitudes toward conception of a child are often significant predictors of later mother-child behavior and interpersonal responses. In exploring the extent to which pregnancy had been planned as well as other attitudes about the coming child, we found a highly significant difference between the alternative and traditional groups. Traditional families were much more likely to have planned and anticipated a baby at that particular time. As expected, the single mothers were the group most unlikely to have consciously planned the baby, although a baby was not inappropriate with respect to their ideological commitments. About one-third of the single mothers consciously planned to have the child without continuing the relationship with the father. The social-contract marriages fell between the traditional and single mother groups with respect to plans for the child. Mothers in alternative family lifestyles were also more likely to have had one or more abortions than women in the traditionally married group. In general, even when the pregnancy was not planned, acceptance came soon afterwards.

Mothers in alternative lifestyles felt far less support from their own parents than mothers in traditional lifestyles. Not only were maternal grandparents perceived as more uncomfortable about the lifestyles their daughters had espoused, but they were also perceived as feeling less positively about the coming grandchild as well.

Aspirations for the Child. The alternative lifestyle parents more often perceived themselves as unhappy as children than the traditional lifestyle parents, and related this to the feeling that their parents had pushed and directed them too much. Thus, they were committed to sparing their children from this pressure. Some tended to look to their own peers and to the natural unfolding of children's own talents to supply the essential basis for children achieving self-fulfillment. Many were far less likely to want their children to identify with parents or grandparents than the traditional mothers, who saw modeling and direct teaching as primary ways of having their children identify with them.

Characteristic of many young adults today in traditional as well as alternative groups, the majority of our mothers were planning to play down sex differences in their children. Most verbalized a nonsexist orientation and planned to emphasize this to their children.

Some alternative parents expressed their own nonconventional intellectual orientation through their knowledge of astrology and reliance upon intuition for personal decisions. These people were frequently found together more often in the alternative than the traditional group. A number of other attitudes and behaviors concerning religion, personal philosophy, and the use of drugs to stimulate creative self-fulfillment supported this finding. In line with this nonrational intellectual perspective, there was less concern with traditional kinds of achievement orientation and goals for children among the alternative groups, although achievement orientation may be expressed in other than usual ways. Most parents related achievement to the child's future capacities and desires; the traditional group seemed to have more defined goals in terms of education and occupation than the alternative group.

Physical Aspects of the Home

Space. The space families have available to them and how this space is used can have important effects on children. Sleeping arrangements, privacy for parents and children, effects of density and crowding, and space available for children's toys and exploration are all important influences. Living-group families often have combinations of private and public areas where space and toys are shared. Many families also use their homes as a kind of refuge, as a way to make a cultural or lifestyle statement, as well as a way of providing functional living space

(Weisner and Martin 1976). Thus, the influence of such variables as the number and kinds of people, opportunities for privacy, and the potential for stimulation and exploration, as well as potential dangers in home environments, needs to be carefully considered.

All the participants in the study drew a floor plan of their dwelling and listed all residents and their relationship to the about-to-be-born child. The census and map data, plus other descriptive materials about the home and community setting, gathered by questionnaires and home visits, provided detailed information on the homes of our families.

Overall, the nonconventional family dwellings did not appear outwardly different from the conventionally married couples' homes. Most lived in single-family dwellings or in apartments which from the street were unremarkable. However, some alternative families did live in very unusual settings. Creedal living groups, for instance, often lived in converted churches or other large buildings. Some of the rural communal groups lived in self-built wood homes, trailers, buses, tents, etc. The strongly committed social-contract couples and the creedal and domestic communal families most often chose such unusual dwellings. More families in these lifestyles lived in rural or small town settings as well, although most families in all lifestyles (74 percent) lived in a large town or metropolitan area in California when their babies were born.

Creedal and domestic living groups lived in the largest and most spacious houses. Nearly one-third of living-group homes had over 2,100 square feet of space, with another one-quarter having between 1,300 and 2,000 square feet of space. This compares with an overall mean square footage for all family dwellings of 1,337 square feet. Single mothers were most likely to live in very small residences of 600 square feet or less; traditionally married couples were more likely to live in large single-family dwellings averaging 1,500 square feet. The data are for the actual space available to the domestic group into which the child was born; the distinction is important when considering the large public spaces and shared areas which were part of communal living areas and some social-contract couples' dwellings.

The communal families had more total space but less space available per person than any other family group. Seventy-five percent of the families in communal settings were below the median of 527 square feet per resident for all families while 65 percent of the traditionally married couples were above the median. None of the other lifestyle categories was unusually high in available space, and almost none of the alternative families lived in the affluent and spacious homes available to some of the traditionally married couples.

People. A number of the domestic communes consisted of five or fewer members; 17 of 51 creedal and domestic living group families were in such small groupings. Many of these groups were scattered in small dwellings on communally owned land or lived in small urban homes. Another 18 families lived in groups of nine to over one hundred members living in apartment complexes. Infants beginning life in a contemporary commune or living group in California may sleep in a separate housing area with the mother or with a small group of other adults; at the other extreme, the baby may awake each morning in a communal nursery, part of a group of one hundred adults and children sharing living quarters and caregiving roles.

Traditionally married couples rarely had any other adults or nonrelated children living with them; social-contract families more often had other adults or nonrelated children in their homes. Many of the older, highly independent, and autonomous "nestbuilder" single mothers lived alone with their babies (80 percent), while 75 percent of the younger, unemployed, least independent single mothers lived with their own parents. Those single mothers who may have preferred marriage were in between: one-half were living alone and one-half were living with one or more others—some with a man (20 percent), and some with sisters, girl friends, or parents.

Social Setting

Social Supports. Parents are influenced by social settings as much as or more than infants, especially in the support the social setting provides for the mother. Cross-cultural studies have repeatedly found that organization of the family's subsistence and household economy and the domestic roles of the mother are important influences on her caregiving practices (Greenfield 1974). For example, mothers who have important functions outside the home must share their domestic and child-rearing tasks with others. Mothers who have support for doing tasks in the home have been reported to be less irritable and more consistent in caregiving than mothers who must bear domestic and child care burdens alone (Bernard 1974). In addition, socioemotional supports and advice are often major aids for primiparous mothers. Thus, we were especially interested in the social supports from kin and non-kin that new mothers had and the help they received in performance of their work.

A wide range of items related to the kinds of social supports mothers might need were combined into a summary social support measure for each family. These items included task support for the mother, amount of contact with her own family or other significant kin and friends, mother's use of or isolation from community services, presence of women or men in the home to help on a regular basis, etc. Single mothers overall had substantially fewer social supports of various kinds than mothers in the other three groups. Certain kinds of single mothers, however, notably the "nestbuilder" (independent, older, employed woman) had a wide range of social supports.

Traditionally married women tended to rely more on their natal and affinal kin than women in the other family groups. Weisner and Martin (1976) compared this pattern of kin and related social supports for communal and traditionally married families; their description generally holds for social-contract and some single-mother families as well.

> We suspected that parents in non-conventional families might themselves have parents less likely to be involved with the mothers or the babies, or have what support they might offer accepted. Living group parents are physically separated from their families of origin much more often than the conventionally married parents are; in addition, some of these grandparents . . . are opposed to the life style their sons or daughters have chosen. . . . Coventionally married mothers had significantly more contact with their own natal kin than did mothers in communal settings. . . . Complete severance of relations is extremely rare. . . . Both conventional and communal mothers were seeing their own mothers more times per month at the baby's sixth month than they were before the birth. (p. 22)

However, the mothers in communal settings reported being closer to and gaining more support from non-kin or others in their living group than did conventionally married mothers. The nature of the support and who provides it distinguishes communal families' support systems. There is no indication that overall social support for alternative groups is any less strong, and it may be stronger in some respects than social support for the traditionally married comparison group.

Assistance with domestic and caregiving tasks in households is another area of maternal support important for new parents. We asked all our new mothers to describe the chores in their homes and who does them. Our primary interests were to measure the mothers' workloads and the degree to which they had help in their domestic work. Weisner and Martin (1976) have reviewed some of these data. Three overall patterns stand out.

First, living-group and communal families do have extensive sharing of domestic work roles in their daily lives, and women in these groups have more help available. However, they also may have more work to do. Living groups, contrary to some popular images, differ widely in their sex-role patterns in domestic activities. Creedal affiliation is a powerful influence on some communes, and religious or philosophical beliefs sometimes favor sex-role differentiation and specialized functions in the domestic and child care sphere. Other living groups have a highly egalitarian atmosphere and may have an elaborate and formalized arrangement to equalize work and domestic roles for each sex.

Second, social-contract couples have considerably more shared roles and tasks in their homes than traditionally married couples. The roles are not typically reversed; both parents report that they do the activities on a shared basis.

Third, single mothers vary widely in their tasks. Some women live alone and therefore do all the chores and tasks themselves. Other single mothers live with their parents and have a great deal of help. In this instance, the independence-responsibility dimension of domestic activities runs counter to the support available: Women who are less autonomous and independent also tend to have more support for tasks and chores.

Infant Socialization after Birth. Birth interviews showed a fairly wide range of birth experiences and attitudes which did not seem to be primarily determined by lifestyle. The parents in our study had 109 boys and 100 girls; 20 percent were born in the home and 80 percent in hospitals. Thirty-four percent of social-contract and 30 percent of living-group parents gave birth at home, compared with 6 percent of the single mothers and 8 percent of the traditionally married women. This outcome was very close to expectations reported in the trimester interviews, the greatest variations being an additional 7 percent of the social-contract mothers and 8 percent of the single mothers who had hospital deliveries instead of the home deliveries they had planned. Midwives or other assistance at birth instead of doctors were used by 11 percent of the living-group mothers, 9 percent of the social-contract mothers, 6 percent of the single mothers, and 5 percent of the traditionally married mothers. In our general population, 37 percent of the mothers reported positive attitudes about the birth experience, 39 percent were neutral or ambivalent, and 24 percent were negative. Single mothers were slightly more negative than mothers in other groups.

Childrearing Practices During Early Infancy. Fathers were present at birth in well over 60 percent of the cases, excluding the single-mother group. Fifteen percent of the single mothers had a male friend present; 30 percent had someone else present, usually another woman. Someone else was present at birth in 21 percent of the social-contract families, 20 percent of the traditionally married families, and 13 percent of the living-group families. Regardless of the status of past relationships, nearly all the new parents contacted their own parents within a few days to inform them of the birth.

Eighty-one percent of our mothers breast-fed their infants; in some cases both breast and bottle were used. Seventy-five percent of all mothers fed their babies "on demand," and 18 percent of the traditionally married mothers and 10 percent of the single mothers reported partially scheduling feedings for their babies; these percentages were slightly lower in other lifestyle groups.

All mothers, both before and after birth, saw physicians when they felt ill* and related this to their new status as parents and their need to maintain health. Sixty-six percent of the mothers did consume some alcohol after the birth period, and 24 percent did smoke at least moderately.

The most significant aspects of the birth experiences of our groups, then, were the high incidence of home deliveries, the increased use of Lamaze and other birth techniques, and the frequent presence of fathers and others at the birth. Lifestyle differences focused primarily on the incidence of home deliveries and the presence of fathers or other individuals at birth; there were also some differences in the incidence of breast-feeding across lifestyle groups. In general, however, we found a wide range of early infant caregiving patterns for mothers across all lifestyles. There were no extreme or unusual practices relating to feeding, parental health, or caregiving patterns for any of our mothers, fathers, or babies.

Socialization Patterns at Five Months of Age

Sleeping Patterns. From questionnaires filled out by parents (usually mothers) five months after their children's birth, we learned that 60 percent of the children had their own rooms for sleeping, 32 percent slept in their own beds in the parents' rooms, and 8 percent slept with the parents. Babies in alternative families did not sleep with their parents more often than babies in traditional families. Fussiness at bedtime was the most common sleep problem, according to the mothers. Incidence and modes of handling sleep problems did not vary a great deal across the groups; all reported ignoring, comforting, and holding children.

Feeding Patterns. Feeding patterns were quite similar for all groups, and were determined primarily by the children's needs. One-fourth of the babies began solid feeding by the first month, another one-fourth by the second month, and one-third by the third month. Fifty-seven percent of the mothers, regardless of lifestyle, reported using prepared

---

*We are frequently asked about the extent to which our Pediatric Incentive Plan influenced the alternative parents' use of pediatric services, because they seem ideologically desirous of using organized medical services as little as possible and depending more on self-help or informal services and "natural" practitioners. It is likely that the extent of use of pediatric services is influenced by the greater financial accessibility that the project provides. However, interestingly, most parents used organized medical services which the project did not cover for themselves, a very small proportion turning to less formal resources. Further, there seems to date to be no significant difference in the extent or kinds of illnesses of children or parents in the various lifestyles.

foods. At five months of age, 42 percent of the babies were already feeding themselves, and 62 percent could pick up a spoon successfully. Nearly 88 percent of all babies were on a daily feeding schedule by five months. Alternative families had their babies eat with them more often than traditional families.

Health Data. Medical and health problems did not vary significantly across alternative and traditional lifestyle groups; 93 percent of the mothers planned to take their children to physicians and 80 percent had already seen physicians and planned baby shots. All the traditionally married mothers had already seen physicians.

Two-thirds of all mothers reported reading "baby books" by the five-month period, but only one-half of the living-group mothers contributed to this figure. This difference might be due in part to the use of assistance from others in the community and/or religious rather than secular written authority. Child bathing practices, frequency of visits and outings, and early childhood illnesses did not vary across lifestyles and were distributed in a normal fashion across all the families. When babies became ill or when treatment was indicated, 67 percent of all families used prescribed or over-the-counter medicines, 12 percent did nothing, and 21 percent used home remedies, herbs, dietary change, or "tender loving care." An interesting lifestyle difference emerged when we asked who determined the medical treatment: In the entire sample, 74 percent reported that physicians determined treatment while 75 percent of the social-contract parents reported that they determined treatment.

It should be emphasized, however, that mothers and babies in all lifestyle groups were seen by doctors when children became ill. No variations across groups were noted in the use of vitamins, likelihood of baby accidents, family illness, or mothers' self-perception of health at the five-month period. In general, 69 percent of the mothers said they felt fine, 12 percent felt somewhat tired, 11 percent had mixed feelings, and 8 percent felt poor, half of these mentioned depression.

About 25 percent of all families used disposable diapers, 50 percent used cloth, and the remainder used some combination of rubber pants or training pants.

In summary, only certain differences in parenting practices at five months approached statistical significance. Reported differences in caregiving styles between lifestyle groups were minimal; normal developmental patterns in sleep and feeding prevailed. Many of the values stressed by the countercultural antecedents of today's alternative groups, such as emphasis on the natural—breast-feeding, natural childbirth—have diffused sufficiently into the mainstream culture and been incorporated into the practices of modern nuclear families. All parents appeared to use institutionalized or organized services when they were judged valuable to their children's health and welfare, e.g., maternal and child health care and preventive medicine.

Fathers' Caregiving Behaviors

One of the critical changes in childrearing in the 1970s identified in our pilot study was the greater desire of fathers to participate actively in parenting. The project tried to involve both parents separately in regard to anticipatory socialization attitudes and behaviors at birth, six months, and one year, and hoped to develop some effective ways of categorizing parenting behaviors to take account of consonance and dissonance in socialization behaviors. Differences among family styles in caregiving attitudes were succinctly stated when we asked fathers whether they anticipated changes in their lifestyles when they became parents: 46 percent of the traditionally married fathers expected no change, compared to 18 percent of the social-contract and 24 percent of the living-group fathers. The difference in ideological perspective expressed here was predictive of other differences in parenting among fathers.

Like mothers, fathers in all groups tended to participate in preparatory programs. They also tended to be present at birth. Traditional fathers preferred to have boys in a larger (but not statistically significant) percentage of cases than alternative group fathers. The conventionally married fathers also looked back on their childhood more positively than the other groups and, therefore, a greater percentage wanted their babies' childhood to be similar to their own. These data are in line with the finding that traditional parents (mothers and fathers) perceived their families as closer emotionally than the alternative lifestyle parents.

Involvement of fathers in caregiving activities did vary by lifestyles, but the differences must be seen within the context of a strong overall pattern for mothers to retain primary caregiving responsibility for infants at six months. Weisner and Martin (1976) reported on the caregiving pattern during visits to the homes of all project participants when babies were six months old. Mothers reported, and observations confirmed, that they were present and involved in child care in nearly all the families. There were striking exceptions in some cases, mostly in creedal living groups which placed group infant and child care in the hands of specially selected members, thereby freeing mothers for other activites. Given this overall high maternal involvement, then,

> differences in caretaking patterns . . . are not due to mother absence in infancy but rather to *additional* support available to the mother in the home. In 71 percent of the conventionally married families there was *no* other primary caretaker of the

infant. This contrasts with . . . 33 percent of the communal babies who experience no additional caretaker. The father was a secondary primary caretaker in 20 percent of the traditionally married families and in 35 percent of the communal babies' home settings. (Weisner and Martin 1976, p. 13)

Fathers and other men were generally more often available to assist in infant care in social-contract and living-group families. The situation for single mothers was more complex. Some of them moved in with their own parents; although these mothers had additional support in child care, men were seldom the ones providing the care. In other cases, single mothers established stable relationships with men after children's birth, and so in some cases men were assisting. Other single mothers, the "nestbuilders," continued to care for their children without men.

Caregiving Patterns and Values

We are presently analyzing the caregiving patterns and values expressed by the parents when children were six months old. Some of the variables we have studied (using home observations and interviews with mothers) included caregiver attentiveness; home stimulation levels, both social and physical; physical contact (touching and holding); proximity; affective tone and expressiveness of caregivers and children; interactions during a standardized morning feeding; arousal and activity levels of babies; activities and tasks engaged in by caregivers and others in the home; vocalizations and mutuality of vocal responsiveness by caregivers and babies; and others. We are breaking down our initial lifestyle categories into subsets and specific sources of home influence likely to lead to differences in home settings and/or caregiving in order to look at subsequent influences on early socialization.

An example from the home setting data will illustrate this process. From the child's point of view, "lifestyle" influences during the child's day can be broken down into a number of categories. One important dimension is the quality of the home setting and home stimulation in terms of its variability, diversity, and mode (social, physical, etc.). Preliminary data indicate that babies in living groups and in some social-contract households are exposed to more different kinds of caregivers and their days are less routinized. Thus, *some* early physical and social stimulation levels clearly appear to differ based on the parents' lifestyle choice, but others do not. We are concentrating our current efforts on identifying which aspects of children's settings and behaviors differ across and within groups, and on looking more closely at the "child's-eye view" of alternative family life and its consequences.

Differences in Babies' Behaviors at Six Months by Family Lifestyle

Babies influence caregivers and their physical environments. We were interested in exploring babies' behaviors in the home setting to see if there were very early differences which might be attributable to family lifestyles as a global variable. We did not expect six-month-old infants' behaviors to vary strongly in the absence of any clear neurological, nutritional, or medical deficits, which were rarely present and were unrelated to family lifestyles. Data on arousal level of the baby, fussing, crying, active and alert play, and smiling did not generally differ according to our four initial lifestyle groups when the baby was observed at six months of age.

We also examined the amount of change and variability in these dimensions during the six-month visit. In general, the amount of change and variability in babies' behaviors, although considerable across the entire population, did not differ according to the families' lifestyles. We also examined the extent to which affect and expressiveness are differentiated in babies; again, there were no striking general differences by lifestyles. Thus, initial parental lifestyle does not appear to be directly associated with a great many differences in six-month-old babies' behaviors such as levels of alertness, crying, smiling, fussiness, neutral periods, and changes and variability of these states.

Developmental Outcome Data

One of the critical issues in this research program is, of course, the question of how growing up in an alternative lifestyle affects the child's cognitive and physical development. Our data are too preliminary to say much about this yet because the children are so young. We are cautious about judging future growth and development from early data since there is so much evidence that growth patterns during the earliest years are not necessarily predictive of later personality and intellectual characteristics. Also, we have purposely adopted a longitudinal strategy, knowing that assessments at any single age period—and especially during early childhood—may reflect behaviors that are transitory, rather than representing indexes of functioning that are stable or reflect continuous trends in the individual. Our periodic evaluations have been aimed, from the project's inception, on aspects of physical, cognitive, and socioemotional patterns of growth. Data collected to date are too detailed to present here, but the trends during the first year are of sufficient interest not only to provide us with basic information but also to give a picture of the early developmental features of our population.

Physical Status of Mother and Baby

The outcome of the cumulative Obstetrical Complications Scale (OCS) and the Newborn Neurological Examination (NNE) risk scores on our babies compares favorably with scores compiled on the populations on which these instruments were developed (Parmalee and Michaelis 1972). Our mean OCS risk score was 111 with a standard deviation of 27.4 and a total range of 52 to 160. Our mean NNE raw score was 101.86, with a standard deviation of 21.5 and a range of 65 to 110. These scores suggest that, at birth, the population was essentially normal. Only 3 percent of the babies were premature. OCS scores which were two standard deviations or more below the mean were usually due to a cumulative or combinatory series of adverse factors during pregnancy and delivery.

When children were considered by sex, there was a slight difference in OCS scores: Mothers of girls had scores surpassing mothers of boys (114 versus 108, p = .06). There were no significant differences in complications at birth on the basis of lifestyle at the trimester. However, because the scores of single mothers were 8 to 11 points lower than those of the other groups, differences on the basis of lifestyles at the time of birth approached a significance level of .07. When scores are rank ordered, living-group mothers had the highest mean score, with traditionally married mothers next, closely followed by social-contract mothers.

Bayley Scale Data. At eight months, cognitive and motor development of infants was assessed in the home, using the Bayley Scales of Infant Development. The babies were generally normal, with scores closely approximating the standardization sample (MDI = 103.5 ± 15.91; PDI = 105.5 ± 12.62). Differences in Mental Scale scores approached significance as a function of lifestyle (p = .07). Infants of traditional mothers achieved a mean of 108, considerably above the mean of 100 for infants whose mothers were in living groups. Social-contract infants ranked closer to the traditional infants, while babies in single-mother households were closer to the living-group infants. Among the behaviors that seemed important in differentiating living-group infants were items covering the five- to seven-month period, involving reaching, transferring, and scribbling. On performance items, differences among infants in various lifestyles approached significance (p = .07). Social-contract infants seemed to do a bit better than infants in other groups on gross motor behaviors. On the Bayley test, sex differences were minimal, in line with the literature in this area (Maccoby and Jacklin 1974). Language items, although few at this age, showed no tendency to favor girls over boys.

When the Bayley tests were readministered at one year, we found a significant relationship between the eight-month and one-year measures—MDI: r = .45, p = .01; PDI: r = .33, p = .01. However, neither the mental nor motor scores differentiated children who were living in different lifestyles, for there were fewer than 2 points difference among the groups. The only dimension in which family lifestyle showed a significant difference was in terms of the change of scores from eight months to one year. In general, mental scores increased by 6 points for the 200 babies as a group while performance scores decreased by 7 points; differences were significant at the .001 level.

Mental scores increased most for infants in living groups and for children of single mothers, less for social-contract children, and not at all for infants in traditional homes. Differences here are largely attributable to a regression to the mean rather than to inherent differences among groups. The PDI scores decreased slightly for all infants.

Only six children had been identified as "at risk" on both OCS and NNE scores. Bayley scores were apparently not related to such findings: Of the six children, at eight months three were below the median on the MDI and one on the PDI; by one year, three were below the median on the MDI and four on the PDI.

Attachment Behaviors. The Strange Situation Test is a measure of attachment to the parent, exploration, separation reactions, and fear of strangers. The 24-minute test involves separation from the parent, brief isolation, and exposure to a stranger in a free play situation. This test was given to all children at one year (and is being given again at three years). In general, children in various lifestyles at one year of age did not show significant differences on the Strange Situation Test, supporting the hypothesis that stranger anxiety and separation anxiety are probably developmental phenomena rather than environmentally-determined behaviors at that age period (Bowlby 1969).

On this test, we noted that one-year-old children were able to be somewhat differentiated by their mobility in this new situation in which they were close to the mother and exposed to new toys ($p = .08$). To the extent that mobility or its absence could relate to exploration of the environment or attention to toys on the mat, living-group children were most inactive—one-half of these children never left the mat where they were initially placed. In contrast, over one-half of the social-contract children moved about four or more squares, and were the most active of all groups. The other two samples were more randomly distributed. Children of traditionally married parents were more apt to hold toys most continuously, while social-contract and single-mother children were less apt to do this.

When the stranger first appeared in the test situation, social-contract and single-mother children seemed most preoccupied with the stranger's presence, looking at her more frequently than the traditionally married and living-group children. Relatively few children approached the stranger, but the traditionally married group were least likely to do so. These children were most likely to resist when the stranger approached; living-group children were least wary.

When the test called for the child to be alone with the stranger, children of single mothers were least inhibited in play and moved about freely, as did social-contract children. Crying at being left alone with the stranger was most prominent among living-group children. Children of single mothers cried least; children of social-contract and traditionally married parents cried about the same. More children from traditional households allowed themselves to be held while separated from the mother; fewer living-group children permitted this way of coping with their distress.

Reunion with the mother after separation is considered a measure of attachment to the mother. Social-contract children were the most complacent, rarely crying or fussing, and the crying or fussing stopped once the mother appeared; only 27 percent could not be soothed immediately. Children of traditional parents were the reverse: One-half continued to cry or fuss when the mother reappeared, while one-half were either originally calm or quickly comforted.

None of these data suggest major differences in responses to new situations or persons, or in attachment behaviors among infants who at the trimester lived in family environments differing in size or structure. The parent-child unit remains the "first family unit" of most children in the project, regardless of how much more elaborated or differently organized the more extended family structure is.

Conclusion

The important issue for this family styles project is the implication of alternative lifestyles for child growth and development, particularly socioemotional and intellectual growth. We were struck by the importance of ideological and value commitments of so many parents in their experiments with the family. We were also struck by the way these values and beliefs are heavily modified within the family setting following childbirth. These modifications of anticipatory socialization values stem from social-ecological factors relating to personnel available in the household and the mother's social and economic support mechanisms, as well as the influence of the child and the effects on the daily routine and lifestyle of the family unit.

Many of the most powerful issues in socioemotional and intellectual development will occur at the point when children enter nursery school and, ultimately, public school. These critical periods will be the focus of our longitudinal data collection efforts in hopes of identifying the pathways of influence between experimental family lifestyles and child socialization.

In some respects we are rediscovering variations in conjugal and domestic relationships and family ecologies that have been around for a long time. Many of the variables we are looking at have not occurred in Caucasian, middle- and working-class populations, however, nor have they been concentrated and focused in all of the value and situational dimensions we have identified. For example, multiple- versus single-parent caregiving is a critical dimension of importance for child socialization. What we are seeing is that the number of caregivers per se is far from the only issue involved. As we have suggested, availability, who the caregivers are, their caregiving style, the number of other children in the setting, and a variety of other issues must be taken into account as well. The interrelationships of these various dimensions are of critical importance. Many of these families face trade-offs in applying their values and beliefs about lifestyle and family to childrearing issues. Parents discover soon enough that there is a need for compromise and that some values, when applied to childrearing, are inconsistent with one another. For example, many parents felt very strongly that they wanted close and strong ties with their children early in life, but many parents also felt strongly about egalitarian sex roles, breast-feeding, and working outside the home. Men and women may be able to juggle these effectively, but it is a difficult set of ideals to put into practice with a child on the scene. Thus, we have found repeatedly a period of compromise and shuffling of the hierarchy of values in the face of the realities of rearing an infant. Similarly, changes in lifestyle and mobility continue after the birth, just as they did before the birth. We would expect this kind of diversity and flux in family patterns, as they are in line with the experimental perspectives and behaviors that brought these families to our attention in the first place.

This work is supported in part by the National Institute of Mental Health Research Scientist Career Award No. 5 K05 MH 70541-05 to Bernice T. Eiduson, and by the United States Public Health Service Grant No. 1 R04-05 MH 24947 and Carnegie Corporation Grant B-3694-04.

An earlier version of this chapter was prepared for the Western Meeting of the Society for Research in Child Development, April 2-3, 1976, Emeryville, Calif. We would like to thank senior project investigators Irla Lee Zimmerman, who directed the analysis of the psychological test data, and Jerome Cohen and Jannette Alexander, who directed the development of the questionnaires and interview schedules, for their assistance in preparing materials for inclusion in this chapter. Joan Martin and Mary Bausano were important contributors in the development of the home observations. Max R. Mickey has taken major responsibility for the data analytic aspects of the project, and Cathryn Wechsler for the pediatric aspects. Computing assistance was obtained from the Health Sciences Computer Facility, University of California at Los Angeles, supported by the National Institutes of Health Special Research Resources Grant RR-3.

References

Ainsworth, M. D. S. "Object Relations, Dependency, and Attachment: A Theoretical Review of the Infant-Mother Relationship." *Child Development* 40 (1969): 969-1025.

Berger, M.; Hackett, B. M.; and Millar, R. M. "Child-Rearing Practices in the Communal Family." In *Intimacy, Family and Society*, edited by A. Skolnick and J. Skolnick. Boston: Little, Brown, 1974.

Bernard, J. *The Future of Motherhood*. New York: Penguin Books, 1974.

Bowlby, J. *Attachment*. Attachment and Loss, vol. I. New York: Basic Books, 1969.

Cohen, J., and Eiduson, B. T. "Changing Patterns of Child Rearing in Alternative Life Styles: Implications for Development." In *Child Personality and Psychopathology: Current Topics*, edited by A. Davids. New York: John Wiley & Sons, 1975.

Eiduson, B. T. "Looking at Children in Emergent Family Styles." *Children Today* 4 (1974): 2-6.

Eiduson, B. T.; Cohen, J.; and Alexander, J. "Alternatives in Child Rearing in the 1970's." *American Journal of Orthopsychiatry* 43 (1973): 720-731.

Greenfield, P. M. "What We Can Learn from Cultural Variation in Child Care." Paper presented at the meeting of the American Association for the Advancement of Science, San Francisco, November 1974.

Keniston, K. *Young Radicals*. New York: Harcourt, Brace & World, 1968.

Kornfein, M.; Weisner, T. S.; and Martin, J. C. "Women into Mothers: Experimental Family Life Styles." In *Women into Wives: The Legal and Economic Impact of Marriage*, edited by R. Chapman and M. Gates. Beverly Hills, Calif.: Sage Publications, 1977.

Maccoby, E., and Jacklin, C. N. *The Psychology of Sex Differences*. Stanford, Calif.: Stanford University Press, 1974.

Parmalee, A. H., and Michaelis, R. "Neurological Examination of the Newborn." In *Exceptional Infant, Vol. 2, Studies in Abnormalities*. New York: Brunner/Mazel, 1972.

Weisner, T. S. "Experimental Families: The Child's-Eye View." In *Alternative Families*, edited by J. Gagne. Ottawa, Canada: Vanier Institute, forthcoming.

Weisner, T. S., and Martin, J. C. "Learning Environments for Children in Conventionally-Married Families and Communes in California." Paper presented at the meeting of the American Anthropological Association, Washington, D.C., November 1976.

Whiting, B., and Whiting, J. W. M. *Children of Six Cultures: A Psycho-Cultural Analysis*. Cambridge, Mass.: Harvard University Press, 1975.

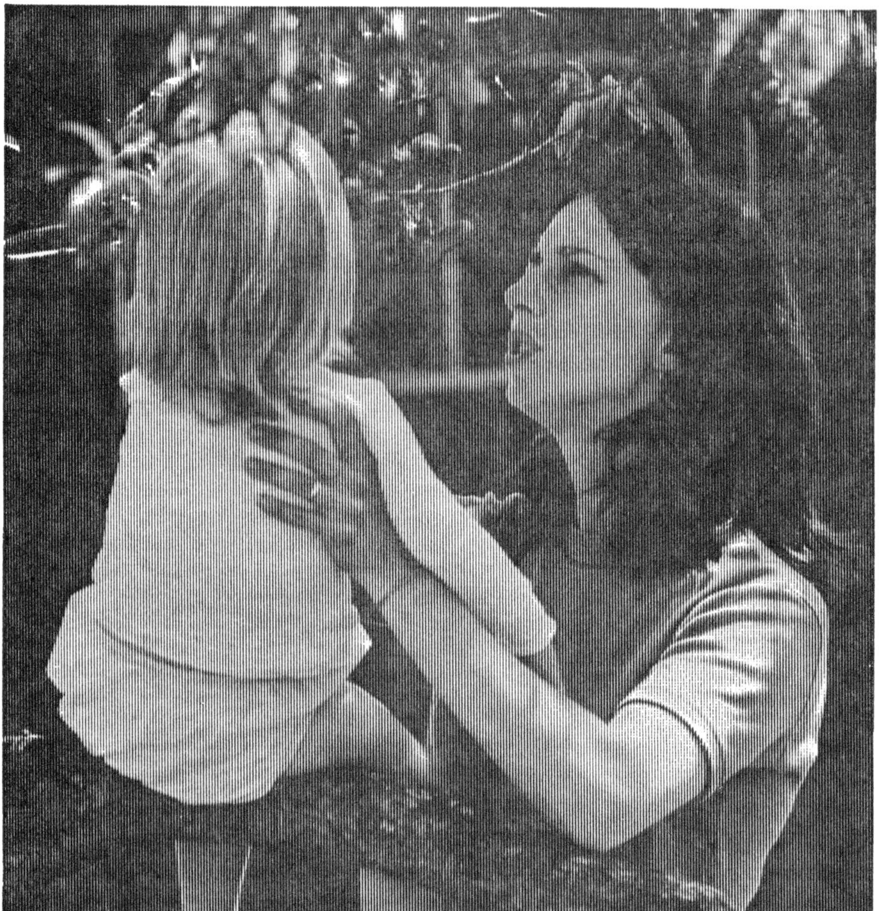

IV

Methodological Issues and the Problem of Application

Since the emergence of the science of child development early in this century, a continuing differentiation and elaboration of inquiry strategies has occurred. Methodologies such as diaries, interviews, testing, direct and systematic observation, laboratory experimentation, and ecological/ethological approaches have emerged, dominated inquiry, and have been assimilated to the researcher's investigative resources. Principles validated by several methodological approaches have strengthened our trust in the validity of these findings. We have clearer understanding about which persons in what situations are characterized by these principles, relationships, or facts. As we examine the implications of research about child development and parent-child relationships for early education, parent education, and childrearing, such careful delimitation is critical. This knowledge does influence whether public funds are used to support programs like day care, parent-child centers, Head Start, and mother-infant nutrition programs.

Many researchers argue that the type of knowledge required by policymakers is not usually available. Bronfenbrenner and others point out that much of what we know about child development has been derived on small numbers of people who are unreflective of the diversity of our country, and about their behavior in a very small percentage of the settings and environments they usually inhabit. In the final chapter in this book, Carew discusses some of these issues substantively and provocatively. She argues that in studying caregiving, different questions need to be asked and researched from culturally-sensitized perspectives. She points out the increased validity of naturalistic observation as well as its vulnerability to the value-laden and culture-bound filters of the researcher. Carew suggests that a child-centered perspective rather than our usual adult-centered perspective may provide more valuable understandings and knowledge. Future research, Carew argues, will need to account more carefully for environmental presage for particular styles of caregiving.

Jean V. Carew

11 The Care of Young Children: Some Problems with Research Assumptions, Methods, and Findings

The popular literature as well as most research on childrearing make several critical assumptions as to the structure and functions of the American family that are obsolete and misleading as well as insulting and dangerous to the families who do not fit the model implicit in this writing. The crucial suppositions are that the White, middle-class, nuclear family—father at work, mother and children at home—represents the vast majority of American families, and research and advice-giving to parents still proceed as if certain major demographic changes in the American family that have taken place in the last twenty years had never come about. But fundamental changes have occurred—notably dramatic increases in the number of working mothers, in the number of female heads of households, and in the percentage of minority children in the population—so that it is probably true to say that currently only a *minority* of children live in the kind of family conjured up by this literature. The majority of American children are not middle class, and a substantial number are from minority groups. More than 30 percent of married mothers with children under age three work outside the home and 12 percent of families are headed by females, most of whom also hold jobs (Bronfenbrenner 1976; Hoffman and Nye 1974; Snapper et al. 1975).

The purpose of this chapter is to examine critically some of the assumptions, methods, and findings of research on effective caregiving of the young child. My main thesis is that in order to understand the fundamentals of effective childrearing, even within just the American culture, one must examine the influence of caregivers other than the mother, the effects of environments other than the home, and families other than those belonging to the White, middle-class mainstream.

In the following sections I shall first consider some newer methods being used in research—in particular the trend toward direct observation of the caregiver and child in natural day-to-day contexts. Although

I welcome this new direction, I see certain dangers in the observation method that have not yet been squarely confronted. Second, I shall briefly summarize the research literature on effective parenting of the young child by the mother in the home. Although some of this research includes families of many social classes and ethnic groups, it is always designed, executed, and interpreted by middle-class researchers. This fact alone compels serious questions concerning the validity of results. This research is also always carried out by adults, and preposterous though it may seem, similar problems arise as to the validity of adult perceptions, interpretations, and assessment of child behavior. Next, I shall turn to research on two nontraditional caregivers: the teacher in the day care center and the working mother who shares her caregiving responsibilities with someone else in or out of the home. The consensus that research has come to regarding effective parenting by *full-time* mothers may or may not apply to effective caregiving by these two *part-time* caregivers—the professional teacher and the working mother. Finally, I shall examine what we know about effective caregiving in minority families. I shall limit my remarks to Black families, but the tenor of my argument applies to families of many other oppressed minorities.

Direct Observation in Natural Contexts: The Functional, Microanalytic Approach

The last ten years have witnessed a welcome trend in research toward the study of the child in "natural" day-to-day contexts. This new strategy relies heavily on direct observation of caregiver behavior and caregiver-child interaction to provide a *functional* analysis of the child care environment. By focusing on the relationship between child development outcomes and observed caregiver *behavior,* this approach often achieves considerably more explanatory power than traditional strategies which typically merely relate dissimilarities in outcomes to differences in gross classifications such as socioeconomic status (SES) and ethnicity, ignoring both the behavior process mediating these outcomes and the enormous variation in process within SES and culture categories.

In my own work, I have developed and applied a microanalytic approach to the study of the home care environment of the child between ages one and three. However, although I remain a strong advocate, I see several dangers in the growing use of this method. First, the microanalytic approach tends to encourage a "conceptual disconnection of functional systems from broader societal systems" (Fein 1976). Studies of this type seldom go beyond child development considerations to address issues that sociologists, economists, and anthropologists might think vital to the interpretation of results (e.g., differences in economic, social, and political resources and differences in cultural norms, expectations, and values as factors influencing parental behaviors). Second, there are problems inherent in the observation and interpretation of behavior that few investigators employing the new method have squarely faced. Are the "same" behaviors equivalent in meaning or consequence for the child from one person, family, cultural group to another? Do observers see the "same" behaviors emitted by members of distinct social classes or cultural groups differently? Do observers from different social classes or cultural groups interpret the "same" behaviors the same way?

All such studies after all apply a common behavior coding system to all of their adult or child subjects. A different system is not used for middle-class and working-class parents or for Black and White children in the same study. This recording framework necessarily reflects its designer's cultural background, life experiences, education, and values, which are nearly always strikingly dissimilar from those of the subjects. Thus, males study females; Whites study Blacks; the rich study the poor; professors study the illiterate; childless women study mothers; working mothers study females who stayed at home to rear their children. Seldom are the subjects or people like them brought in to collaborate on the design of the research or to voice their views as to the interpretation of behavior. This practice is only defensible if we believe that behavior is constant in its meaning and consequence for child development through time, space, culture, and a myriad of life circumstances—a thesis in which few of us, I am sure, would be willing to place much faith.

Until these fundamental problems are overcome, we should treat skeptically research results such as those I shall soon be reviewing. Terms such as *restrictiveness, responsiveness, stimulation,* and *warmth,* even when concretely defined in terms of specific behaviors, still inevitably reflect the study designer's and observer's values and understandings of what constitute their behavioral manifestations. Critically needed are studies designed to show in what ways behavior in natural contexts is spontaneously perceived and interpreted differentially by participants, by people like them, and by researchers. Quite different "psychologies"—different concepts, different ways of perceiving and interpreting behavior—might emerge from such a study with salutary results if it persuades the research elite to question its own sometimes self-serving biases.

Another humbling experience is to ponder how valid can be analyses of **child** behavior that are based solely on **adult** perceptions and interpretations. Researchers are virtually always adults. They are disposed to examine children's activities through the eyes of an adult.

Child behavior that is like an adult's in its rhythm, concentration, systematic approach, and verbal quality is more easily understood, coded, and evaluated; hence the kind of behaviors that are accorded high scores in cognitive tests. Similarly, experiences which adults help to structure for the child are even more easily recognized as "intellectually stimulating" and assimilated to the researcher's recording and evaluating schemes. By comparison, "intellectually valuable" activities that the *child* fashions may not be detected so easily.

Research evidence on these points is scarce because the question itself has seldom been raised. However, in two independent studies (Carew et al. 1976, 1977), my colleagues and I have examined longitudinally the functional environments of one- to three-year-old children reared at home and attending day care centers. Both studies used the same observational procedures and focused on the relationship between the child's day-to-day experiences, in which the caregiver played a more or less active, structuring, participatory role, and the child's later cognitive development. The major results pointed to the critical and very similar role played by mothers at home and teachers in centers in creating, guiding, and sustaining "intellectually valuable" activities for the young child. In both studies, a large portion of the variance in test scores at age three could be predicted from knowing how often the child had had "intellectually valuable" experiences (especially those focused on language acquisition) in the preceding two years in which the child's caregiver had been actively involved as teacher, helper, playmate, or conversation partner.

These findings are very much in line with the many studies of mother-child interaction that highlight the key role of mothers in providing children with intellectual stimulation and influencing children's intellectual competence. However, an equally important finding in these two studies was the very *weak* relationship between "intellectually valuable" activities that children created *for themselves* in their independent play and their later test scores. These activities, by definition, required highly competent, well-organized, mastery-oriented behavior on the part of the children. For example, a child might build a tall tower of blocks, or undertake an experiment in flotation, or pretend to be a dinosaur eating up imaginary prey. These activities—clearly the kinds of experiences in which children manifest and build their intellectual competence—were nevertheless essentially unrelated to their later test scores and especially not to their Binet IQs. High scores on the Binet were correlated almost exclusively with well-structured *language* experiences that adults provided for children and hardly at all to the large variety of intellectually stimulating experiences that the children created for themselves.

Perhaps the reason for these contrasting findings is the similarity between the test situation and the adult-structured natural experience.

Some Problems with Research

In both cases a principal component of the child's task is to listen to language input from adults and to carry out their directions. The point I wish to stress however is that it is *adults* who define children's "intelligence" in the test situation (e.g., attentive listening and the carrying out of the adult's direction earn high scores) and similarly it is *adults* who perceive certain types of everyday experience (e.g., the teaching of language) as "intellectually stimulating." Adults have difficulty conceiving of other forms of child behavior in the test situation (e.g., originality, resisting the tester, tuning out) as intelligent, and similarly they have difficulty in perceiving child-generated experiences in the natural situation as intellectually self-stimulating. Thus, one would do well to be somewhat skeptical about the very research studies soon to be reviewed which claim that the caregiver's interactions are the key factor in the child's cognitive development. Until more valid "child-centric" measures of children's everyday experiences and intellectual competence are employed, the findings of such research are likely to be biased in favor of precisely this comfortable conclusion.

Full-Time Mothers

Direct observational studies of the home caregiving environment are difficult and expensive to undertake. Thus, relatively few studies provide detailed functional analyses of the home environment, and fewer still pertain to the very young child. Available research supports the following conclusions.

Birth to Six Months

Before the age of three months, babies seem to develop normally even under extremely "deprived" home or institutional conditions in which they are seldom spoken to, played with, responded to, or cuddled. After this point, depriving circumstances may begin to exert effects which are latent and cumulative, although reversible through appropriate intervention (Ainsworth 1962; Dennis and Najarian 1957; Dennis and Sayegh 1965; Skeels 1949.)

Some researchers see similarities between the radical forms of deprivation just referred to and that implied by low socioeconomic status. Social class comparisons of maternal behavior, however, yield few differences in responsiveness, talkativeness, or affection to the infant. If anything, the environment of the average low-income home may be the more adequate in that some studies show that mothers in this group touch, hold, smile, and look at their infants more than do middle-class mothers, and that their babies tend to be more active, motorically advanced, and socially responsive. The main difference favoring the middle class has to do with the vocal interchange between mother and infant. Middle-class mothers are more likely to talk to their infants at close range, to respond to their babbles with speech, and to elicit "listening" behavior from them (Caldwell 1967; Deutsch 1973; Golden and Birns 1968; Kagan 1968; Lewis and Freedle 1972; Wachs et al. 1971).

These differences remind me of the effects of adult-structured language experiences demonstrated in my own research and may very well be the earliest antecedents of later differences in language acquisition between children from low and middle SES levels.

The main point, however, is that both within and across social classes there is substantial evidence indicating that the infant's perceptual and cognitive development is significantly shaped by maternal behavior. The more the mother looks at, talks to, and plays with the baby, and the more age-appropriate, various, and responsive her stimulating behavior, the better the infant's performance on standard perceptual and cognitive tests (Gallas and Lewis 1977). The mother's interactive behavior with the infant also strongly affects the baby's social and emotional development—a truism that much research has established as scientific fact. Infants of mothers who promptly respond to their babies' crying; who smile at, hold, and cuddle them frequently; who make eye-to-eye contact with them often; seem happier, less fretful, more socially responsive, and more securely attached to their mothers (Ainsworth 1973; Bell and Ainsworth 1972; Robson and Moss 1970; Zelazo 1971). These changes in the child's development, both cognitive and social, may very early influence the mother's perceptions of and behavior toward the child so that almost from the beginning the mother-child relationship is best described as a *reciprocal*, interactive dynamic in which the behavior of each member of the dyad is continually adapting to the other's.

Six Months to Three Years

There is substantial research evidence demonstrating that children who spend much of the first three years of their lives in depriving institutional environments may consequently be severely retarded in cognitive, language, social, and motor development. Normal development of particular children in such institutions can usually be attributed to exceptional attention they received from a caregiver (Ainsworth 1962; Dennis and Najarian 1957; Skeels 1949; Spitz 1965).

Several studies report striking social class differences in the behavior of mothers of children of this age. Again, the most pronounced differences are in the quality of verbal interaction, with middle-class mothers being seen as more verbal. Even with these very young children, middle-class mothers more often deliberately teach the use of language and symbols through labeling and explanation. They more often elaborate and expand their children's statements, explain events and functions, read, converse, and comment interpretatively on television programs. Their speech is also found to be more "distinctive." It contains more questions and references to objects, fewer commands and rejecting statements, and is more complex and varied. Middle-class mothers also exercise greater control over the television programs their children are allowed to watch. They turn on programs like "Sesame Street" and switch off soap operas and Saturday morning cartoons. Middle-class mothers more often play with their children, use educational toys and creative materials, and exploit these occasions to teach the child skills similar to those assessed in cognitive tests. They also tend to put fewer restrictions on the child's exploratory activities and are more likely to sweeten commands and requests with explicit, verbal rationales (Carew et al. 1976a,b, and 1977; Clarke-Stewart 1975; Kagan 1968; Kessen et al. 1975; Schachter et al. 1977; Tulkin and Cohler 1973; White et al. 1973).

Thus, a composite of highly correlated behaviors seems to distinguish mothers of high and low socioeconomic status. These differences apparently influence a number of competencies or dispositions which children acquire between six and thirty-six months, including language comprehension and expression, problem solving skills, social sensitivity, the ability to express and control emotions, and the willingness to trust adults and to have confidence in oneself. Differences among children of different social classes on measures of intellectual development usually are not apparent until age eighteen or twenty-four months although the corresponding differences in maternal behaviors are discernible much earlier. In fact, at about age one, children from lower socioeconomic groups may be relatively advanced on cognitive tests. By eighteen months however, this difference typically attenuates, and by thirty months it is reversed. Although many of these studies are correlational in design, the very high reported relationships between prior maternal behavior and later child outcomes make a causal hypothesis irresistible to many. This interpretation finds further support in the findings of the more successful intervention studies in which mothers were encouraged to adopt strategies of interaction with their children very similar to those referred to above, and positive changes in child functioning were observed.

Before ending this section, I should point out that the mother is typically not the only significant person in the child's life, even when she is the primary caregiver. Father, grandmother, siblings, the sitter, and even the ubiquitous television set may all play roles in the child's day-to-day experiences which may well rival in impact that of the mother. However, research has given very little attention to these "significant others" although they may often play a central caregiving role in some ethnic groups and among working mothers (Kotelchuck 1973; Lamb 1975; Lewis et al. 1972; Spelke et al. 1973; Wachs et al. 1971).

Finally I want to stress again the caveats previously introduced. As I mentioned, neither the framework used to record and interpret behaviors nor the measures employed to assess child development can be assumed to be equally valid for all the subjects involved in these studies. In fact, both observations and tests are virtually always designed by researchers whose education and cultural background approximate those of some subjects (e.g., middle-class parents) and are entirely alien to others (e.g., welfare mothers). Moreover, the recording of children's everyday experiences and assessments of their cognitive development may also be fundamentally biased in the adult-centric sense that the research by Carew et al. (1976a,b, 1977) described in the previous section seems to suggest. So again it is wise to be suspicious about research results. One can easily be beguiled by the apparent high agreement among researchers into thinking that the answers are already in. But in fact the consensus may be a spurious one traceable to the similarity of conceptualization and methods used by most investigators whose cultural background and training tend to be highly similar rather than to a convergence on the same conclusions by researchers with very different life histories and perspectives.

Day Care Teachers

We turn now to research on another type of caregiver and environment, the teacher in the day care center. Although most nonmaternal care of young children is provided in the child's home by relatives or nonrelatives or in the homes of other people rather than in centers, the former settings have seldom been studied. Most research on nonmaternal caregiving focuses on teachers in day care centers perhaps because it is easier to study a few caregivers and many children in one site than each caregiver-child dyad in a different home.* We note that most day care centers for young children are set up simply to provide good substitute care outside the home and are not concerned with accelerating development. Thus, studies on the effects of day care are typically

---

* Some large-scale comparative studies of caregiving environments are now in progress. For example, at the national level, ACYF is sponsoring a large-scale study of caregivers and three- to four-year-olds in day care centers in three cities, and a similar study of children under five in day care homes (Abt Associates and Stanford Research Institute 1977). A similar study is now being carried out in New York City investigating the environments and development of six- to thirty-month-old children in day care centers, day care homes, and "natural" homes (Golden 1977), and another in Chicago examining the social development of 2½- to 4-year olds in six different child care arrangements (Clarke-Stewart 1976). These three studies are still in progress, and final reports are not due for some time.

designed to consider whether the day care experience has *detrimental* effects on development—the explicit or implicit comparison being with children reared at home by their mothers.

Adverse Effects

Strident claims that day care adversely affects the young child find little support from existing research. There is little or no evidence indicating unfavorable consequences, whether one considers intellectual development, peer relationships, responsiveness to adult socialization, or affective relationships between child and parent. However, this conclusion must be tempered with the realization that most research has been carried out in "high quality" centers (Caldwell 1970; Kagan et al. 1976; Keister 1970; Lally 1974; Lewis 1975; Ragozin 1976; Ramey and Smith 1976; Willis and Ricciuti 1974). Only now are major research studies being implemented involving children enrolled in the broad range of centers characterizing the day care market.

Beneficial Effects

"High quality," cognitively-structured day care programs probably do not enhance the development of children whose home environments are already supportive of normal development (that is, these children do not do better on assessments than control children from similar home backgrounds). On the other hand, such day care programs may prevent the decline in intellectual functioning reported for children from considerably less favorable home environments or those judged to be at substantial developmental risk (Fowler and Khan 1975; Heber et al. 1972; Garber et al. 1976; Robinson and Robinson 1971). High quality day care may also have positive social consequences in the sense of fostering the child's ability to play harmoniously and productively with peers, to adapt to strange adults, and the like, but research on these issues is scant.

Quality of Care

Day care centers vary widely in a number of aspects that have to do with "quality of care." These features include: caregiver/child ratios at different ages and group size; staff qualifications and turnover; the nature of the child's day-to-day experiences or "program" and available play materials; provisions for ensuring adequate health, nutrition, and safety; and communication with, support, and involvement of parents. "High quality" care refers to desirable components of variables which are thought to facilitate the children's intellectual, social, and emotional development and the relationship with their families. The problem is that not enough is now known as to the effects of variation on each of these characteristics and still less as to the many combinations that might define "high" and "poor" quality care.

In defining quality of care, Ricciuti (1976) suggests that the day care center should approximate a "good" natural home environment in the kinds of daily experiences it provides for children and that its goals for children should be the same as most parents'. Thus, the center should not only provide for children's basic physical, health, safety, and nutritional needs, but should also ensure that they are "cared for by familiar, responsive, and affectionate caregivers who (a) foster through their interactions with the child an early sense of trust and confidence in salient, caring adults; (b) frequently create mutually enjoyable opportunities for learning through play and social interactions in the natural context of daily caregiving; and (c) are sensitive in dealing with the individual needs and characteristics of particular babies" (p. 44-46).

There are some obvious problems with this definition of quality day care. What is a "good" natural home environment? What are the goals that most parents want for their children? Should the comparison be with a general norm or with the home environments and goals of most of the center's actual *clients*? This definition also glosses over some intrinsic differences between centers and homes which compel different strategies and goals for the two settings. The day care center is intrinsically a *group* setting. The child in this setting usually has to learn to relate to more than one primary caregiver (at a time and over time) and to many children similar in age who also tend to come and go. Therefore, one of the most important aspects of effective caregiving must be the caregiver's skill in helping children relate to many different people in cognitively, socially, and emotionally productive ways. Again, because it is a group setting, the individual child's experience in day care nearly always will include more accommodation to routine and rules, more waiting time, less privacy, more interruptions, more direction of activity from adults, more doing things in a group and with other children, and perhaps less one-to-one interaction with adults than in the average home. We are very far from being able to say how these obvious differences between center and home settings relate to development in children, but it would be a mistake to bias our answers in advance by assuming that the child's experience in a "good" home is the norm by which quality of care in centers should be measured.

The Working Mother

In their recent book, Hoffman and Nye (1974) review many studies concerned with maternal employment as a factor relating to development in children. However, as the authors acknowledge, virtually none of these studies considers the very young child, and in most of the studies maternal employment is so confounded with other variables such as social class, type of job relative to qualifications, approval of mother's employment by family members and so on, that few generalizable conclusions can be drawn. The data as a whole suggest that the children of working mothers who obtain personal satisfaction from employment, whose decision to work is supported by family members, who do not feel guilty or anxious about working, and who have been able to make adequate household and child care arrangements, develop at least as well as children of nonworking mothers, and possibly better in certain areas such as sex-role attitudes. As we have already seen, this general conclusion was also supported by the research on children in day care, most of whom are children of working mothers.

Research on maternal employment, however, is sorely in need of redirection. Urgently needed are studies directly focused on the resources and skills required by the working mother for effective parenting. The problems a working mother faces, after all, are quite different from those of the mother rearing her children at home. First, the working mother is basically buying a service rather than performing one for her child. She must weigh the value of the service in terms of costs, convenience, quality, suitability to her child's needs, and so forth, and typically she has few options, little knowledge about alternatives, and must reach a decision rapidly. Even when the working mother has the luxury of time and the choice of many alternatives, she is often unable to judge quality or suitability because few guides are available to help her distinguish poor from good centers or to discern differences between center and home care. Research on how mothers make this critical decision should be done because the choice of a center is likely to affect the daily fabric of the child's life and consequent development. Moreover, the mother's perceptions of the child's day care world may (and should) consciously affect how she spends her time with the child at home and our definition of her parenting skill.

Most working mothers of children in day care see them only for a few hours each work day. In most homes these are hectic hours. Meals must be prepared, children fed, washed, dressed, and transported, and a multitude of housekeeping chores accomplished. The organizational, managerial, and interpersonal skills and attitudes required to get these tasks carried out efficiently are therefore as much a part of the working mother's parenting skill as the quality of her specific interactions with the young child. Where other adults or older children are available, her skill must include the ability to obtain adequate help from them in the routine performance of domestic responsibilities. It is estimated that full-time employment coupled with sole responsibility for domestic family needs demands a weekly investment of 105 hours of work—a burden few women can shoulder and still find the time, energy, and psychological resources to engage in positive interactions with young children (Howell 1973). Again, research is sorely needed on this issue because, for the working mother, the carrying out of essential domestic tasks in a few crowded hours before or after a full day of work necessarily sets the main context in which interactions with young children can take place (Goldberg 1977; Peters 1976; Powell 1977).

There is also a need for research to determine what aspects of mother-child interaction are important to the development of children when the mother works and the children spend most of their day with another caregiver. It cannot be casually assumed that the same variables defining effective caregiving for the mother at home or the teacher in day care apply to the working mother. In fact, it is plausible that a different composite of behaviors describes effective parenting for the working mother. For example, if she knows that the child is already bombarded with "intellectual stimulation" in day care, the working mother might profitably forego duplicating these experiences at home and concentrate instead on meeting needs that the other setting inadequately reaches. Obvious candidates might be the child's needs for overt affection and for experiences through which the child can learn to understand the personalities of family members, and achieve a sense of belonging and interdependence with others. Thus, for working mothers, the sociocultural aspect of interactions with young children is likely to be far more important than the cognitive if the child's intellectual needs are already well satisfied in day care. It is not sensible to assume that whatever defines good caregiving in one context also defines good caregiving in another.

Black Mothers

The themes I have touched on so far provide essential background for examining effective parenting in Black families. Proportionately more than in White families, Black mothers are employed, Black children attend day care, Black mothers are single heads of family, and Black families are poor. These features do **not,** however, describe the majority of Black families. The modal Black family is still the hardworking blue collar and white collar family in which two parents are present and the mother stays at home to rear her children when they are young. Thus each of the several bodies of research that I hav summarized apply to some Black families *if we disregard their race*.

To be Black in America, however, is to be part of a culture that is different from and defensively resistant to the dominant Euro-American culture. These facts render invalid the application to Black families of analytic and interpretative frameworks designed by non-Blacks. As Pierce (1974), Nobles (1974), and others have pointed out, social science knowledge is rooted in social relations, and the predominantly race and class segregated society of the United States severely limits what a non-Black knows or can learn about the thoughts, feelings, and behavior of Blacks. (It also severely distorts what a Black, trained and educated in White institutions, can know about Blacks not so acculturated.) The history of the Black family vividly illustrates this point.

Traditionally, the Black family has been studied as a pathological social organization, the perspective being that of a "sick" White family. Years ago, Du Bois (1908) and then Frazier (1932) focused on "disorganization" in the Black family which they related to oppressive economic conditions. More recently Moynihan (1965) claimed that the cause of Black community deterioration was no longer its political and economic subjugation by a hostile wider society but the structure and nature of Black families themselves. Other researchers have contended that the root causes of differences between Black and White families lie in three centuries of slavery, servitude, economic oppression, and racism. Whether with benign or malevolent intentions however, researchers continue to view the Black family as a social "problem." Their perspective is nearly always one that glosses over the uniqueness of the Black family, ignores its strengths, and emphasizes its weaknesses. Only recently have scholars (Billingsley 1966; Gutman 1976; Hill 1972; Ladner 1971; Nobles 1974, 1976; Peters 1976; Staples 1973, 1974) seriously turned to considering the coping strategies of Black families that have enabled them to survive through centuries of economic, political, and cultural oppression.

In an insightful paper, Nobles (1974) emphasizes that the Black family's "definition, character, form, and function did not begin with the American experience of slavery and that as a system it has an historical continuation extending back in history to traditional Africa and its culture" (p. 37). The analysis of Black family life must therefore take seriously its *Afro*-American heritage. Black family systems are "African in nature and American in nature." Nobles presents several examples of structure, roles, and behavior in Black families that can be traced to their African heritage. These include parakinship ties where boys and girls have "play" brothers and sisters who have the same loyalties and responsibilities as blood relations; the extended family and the practice of informal adoption; flexible family roles in which Black men and women more easily interchange the expressive/domestic and economic/instrumental roles that are normally sex-specific in White society; the more egalitarian pattern of relations between Black men and women (which non-Blacks often regard as evidence of female dominance). Knowing little of traditional African culture and histo y, I cannot say whether these features are truly African in origin.

But certainly they are distinctive features of many Afro-American families that research usually ignores.

Pierce (1974; 1975a,b) has presented a psychological analysis of the effects of racism and "the mundane extreme environment" on the behavior of Black people which has enormous implications for how research is conducted and data are interpreted. First, he points out that Black people have always lived in the United States under conditions of segregation and restricted mobility. Much of the life of a Black individual is spent in all-Black groups. Most Black children spend the bulk of their time in an all-Black family, neighborhood, and school setting, and for many, this pattern of minimal contact with Whites continues all through adulthood.

Pierce defines racism as both a perceptual problem and a *"folie à deux"* in which both Blacks and Whites engage in complementary delusional beliefs. Racism is so pervasive in Black-White relations that its effects are similar to terrorism. Blacks must constantly mobilize resources of body and mind to defend themselves against "microaggressions" by Whites that are so routine and habitual as to be typically unconsciously committed by the White and unconsciously perceived by the Black. This self-protective posture inevitably involves defensive thinking and defensive behaviors by Blacks in the presence of Whites.

Pierce couples his analysis of the effects of racism with an analysis of the effects of extreme environments on behavior. An extreme environment is one in which the magnitude of stress or wear and tear on the body is abnormally high. The urban ghetto is an excellent example of a *mundane* extreme environment; the South Pole or the moon are examples of *exotic* extreme environments. According to Pierce, both exotic and mundane extreme environments share the following stress-producing characteristics: forced socialization, density clustering, spatial isolation, inability to escape, fears of abandonment, noise/silence extremes, lack of information, and increased "empty" time. These stresses have discernible effects on thinking and behavior, requiring the victim to engage in greater than ordinary surveillance of the environment and constant mobilization against threat and hopelessness. The extreme environment also engenders problems of leadership and followership, time usage, planning, and decision-making. Dependency is increased and self-confidence is decreased as threats to one's survival multiply.

The behavior of most Blacks then is fundamentally affected by their experience of racism and the stress of the mundane extreme environment in which they live. What does this imply for observational research on Black families? The first implication is that Blacks are likely to act differently in the presence of Whites or of other Blacks whom they may see as similar to Whites or as carrying out their purposes.

Some Problems with Research

Indeed, the behaviors of parents toward young children are among those *most likely* to be affected by the presence of such an outsider in the home because this is the first context in which defense, wariness, and vigilance must be taught. Intensification of defensive behavior is automatic and is not likely to be much mitigated by the customary training of observers "to be friendly and respectful" because it is triggered as much by the Black person's prior experience of racism and the mundane extreme environment as by the particular behavior of the observer/interviewer.

A second implication to be drawn from Pierce's analysis is that when the research instruments for recording/interpreting behavior have been conceived and designed by Whites (or imitatively by Blacks), these instruments are not likely to "fit" the behaviors of Blacks. The basic concepts and definitions of behavior and the underlying values are likely to be inappropriate. For example, "control" is a category of behavior often used in observational research. Most middle-class White researchers regard "frequent" and "harsh" control of children as a bad thing, whether this takes the form of imposing ideas or controlling behavior. Pierce's analysis, however, suggests that in Black families a high level of control over children may be critical to effective parenting insofar as it may protect the child from a hostile wider environment.

A third implication is that Black and White observers, using the same recording and analytic framework, are likely to perceive and interpret the "same" behavior of a Black person differently. No observation system can specify in advance how the large variety of behaviors observable in natural contexts should be recorded. Much must be left to the judgment of the observer who ultimately must rely on his/her own culturally and idiosyncratically determined ways of perceiving and interpreting behavior. Such basic categories as whether or not the mother "interacted with" the child are likely to be recorded dissimilarly by Black and White observers who are differentially attuned to the meanings of nonverbal behavior. Similarly, "aggression," "affection," "responsiveness," "rejection" are categories of behavior that Black and White observers are likely to define operationally in quite different ways.

One looks in vain for research on Black families in which these all too real possibilities of bias are seriously assayed and finds instead only perfunctory attempts to train White observers to respect differences or to use Black observers in Black homes. The fact of the matter is that the research instrument, its designers, and users control the data, not the other way around. Until more valid concepts and methods for studying Black families are created by those who know and have experienced Black culture firsthand, it is fair to say that the accumulated research on Black parenting is of limited authenticity and value.

Summary

This chapter examines some problems with the assumptions, methods, and findings in research on the care of the young child. A major premise is that in order to understand the fundamentals of effective childrearing, one must examine the influence of caregivers other than the mother, the effects of environments other than the home, and families other than those belonging to the White middle-class mainstream. At the same time a major thesis of the paper is that the assumptions, methods, and findings of currently available research leave much to be desired. Observation instruments and tests are virtually always adult-centric, ethnocentric, class-biased, and designed with the now outmoded model of the conventional nuclear family in mind. These biases are so strong and pervasive as to compel serious doubts about the validity of investigations involving lower-class children, children of working mothers, children in day care, perhaps *all* children studied by adult researchers. These doubts will not be allayed until researchers learn to take the perspective of the research subject more seriously into account and ensure that this perspective truly influences the research at every stage: conceptualization, design, execution, analysis, and dissemination.

References

Abt Associates, Inc., and Stanford Research Institute. National Day Care Center Study, in progress 1974-1977.

Abt Associates, Inc., and Stanford Research Institute. National Day Care Home Study, in progress 1976-1978.

Ainsworth, M. D. S. "The Effects of Maternal Deprivation: A Review of Findings and Controversy in the Context of Research Strategy." *Public Health Papers* 14 (1962): 97-165.

Ainsworth, M. D. S. "The Development of Infant-Mother Attachment." In *Review of Child Development Research,* vol. 3, edited by B. M. Caldwell and H. N. Ricciuti. Chicago: University of Chicago Press, 1973.

Bell, S. M., and Ainsworth, M. D. S. "Infant Crying and Maternal Responsiveness." *Child Development* 43 (1972): 1171-1190.

Billingsley, A. *Black Families in White America*. Englewood Cliffs, N.J.: Prentice-Hall, 1966.

Bronfenbrenner, U. "Research on the Effects of Day Care on Child Development." In *Toward a National Policy for Children and Families*. Washington, D.C.: National Academy of Sciences/National Research Council, 1976.

Caldwell, B. M. "Social Class Level and Stimulation: Potential of the Home." *Exceptional Infant* 1 (1967): 455-466.

Caldwell, B. M.; Wright, C. M.; Honig, A. S.; and Tannenbaum, J. "Infant Day Care and Attachment." *American Journal of Orthopsychiatry* 40 (1970): 397-412.

Carew, J. V.; Chan, I.; and Halfar, C. *Intelligence and Experience in Day Care*. Final report to National Institute of Mental Health, August 1976a.

Carew, J. V.; Chan, I.; and Halfar, C. "Observed Intellectual Competence and Tested Intelligence: Their Roots in the Young Child's Transactions with His Environment." In *Child Development: A Study of Growth Processes*, edited by S. Cohen and T. J. Comiskey, 2nd ed. Itasca, Ill.: F. E. Peacock, 1977.

Carew, J. V.; Chan, I.; and Halfar, C. *Observing Intelligence in Young Children: Eight Case Studies*. Englewood Cliffs, N.J.: Prentice-Hall, 1976b.

Clarke-Stewart, A. *Child Care in the Family. A Review of Research and Some Propositions for Policy*. Report to the Carnegie Council on Children, 1975.

Clarke-Stewart, A. "Early Child Care Arrangements: Variations and Effects." A research proposal presented to the Bush Foundation, 1976.

Cochran, M. "A Comparison of Group Day Care and Family Childrearing Patterns." Unpublished manuscript, Cornell University, 1976.

Dennis, W., and Najarian, P. "Infant Development Under Environmental Handicap." *Psychological Monographs* 71 (1957).

Dennis, W., and Sayegh, Y. "The Effect of Supplementary Experiences upon the Behavioral Development of Infants in Institutions." *Child Development* 36 (1965): 81-90.

Deutsch, C. P. "Social Class and Child Development." In *Review of Child Development Research*, vol. 3, edited by B. M. Caldwell and H. N. Ricciuti. Chicago: University of Chicago Press, 1973.

Doyle, A. "Infant Development in Day Care." *Developmental Psychology* 11 (1975): 655-656.

Du Bois, W. E. B. *The Negro American Family*. Atlanta: Atlanta University Press, 1908.

Fein, G. "The Changing Ecology: Economic Uncertainty, Families and Children." Proposal submitted to the National Science Foundation, 1976.

Fowler, W., and Khan, N. "The Development of a Prototype Infant and Child Day Care Center in Metropolitan Toronto." Year IV Progress Report, 1975.

Frazier, B. F. *The Negro Family in Chicago*. Chicago: University of Chicago Press, 1932.

Gallas, H., and Lewis, M. "Mother-Infant Interaction and Cognitive Development in the 12-Week-Old Infant." Paper presented at the Society for Research in Child Development meeting, New Orleans, March 1977.

Garber, H.; Heber, R.; Hoffman, C.; and Harrington, S. "Preventing Mental Retardation Through Family Rehabilitation." *TADS Infant Education Monograph*. Chapel Hill, N.C.: TADS, 1976.

Goldberg, R. "Maternal Time Use and Preschool Performance." Paper presented at the Society for Research in Child Development meeting, New Orleans, March 1977.

Golden, M. "The New York City Infant Day Care Study." Symposium presented at the Society for Research in Child Development meeting, New Orleans, March 1977.

Golden, M., and Birns, B. "Social Class and Cognitive Development in Infancy." *Merrill-Palmer Quarterly* 14 (1968): 139-149.

Gutman, H. *The Black Family in Slavery and Freedom: 1750-1925*. New York: Pantheon Books, 1976.

Heber, R.; Garber, H.; Harrington, S.; Hoffman, C.; and Falender, C. *Rehabilitation of Families at Risk for Mental Retardation*. Rehabilitation Research and Training Center, University of Wisconsin, 1972.

Hill, R. *The Strengths of Black Families*. New York: Emerson Hall, 1972.

Hoffman, L. W., and Nye, F. I. *Working Mothers*. San Francisco: Jossey-Bass, 1974.

Howell, M. "Employed Mothers and Their Families (I)." *Pediatrics* 2 (1973).

Kagan, J. "On Cultural Deprivation." In *Environmental Influences*, edited by D.C. Glass. New York: Rockefeller University Press, 1968.

Kagan, J.; Kearsley, R.; and Zelazo, P. "The Effects of Infant Day Care on Psychological Development." Paper presented at the American Association for the Advancement of Science meeting, Boston, February 1976.

Keister, M. *A Demonstration Project: Group Care for Infants and Toddlers.* Final report. University of North Carolina at Greensboro, 1970.

Kessen, W.; Fein, G.; Clarke-Stewart, A.; and Starr, S. "Variations in Home-Based Infant Education: Language, Play, and Social Development." Final report to the U.S. Office of Child Development, 1975.

Kotelchuck, M. "The Nature of the Infant's Tie to His Father." Paper presented at the Society for Research in Child Development meeting, Philadelphia, 1973.

Ladner, J. *Tomorrow's Tomorrow: The Black Woman.* Garden City, N.Y.: Doubleday, 1971.

Lajewski, H. C. *Child Care Arrangements of Full-Time Working Mothers.* Washington, D.C.: Children's Bureau, 1959.

Lally, R. *The Family Development Research Program.* Syracuse University Progress Report, 1974.

Lamb, M. E. "Fathers: Forgotten Contributors to Child Development." *Human Development* 2 (1975): 245-266.

Lewis, J. *Family Developmental Center: A Demonstration Project.* San Francisco: Family Services Agency Final Report, 1975.

Lewis, M., and Freedle, R. "Mother-Infant Dyad: The Cradle of Meaning." Paper presented at University of Toronto Symposium on "Language and Thought," March 1972.

Lewis, M.; Weinraub, M.; and Ban, P. "Mothers and Fathers, Boys and Girls: Attachment Behavior in the First Two Years of Life." Princeton, N.J.: Educational Testing Service, 1972.

Low, S., and Spindler, P. B. *Child Care Arrangements of Working Mothers in the United States.* (Publication 461) Washington, D.C.: Children's Bureau, 1968.

Moynihan, D. "Employment, Income and the Order of the Negro Family." *Daedalus* 94 (1965): 745-770.

Nobles, W. "Africantry in Black Families." *The Black Scholar,* June 1974.

Nobles, W. "A Formulative and Empirical Study of Black Families." Final report to the U.S. Office of Child Development, 1976.

Peters, M. "Nine Black Families: A Study of Household Management and Childrearing in Black Families with Working Mothers." Doctoral dissertation, Harvard Graduate School of Education, 1976.

Pierce, C. M. "The Mundane Extreme Environment and Its Effects on Learning." In *Learning Disabilities: Issues and Recommendations for Research,* edited by S. Brainard. Washington, D.C.: National Institute of Education, DHEW, 1975a.

Pierce, C. M. "Poverty and Racism as They Affect Children." In *Advocacy for Child Mental Health,* edited by I. Berlin. New York: Brunner/Mazel, 1975b.

Pierce, C. M. "Psychiatric Problems of the Black Minority." In *American Handbook of Psychiatry,* vol. 2, edited by S. Arieti. New York: Basic Books, 1974.

Powell, D. "The Coordination of Preschool Socialization: Parent-Caregiver Relationships in Day Care Settings." Paper presented at the Society for Research in Child Development meeting, New Orleans, March 1977.

Prescott, E. "A Comparison of Three Types of Day Care and Nursery School-Home Care." Paper presented at the Society for Research in Child Development meeting, Philadelphia, 1973.

Ragozin, A. "Attachment in Day Care Children: Field and Laboratory Findings." Paper presented at the Society for Research in Child Development meeting, Denver, April 1975.

Ramey, C., and Smith, B. "Learning and Intelligence in Disadvantaged Infants: Effects of Early Intervention." Paper presented at the Council on Exceptional Children meeting, Chicago, April 1976.

Ricciuti, H. N. "Effects of Infant Day Care Experience on Behavior and Development: Research and Implications for Social Policy." Unpublished manuscript, Cornell University, 1976.

Robinson, H., and Robinson, N. "Longitudinal Development of Very Young Children in a Comprehensive Day Care Program: The First Two Years." *Child Development* 42 (1971): 1673-1683.

Robson, K. S., and Moss, H. A. "Patterns and Determinants of Maternal Attachment." *Journal of Pediatrics* 77 (1970): 976.

Schachter, F.; Marquis, R.; Bundy, C.; and McNair, J. "Everyday Speech Acts of Disadvantaged and Advantaged Mothers to Their Toddlers." Paper presented at the Society for Research in Child Development meeting, New Orleans, March 1977.

Skeels, H. "Adult Status of Children with Contrasting Early Life Experiences." *Monographs of the Society for Research in Child Development* 31, no. 3 (1966).

Snapper, K.; Bariga, H.; Baumgarner, F.; and Wagner, C. *The Status of Children 1975*. Washington, D.C.: George Washington University Social Research Group, 1975.

Spelke, E.; Zelazo, P.; Kagan, J.; and Kotelchuck, M. "Father Interaction and Separation Protest." *Developmental Psychology* 9 (1973): 83-90.

Spitz, R. A. *The First Year of Life*. New York: International Universities Press, 1965.

Staples, R. "The Black Family Revisited: A Review and Preview." *Journal of Social and Behavioral Sciences* 20 (1974): 65-78.

Staples, R. *The Black Woman in America*. Chicago: Nelson-Hall, 1973.

Tulkin, S. R., and Cohler, B. J. "Child Rearing Attitudes and Mother-Child Interaction in the First Year of Life." *Merrill-Palmer Quarterly* 19 (1973): 95-106.

Wachs, T. D.; Uzgiris, I. C.; and Hunt, J. McV. "Cognitive Development in Infants of Different Age Levels and from Different Environmental Backgrounds: An Exploratory Investigation." *Merrill-Palmer Quarterly* 17 (1971): 283-317.

White, B.; Watts, J. C.; Barnett, I.; Kaban, B.; Marmor, J.; and Shapiro, B. *Environment and Experience: Major Influences on the Development of the Young Child*. Englewood Cliffs, N.J.: Prentice-Hall, 1973.

Willis, A., and Ricciuti, H. N. "Longitudinal Observations of Infants' Daily Arrivals at a Day Care Center." Research Program in Early Development and Education, Cornell University. Technical Report, 1974.

Zelazo, P. "Smiling to Social Stimuli: Eliciting and Conditioning Effects." *Developmental Psychology* 4 (1971): 34-42.

Contributors

Patricia Teague Ashton, Assistant Professor, Department of Educational Foundations, University of Florida, Gainesville, Florida.

Jean V. Carew, Senior Research Associate and Lecturer, Graduate School of Education, Harvard University, Cambridge, Massachusetts.

Martha J. Cox, Assistant Professor, Department of Psychology, University of Evansville, Evansville, Indiana.

Roger D. Cox, Assistant Professor, Department of Psychology, Indiana State University, Evansville, Indiana.

Sandra Kanu Dunn, Executive Director, Women's Community Health Center, Clearwater, Florida.

Bernice T. Eiduson, Professor, Department of Psychiatry, and Principal Investigator, Family Styles Project, University of California, Los Angeles, California.

Muriel E. Hamilton, Doctoral Student, Department of Educational Administration, Atlanta University, Atlanta, Georgia.

Michael L. Hanes, Director, Preschool Education Department, High Scope Educational Research Foundation, Ypsilanti, Michigan.

E. Mavis Hetherington, Professor, Department of Psychology, University of Virginia, Charlottesville, Virginia.

John H. Kennell, Professor, Department of Pediatrics, Rainbow Babies and Children's Hospital, Case Western Reserve University, Cleveland, Ohio.

Marshall H. Klaus, Professor, Department of Pediatrics, Rainbow Babies and Children's Hospital, Case Western Reserve University, Cleveland, Ohio.

Michael E. Lamb, Center for Human Growth and Development, and Department of Psychology, University of Michigan, Ann Arbor, Michigan.

Harriette Pipes McAdoo, Professor, School of Social Work, Howard University, Washington, D.C.

Ervin Staub, Professor, Department of Psychology, University of Massachusetts, Amherst, Massachusetts.

Marsha Weinraub, Assistant Professor, Department of Psychology, Temple University, Philadelphia, Pennsylvania.

Thomas S. Weisner, Assistant Professor of Anthropology, Department of Psychiatry, University of California, Los Angeles, California.

James C. Young, Associate Professor, Early Childhood Education, Georgia State University, Atlanta, Georgia.

Author Index

Aberle, D. F. 116
Abt Associates 232
Adamson, L. 39, 98
Adelson, J. 110
Ainsworth, M. D. S. 31, 32, 33, 34, 35, 36, 39, 40, 43, 58, 59, 88, 89, 90, 93, 98, 99, 101, 136, 229, 230
Aldous, J. 112, 116
Alexander, D. 6
Alexander, J. 197, 203
Alpert, R. 138, 152
Als, H. 38, 39, 98
Altucher, N. 111
Alvirez, D. 186
Ambrose, J. A. 39
Ambuel, J. 6
Ames, B. L. 139
Ames, L. B. 139
Anastasiow, N. J. 60
Anderson, B. J. 103, 127
Anderson, J. E. 61
Angrilli, A. F. 110
Aquilar, L. 186
Archuleta, N. 186
Arcimega, T. 185
Armentrout, J. A. 116
Aronfreed, J. 73

Babigan, H. 80
Bach, G. 110
Badaines, J. 110
Baldwin, J. 6
Bales, R. F. 115
Ban, P. 40, 114
Banet, B. 56
Barber, L. 101
Barbero, G. 6
Barbrack, C. R. 136
Barnett, C. R. 7, 8
Baruch, G. K. 52
Baskiewicz, A. 25
Baumrind, D. 74, 118, 121, 135, 152
Bean, F. 186
Becker, W. 60
Beckwith, L. 32, 34, 59
Bell, R. Q. 37, 57, 59
Bell, S. M. 31, 32, 34, 35, 36, 43, 58, 59, 98, 101, 230

Bem, S. 120, 123
Bernal, J. B. 55
Bernard, J. 209
Bibring, G. 19
Biller, H. B. 33, 92, 102, 110, 111, 124, 125, 138, 149, 163
Billingsley, A. 137, 189, 190, 237
Bing, E. 112
Birch, H. G. 38
Birns, B. 230
Blanchard, R. W. 111, 163
Blank, M. 57
Blehar, M. C. 43, 98, 100
Block, J. H. 116
Bloom, B. 24
Boll, E. S. 77
Bond, J. T. 60
Borstelmann, L. J. 111
Bossard, J. H. S. 77
Bowlby, J. 5, 18, 31, 33, 40, 99, 119, 124, 218
Brazelton, T. B. 12, 14, 38, 39, 62, 98, 103
Brody, S. 58, 61
Bromwich, R. M. 35, 45
Bronfenbrenner, U. 77, 92, 102, 114, 116, 149, 190, 225
Bronson, G. W. 43
Bronson, W. C. 58, 111
Brookhart, J. 43
Brooks, J. 109
Brophy, J. E. 135
Broussard, E. R. 56
Broverman, D. 120
Broverman, I. K. 120, 121
Brown, D. G. 92
Bryan, J. 74, 75
Budin, P. 6
Burchinal, L. 190
Burger, G. K. 116
Burnstein, E. 111
Busse, T. V. 111

Cain, R. L. 103, 127
Caldwell, B. M. 42, 59, 60, 61, 104, 136, 230, 233
Cameron, P. 56
Campbell, F. 60

Author Index

Campos, J. J. 33, 89, 90
Caplan, G. 62
Carew, J. V. 228, 231, 232
Carlsmith, L. 111
Carr, D. L. 116
Castle, R. 6
Cava, E. L. 92
Chan, I. 185
Chandler, M. J. 76
Chapman, L. 185
Chase, A. 187, 188
Chess, S. 38
Church, J. 139
Clarke-Stewart, A. 117, 231, 232
Clarke-Stewart, K. A. 34, 35, 37, 38, 57, 103
Clarkson, F. E. 120
Cleaves, W. T. 102
Cobb, J. A. 153
Cohen, J. 197, 203
Cohen, L. J. 33, 89, 90
Cohen, S. E. 34
Cohler, B. J. 53, 54, 135, 231
Coleman, J. 184, 188
Comer, J. P. 139
Committee on the Infant and Preschool Child 41
Condon, W. S. 12, 59
Conger, J. J. 139
Coopersmith, S. 74
Cowen, E. L. 80
Cox, J. 6
Crain, A. J. 127
Crandall, V. 112
Cross, H. J. 111, 112, 113

Danzger, B. 57
David, J. 101
Davids, A. 136
de Berlin, A. 186
de la Garza, R. O. 185
Dennis, W. 229, 230
Department of Commerce 113
Department of Health, Education, and Welfare 188
Deur, J. L. 92, 149
Deutsch, C. P. 55, 230
Dewey, R. 112
Distler, L. 111
Dixon, S. 98
Dlugokinski, E. L. 74
Dodson, F. 139
Dollard, J. 89, 100
Donovan, W. L. 101

Dorman, L. 139
Douvan, E. 110
Doyle, A. B. 42, 100
Drotar, D. 25
Du Bois, W. E. B. 237
Dubanoski, R. A. 60
Duchowny, M. S. 59
Dyk, R. B. 111

Eggan, F. 181
Ehrhardt, A. A. 92
Eiduson, B. T. 197, 203
Elmer, E. 6
Emerson, P. E. 34, 58, 87, 88, 89, 100, 101
Emmerich, W. 116
Epstein, A. S. 111, 112
Epstein, S. 71
Eron, L. 73
Escalona, S. K. 62
Evans, E. D. 139
Evans, S. 6

Fagot, B. I. 115, 116, 117
Fanaroff, A. A. 23
Fargo, J. 136
Faterson, H. F. 111
Fein, G. 226
Feinberg, H. 78, 79
Feiring, C. 102, 127
Feldman, S. S. 41, 42, 100, 114
Ferree, M. M. 52
Firestone, I. J. 74
Fishbein, M. 62
Fitzgerald, M. P. 116
Flaherty, D. 33, 100, 114
Fling, S. 116
Foster, J. C. 61
Fotta, M. 78
Fowler, W. 233
Frankel, J. 114, 117
Frazier, B. F. 237
Freeberg, N. E. 135
Freedle, R. 230
Freud, S. 88, 98, 100
Friedman, S. B. 24
Friedrich, L. K. 76
Frodi, A. M. 101
Frost, M. A. 80

Gallas, H. 230
Garber, H. 233
Gewirtz, J. L. 34, 57, 88
Geleerd, E. R. 24

Gildea, M. C. 51, 60
Gillard, B. J. 111
Gilmer, B. R. 136
Giordano, J. 189
Glidewell, J. C. 51
Goldberg, R. 236
Goldberg, S. 32, 34, 39
Golden, M. 80, 230, 232
Good, S. 112
Goodenough, D. R. 111
Goodenough, E. W. 92, 116
Gordon, I. J. 57, 59, 61, 62
Gordon, T. 139, 188, 189
Gorsuch, R. L. 152
Gough, H. G. 152, 173
Gray, S. W. 136
Grebler, L. 191
Green, M. 139
Greenberg, M. 18
Greenfield, P. M. 57, 209
Gregg, D. 6
Greif, E. B. 33
Grimm, E. 55
Grimm, R. 55, 56
Grobstein, R. 7, 8, 59
Grote, B. H. 43, 44
Grusec, J. E. 75
Gutman, H. S. 182, 190, 237
Guzman, R. C. 186, 191

Haley, A. 182, 183
Hanes, M. L. 60, 62
Hanks, C. 37, 113
Hare, E. H. 23
Harlow, H. F. 89
Harrell, S. N. 111
Harris, B. 6
Hartley, R. E. 114
Hartner, M. S. S. 56
Havighurst, R. J. 55
Heaton, C. 33, 100, 114
Heber, R. 233
Heilbrun, A. B. 111, 112, 138, 152, 173
Heiss, J. 190
Herbert-Jackson, E. 44
Herrnstein, R. 187
Hersher, L. 11, 59, 136
Herzog, E. 102, 110, 111, 149, 157
Hetherington, E. M. 92, 110, 111, 149, 152
Hill, R. 182, 190, 237
Hirsch, J. 186, 187, 189
Hock, E. 43

Hoffman, L. W. 53, 225, 234
Hoffman, M. L. 73, 74
Hogan, R. 32, 34, 59
Honig, A. S. 42
Hornstein, H. A. 75
Horton, D. M. 136
Hosken, B. 116
Howell, M. 236
Huang, L. 184, 185
Hudgins, B. B. 51
Hurley, J. 111
Hurlock, E. B. 139

Ilg, F. L. 139
Ingham, M. E. 100, 114
Irvin, N. 25
Izzo, L. D. 80

Jacklin, C. N. 115, 217
Jacoby, A. P. 61
Jankowski, J. J. 35
Jensen, A. 187
Johns, N. 23
Johnson, M. M. 111
Jones, B. F. 182

Kagan, J. 36, 40, 41, 42, 43, 89, 116, 135, 138, 139, 230, 231, 233
Kantor, M. B. 51
Karnes, M. B. 58, 62
Karp, S. A. 111
Katkovsky, W. 112
Kearsley, R. B. 41
Keister, M. 233
Keniston, K. 200
Kennell, J. H. 16, 18, 25, 56, 62
Kenney, D. A. 171
Kessen, W. 231
Khan, N. 233
Klaus, M. H. 7, 8, 11, 15, 16, 25, 62
Klaus, R. A. 136
Klein, M. 6
Klein, R. E. 37
Klopfer, P. 14
Kohn, M. L. 60
Kopf, K. E. 124, 125
Kopp, C. B. 34
Korner, A. F. 59
Kornfein, M. 201, 202
Kosdilsky, M. L. 56
Koslowski, B. 14, 38
Kotelchuck, M. 33, 36, 37, 89, 90, 91, 93, 101, 109, 114, 115, 232
Kruszewski, Z. 185

Author Index

Ladner, J. 190, 237
Lally, R. 62, 233
Lamb, M. E. 33, 36, 52, 89, 90, 91, 92, 93, 98, 99, 100, 101, 102, 103, 105, 109, 114, 115, 117, 141, 232
Lambie, D. Z. 60, 136
Lamme, L. L. 62
Lang, R. 12, 13
Lansky, L. M. 116
Lavatelli, C. S. 139
Leavitt, L. A. 101
Lefkowitz, M. M. 73
Leichter, H. J. 189
Leiderman, G. F. 44
Leiderman, P. H. 7, 8, 44
Leifer, A. 15
Leite, J. 114
Lemkin, J. 116
Lester, B. M. 37
Levenstein, P. 136
Levin, H. 55, 111
Levine, I. 189
Levy, J. M. 55
Levy, R. 78
Lewis, J. 233
Lewis, M. 32, 33, 34, 37, 38, 40, 41, 59, 102, 109, 113, 114, 119, 120, 125, 126, 230, 232
Liberty, P. G. 111
Lind, J. 13, 18
Lippman, M. Z. 43, 44
Lipton, E. 59
Litwak, E. 189
Lushene, R. 152
Lynn, D. B. 110, 111, 112, 138, 149
Lytton H. 61

Maccoby, E. E. 40, 42, 55, 88, 111, 115, 117, 118, 136, 138, 217
MacFarlane, J. A. 13
Mächtlinger, V. J. 100
Mack, D. 183
Main, M. B. 14, 38, 90
Manosevitz, M. 116
Marcus, R. F. 118
Marcy, T. G. 34
Marecek, J. 123
Margolin, G. 116
Marsden, G. 52
Marsella, A. J. 60
Martin, B. 55, 60, 152, 166
Martin, J.C. 201, 202, 208, 210, 214, 215
Masters, J. C. 88, 136
Matejcek, Z. 56

Maxey, A. 52
Mayeske, G. 188
McAdoo, H. 177, 180, 183, 191
McBryde, A. 18
McCandless, B. R. 139
McCord, J. 110
McCord, W. 110
McCrae, J. 44
McGee, R. K. 55
McQueen, A. 191
Mead, M. 140, 185
Meier, G. W. 15
Mercer, J. 188
Michaelis, R. 217
Michaels, J. 23
Miller, N. E. 89, 100
Mitchell, W. E. 189
Mobley, E. D. 112, 121
Mohs, K. 60
Money, J. 92
Moore, A. 11
Moore, J. W. 191
Moore, T. 43
Moss, H. A. 34, 37, 41, 54, 59, 230
Moulton, R. W. 111
Moynihan, D. 182, 183, 187, 237
Munsinger, H. 139
Mussen, P. H. 111, 139

Naegele, K. D. 116
Najarian, P. 229, 230
National Association for Mental Health 23
Newton, M. 9, 55
Newton, N. 9, 55
Nobles, W. 237
Nye, F. I. 225, 234

O'Connell, E. 117
Olds, S. W. 139
O'Leary, S. 101, 117, 127
Oliver, J. E. 6
Oliver, L. W. 113
Olshansky, S. 23
Oltean, M. 53
Osofsky, J. D. 57, 117

Papalia, D. E. 139
Parke, R. D. 13, 101, 117, 127
Parmalee, A. H. 217
Parmelee, A. H. 34
Parsons, T. 115, 138, 189
Patterson, G. R. 116, 153, 170, 172
Payne, D. T. 135

Pedersen, F. A. 33, 35, 54, 87, 89, 100, 103, 105, 113, 114, 124, 125, 127, 137, 139
Pederson, A. 80
Peters, M. 236, 237
Phares, J. 34
Phelan, H. M. 110
Piaget, J. 31
Pickarts, E. 136
Pierce, C. M. 237, 238, 239
Pintler, M. H. 110
Poresky, R. H. 100
Poussaint, A. F. 139
Powell, D. 236
Poznanski, F. 52
Preston, A. 112
Price, J. A. 180, 181, 182

Radin, N. 33, 111, 112, 135
Ragozin, A. 100, 233
Ramey, C. 60, 233
Raphael, D. 14
Rappoport, L. 24
Rau, L. 138, 152
Rausch, H. L. 92
Ray, R. S. 153
Rebelsky, F. 37, 113, 139
Reinhart, J. 6
Rheingold, H. L. 34, 57
Ricciuti, H. N. 100, 233, 234
Rice, B. 184, 185
Richards, M. P. M. 39, 55
Richmond, J. 11, 59
Ringler, N. M. 16
Ringness, T. A. 112
Ritchey, G. 33, 100, 114
Robey, J. 12
Robinson, H. 233
Robinson, N. 233
Robson, K. S. 12, 33, 34, 37, 54, 87, 89, 100, 113, 114, 230
Roff, M. 80
Rolnick, A. 18
Rosenberg, I. 18
Rosenblatt, J. 11
Rosenblatt, P. C. 102
Rosenhan D. 74
Rosenkrantz, P. S. 120
Roskies, E. 23, 24
Ross, G. 36, 89
Ross, H. W. 34
Rothbart, M. K. 117, 118, 138
Rotter, J. B. 152
Rubenstein, J. L. 35, 139

Rubin, R. 11
Ruppenthal, G. G. 15
Rushton, J. P. 74, 75
Rutherford, E. 111

Sackett, G. P. 15
Saltzstein, H. D. 73, 74
Sameroff, A. J. 38
Sample, W. 182
Sander, L. W. 12, 38, 57, 59
Santrock, J. W. 110
Sawin, D. B. 101
Sawrey, W. L. 110
Sayegh, Y. 229
Schachter, F. 231
Schaefer, E. S. 60, 136
Schaffer, H. R. 34, 58, 87, 88, 89, 90, 100, 101
Schlenker, P. 62
Schneider, D. 180
Schneirla, T. 11
Schoggen, P. 37
Scholl, M. 12
Scott, P. M. 73
Sears, P. S. 110, 111
Sears, R. R. 55, 56, 110, 111, 116, 135, 138, 152
Seashore, M. H. 60
Sellers, M. J. 37
Sells, B. 80
Senn, M. J. E. 52
Shaheen, E. 6
Shaw, D. A. 153
Shipman, V. 188
Shockley, W. 187
Shortsleeves, J. 78
Shucman, H. 23
Skeels, H. 229, 230
Skinner, A. 6
Skubicki, L. 75
Smart, M. S. 139
Smart, R. C. 139
Smith, B. 233
Smith, L. M. 51
Smith, N. 60
Smith, R. 180
Snapper, K. 225
Snyder, C. A. 114
Sollenberger, R. 184
Solnit, A. J. 23, 24
Somers, K. 100
Sousa, P. L. R. 16
Spelke, E. 37, 89, 101, 232
Spielberger, C. D. 152, 171

Author Index

Spitz, R. A. 5, 124, 230
Stack, C. B. 190, 191
Stamm, C. S. 127
Stanford Research Institute 232
Staples, R. 237
Stark, M. H. 23, 24
Staub, E. 70, 71, 72, 75, 77, 78, 79
Stayton, D. J. 32, 34, 35, 43, 59, 90, 101
Stehbens, J. A. 116
Stein, A. H. 76
Stendler, F. 139
Stern, D. 14
Stern, D. N. 37
Stern, G. 59
Stern, L. 6
Stolz, L. M. 115
Stone, L. J. 139
Storr, C. 55
Succop, R. 6
Sudia, C. 102, 110, 111, 149, 157
Sussman, M. 189, 190

Tannenbaum, J. 42
Tasch, R. J. 116, 138
Taylor, A. 6
Teahan, J. E. 113
Thoman, E. 38
Thomas, A. 38
Thomes, M. M. 116
Thompson, S. K. 114
Thurber, E. 110
Thurstone, L. L. 51
Tobach, E. 11
Tronick, E. 98, 39
Truskowsky, M. 6
Tulkin, S. R. 54, 135, 231

Vener, A. M. 114
Venet, W. R. 55, 56
Vogel, S. R. 120
Vuorenkoski, V. 13

Wachs, T. D. 230, 232
Walbeck, N. 74, 75

Walder, L. O. 73
Wall, S. N. 98
Walstedt, J. J. 113
Wandersman, L. P. 55
Wasz-Hoeckert, O. 13
Waterman, J. H. 23
Waters, E. C. 98
Watson, S. 116
Waxler, C. Z. 73
Weikart, D. P. 60
Weinraub, M. 33, 37, 41, 102, 109, 113, 114, 117, 119, 120, 125, 126
Weisner, T. S. 201, 202, 208, 210, 214, 215
Weissbrod, C. 71, 72, 74
Werner, E. E. 61
Werts, C. E. 113
White, B. 231
White, B. L. 121
White, G. M. 74, 75
Whiting, B. B. 77
Whiting, J. M. W. 77
Willemsen, E. 33, 100, 114
Willis, A. 233
Winters, M. 16
Wirth, L. 189
Wise, S. 39
Witkin, H. A. 111
Wittig, B. A. 32, 98
Wolff, P. H. 34
Wortis, R. P. 52
Wright, C. M. 42
Wright, D. 186

Yarrow, L. J. 35, 53, 59, 139
Yarrow, M. R. 73
Yogman, M. W. 98

Zehrbach, R. R. 58, 62
Zelazo, P. R. 36, 41, 89, 101, 230
Zimmerman, R. R. 89
Zuckerman, M. 53
Zuk, G. H. 23, 24
Zunich, M. 54

Subject Index

Achievement motivation, father's role 112–113, 127
Adult behaviors and children's prosocial behaviors 72–73
Adult-centered bias 227–229, 232
Affiliative behavior and attachment 40, 90–91
Afro-American families. See *Black families*.
Aggression by children and physical punishment 73
Alternative family styles. See *family style differences*.
Androgyny 121–122, 123
Animal birth behaviors 11, 14–15
　Early separation 14–15
Attachment (child to parent) 5, 12–14, 18, 31–46, 56, 58, 59, 88–92, 99–101, 104, 218–219, 230
　Affiliative behavior 40, 90–91
　Caregiving 88–89, 100–101
　Child development 31–33
　Cognitive development 31, 32, 45
　Compliance with mother's demands 32
　Contingent responsiveness 32, 34–39, 44
　Cultural differences 41–42
　Day care 41–44, 46, 100
　Distal behaviors 40–41, 59
　Expectancy of control 32–33
　Exploratory behavior 32–33
　Eye contact 34
　Family style differences 218–219
　Fathers 18, 33, 34, 36–37, 88–89, 101
　Infant's feelings of security 32
　Mothers 12–14, 18, 41–44, 46
　Mother's attitudes toward pregnancy 56
　Object permanence 31–32
　Parenting skills 39
　Physical contact 34
　Preferences for either parent 33, 89–92, 99–100
　Proximal behaviors 40–41, 59
　Reciprocal interactions 37–39
　Separation behavior 34, 36, 40, 42, 43, 89–90, 100–101, 218–219
　Sex differences 33, 41, 59, 91–92
　Social development 31
　Time with child 33–34, 45, 100–101
Attachment (parent to child) 5–26
　Behaviors 5, 15–16
　Birth conditions 11–12, 18, 19

Early contact between mother and infant 15–17, 26
　Early separation 5, 15
　Indicators 5
　Influences 7, 9–10
　Malformed infants 23–26
　Premature or sick infants 21–23
　Reciprocal interactions 12–14, 18
Battering 6, 9, 10
　Early separation 6
Biological basis for mother/child relationship 119–120
Birth 9, 11–12, 14–15, 17, 18–26, 55–56, 211–212, 214
　Animal behaviors 11, 14–15
　Attachment 11–12, 18, 19
　Cultural differences 17, 18, 20
　Father's presence 211–212, 214
　Home 11–12
　Hospital 19–26
　Mother's attitudes 55–56, 211
　Family style differences 211
　Species-specific behavior 11, 12
　Support systems 19
Black families 182–184, 236–239
　Characteristics 237–238
　Cultural bias 238–239
　Racism 237, 238, 239
　Research bias 239
　Segregation 238–239
　See also *minority families*.
Brain damage 22
Breast-feeding 6, 13, 16–17, 211–212
　Early contact between mother and infant 16–17

Caregiving 18, 36–37, 44, 46, 88–89, 100–101, 115, 142, 215, 220, 225, 240
　Attachment 88–89, 100–101
　Family style differences 215
　Father's role 18, 36–37, 88–89, 100–101, 115, 142
　　Cultural differences 37
　Monomatric 44
　Mother's role 36, 44, 88–89, 100–101, 115
　Polymatric 44
　Research problems 225–240
　　Adult-centered bias 227–229, 232
　　Cultural bias 226–227, 232, 236–239
　　Social class bias 227, 229–232

Subject Index

Sex differences in parental styles 88–89, 100–101, 115
Variables 46, 220
Child abuse. See *battering*.
Child control 73–75, 117–118, 163–172, 239
  Divorced families 163–172
    Mother's parenting problems 164, 169–171
    Negative behaviors of children 169–170
    Reasoning and compliance 165–167
    Reinforcement 167–169
  Physical punishment and aggression 73
  Prosocial behaviors 73–74
  Sex differences in permissiveness 117–118
  Social class differences 239
Child development 10, 31–33, 38, 45, 51, 57–61, 93, 104, 109–128, 135–139, 141–143, 215–219, 229–231
  Attachment 31–33, 51, 57–61
  Eye contact 59
  Family style differences 215–219
  Father's role 33, 93, 104, 109–128, 137–139, 141–143
    Goal determination 137–138
    Misconceptions 137, 139, 141–142
  Impact of divorce. See *divorced families*.
  Mother's role 10, 38, 51, 57, 61, 93, 104, 136, 229–231
  Sex differences 217
Childbirth. See *birth*.
Childrearing practices 52, 53, 58, 211–216
  Family style differences 211–216
    Caregiving patterns 215
    Father's role 214–215
    Feeding patterns 212–213
    Health of children 213
    Sleeping patterns 212
  Mother's attitudes 52, 58
  Working mothers 53
Chinese-American families 184–185
  See also *minority families*.
Cognitive development 15, 31, 32–33, 34, 35, 44, 45, 59, 111–112, 127, 217–218, 227–229, 231
  Attachment 31, 32, 45
  Contingent responsiveness 34, 35
  Exploratory behavior 32–33
  Eye contact 34
  Father's role 33, 111–112, 127
  Mother's role 32, 34, 35, 45, 59
  Physical contact 34
  Social class differences 44, 231
Competency, mother's feelings of 52

Compliance 32, 164–169
  Mother's demands and attachment 32
  Reasoning 165–167
  Sex differences in parental styles 167–168
Contingent responsiveness 32, 34–39, 44, 45, 58–59, 230
  Attachment 32, 34–39, 44
  Cognitive development 34, 35
  Expectancy of control 34
  Fathers 36
  Mothers 34–36, 37, 45, 58–59
  Object permanence 34
  Sensorimotor development 34–35
  Social development 34, 35
Crying by infants 35, 36
Cultural basis for father/child relationship 119–120
Cultural bias 226–227, 232, 236–239
Cultural differences 14, 17, 18, 19, 20, 37, 41–42, 43, 44, 77, 187–188
  Attachment 41–42, 44
  Birth procedures 17, 18, 20
  Day care effects 41–42, 43, 44
  Father's caregiving 37
  IQ 187–188
  Prosocial behaviors of children 77
  Support systems 14, 19
  See also *minority families*.

Day care 41–44, 46, 100, 228, 232–234, 235
  Attachment 41–44, 46, 100
  Cultural differences 41–42, 43, 44
  Defining quality 233–234
  Different from home care 228, 234
  Effects 41–42, 43, 44, 232–233
  Sex differences 43
  Working mothers 235
Diet during pregnancy, family style differences 206
Discipline. See *child control*.
Discrimination against minority families 177–178
Distal attachment behaviors 40–41, 59
Divorced families 143, 149–175
  Child control 163–172
    Mother's parenting problems 164, 169–171
    Negative behaviors of children 169–170
    Reasoning and compliance 165–167
    Reinforcement 167–169
  Economic stress 156–157
  Emotional adjustments 157–159
  Father/child relationships 143, 162–173
  Household disorganization 156

Interpersonal relationships 159–161
Mother/child relationships 162–173
Relationships between divorced parents 161–162
Remarriage, attitudes toward 162
Research methods 150–155
Self-concepts of parents 157–159
Support systems 173
Domestic work roles 114, 138, 210–211
Family style differences 210–211
Drug use during pregnancy, family style differences 205

Early contact between mothers and infants 15–17, 26
Attachment 15–16, 17
Breast-feeding 16–17
Infant development 16
Early separation 5, 6, 7, 8, 9–10, 14–18, 31, 60
Animals 14–15
Attachment 5, 15
Battering and failure-to-thrive 6
Hospital care policies 9
IQ 15
Mothering disorders 9–10
Mother's attitudes 60
Economic stress in divorced families 156–157
Education and minority families 186–189, 192–193
Emotional adjustment in divorced families 157–159
Employment, mother's attitudes toward 52–53
Environmental variables 60, 207–211, 215
Family style differences 207–211, 215
Mother/child relationships 60
Ethnic diversity 178–181
Expectancy of control 32, 34, 44, 45
Attachment 32
Contingent responsiveness 34
Exploratory behavior 32–33, 218–219
Attachment 32–33
Cognitive development 32–33
Expressive role of mother 115–116, 123, 137, 237
Extended families. See *kin-help systems of minority families*.
Eye contact 12–13, 20, 22–23, 34, 35, 37, 54, 59
Attachment 34
Child development 59
Mother and infant 12–13, 20, 22–23, 54, 59
Social development 34

Failure-to-thrive 6, 10
Early separation 6
Family style differences 197–220
Attachment 218–219
Beliefs 201–205
Child development 215–219
Childrearing practices 211–216
Caregiving patterns 215
Father's role 214–215
Feeding patterns 212–213
Health of children 213
Sleeping patterns 212
Demographic characteristics 200–201
Domestic work roles 210–211
Living groups 140, 203–204
Parents' aspirations for children 207
Physical and social environments 207–211, 215
Pregnancy 205–207, 211
Diet 206
Drug use 205
Mother's attitudes 206–207, 211
Prenatal care 206
Research methods 198–199
Single mothers 202–203
Social-contract families 201–202
Support systems 209–211
Traditional families 204
See also *divorced families, minority families*.
Father absence 60, 92, 102, 110, 111, 125, 127, 157
Mother's attitudes 60
See also *divorced families*.
Father/child relationships 13, 18, 20, 21, 22, 25, 33, 34, 36–37, 41, 42, 87–105, 109–128, 137–139, 141–143, 162–173, 211–212, 214–215, 237
Achievement motivation 112–113, 127
Attachment 18, 33, 34, 36–37, 88–89, 101
Caregiving 18, 36–37, 88–89, 100–101, 115, 142
Cultural differences 37
Family style differences 214–215
Child development 33, 93, 104, 109–128, 137, 142–143
Cognitive development 33, 111–112, 127
Contingent responsiveness 36
Cultural basis 119–120
Divorced families 143, 162–173
Effects of mother/child relationships 101–103
Goal determination 137–138
Initial contact with infant 20, 21, 22, 25
Instrumental role 115–116, 123, 137, 237

Subject Index

Misconceptions 137, 139, 141–142
Perceptions of own childhood 214
Physical contact 41, 93, 96–97, 117
Play 36, 93, 94–95, 117
Preferences for either parent 33, 36, 42, 88–92, 99–100
Presence at birth 211–212, 214
Sex differences in parental styles 88–89, 93–98, 100–101, 104, 113–120, 138–139
Sex role development 33, 92, 104, 110–113, 127, 138–139, 141
Similarities in parental styles 13, 122–123, 126–127
Time with child 34, 113–118
Verbal interaction 34, 37
Father's self-concept in divorced families 157–159
Feeding patterns, family style differences 212–213
Feminine attributes and parenting 120–121

Gender identity. See *sex-role development*.

Head Start 188
Health of children, family style differences 213
Helping behaviors of children 70–71, 72–73
See also *prosocial behaviors of children*.
Hospital birth procedures 9, 19–26
Early separation 9
Household disorganization in divorced families 156

Indirect effects of parents on children 101–103, 126–127
Infants 5–26, 32, 34, 36, 39–40, 57, 60, 61, 101–103
Attachment of parents 5–26
Battering and failure-to-thrive 6
Behaviors and parental attitudes 103
Crying 35, 36
Development and early contact with mother 16
Effects of mother/father relationship 101–103
Feelings of security 32
Initial contact with parents 11–13, 16, 20–22, 25
Malformed 23–26
Premature or sick 6, 7, 11, 12, 15, 21–23, 60
Reciprocal interactions with mother 12–14, 57, 61
Smiling 34, 35, 39–40

See also *attachment, father/child relationships, mother/child relationships*.
Instrumental role of father 115–116, 123, 137, 237
Interpersonal relationships in divorced families 159–161
IQ 15, 187–188
Cultural differences 187–188
Early separation 15
See also *cognitive development*.

Kin-help systems of minority families 178, 180, 189, 190–192, 237
See also *support systems*.

Living groups 140, 203–204
See also *family style differences*.

Malformed infants 23–26
Initial contact with parents 25
Maximizing parents' attachment 23–26
Parents' reactions 23–24, 25
Masculine attributes and parenting 120–121
Maternal deprivation. See *early separation*.
Maternal role. See *mother/child relationships*.
Minority families 177–193, 237
Blacks 182–184
Characteristics 179–180
Chinese-Americans 184–185
Discrimination 177–178
Education, role of 186–189, 192–193
Ethnic diversity 178–181
Kin-help systems 178, 180, 189, 190–192, 237
Misconceptions 187
Native Americans 181–182
Parenting stresses 177–178
Spanish-speaking Americans 185–186
Structure 189–190
Modeling and prosocial behaviors of children 75–76
Monomatric caregiving 44
Mother/child relationships 5, 6, 7, 9–10, 11–14, 15, 16, 18, 19, 20, 21, 22–23, 25, 32, 33, 34–36, 37, 38, 41–44, 45, 46, 51, 53, 54–56, 57–61, 62, 88–92, 93–97, 99–103, 104, 113–118, 119–120, 122–123, 126–127, 136, 137, 162–173, 229–231, 237
Attachment 5, 7, 9–10, 11–14, 15, 18, 41–44, 46
Birth conditions 11–12
Early separation 5, 15
Influences 7, 9–10

Subject Index

Biological basis 119–120
Caregiving 36, 44, 88–89, 100–101, 115
Child development 10, 38, 51, 57, 61, 93, 104, 136, 229–231
Cognitive development 32, 34, 35, 45, 59
Contingent responsiveness 34–36, 37, 45, 58–59
Divorced families 162–173
    Parenting problems 164, 169–171
Early contact and infant development 16
Early separation and mothering disorders 9–10
Effects of father/child relationships 101–103
Environmental variables 60
Expressive role 115–116, 123, 137, 237
Eye contact 12–13, 20, 22–23, 54, 59
Initial contact with infant 11–13, 16, 20, 21, 25
Mothering disorders 6, 9–10, 14, 23, 53
Mother's attitudes 53, 54, 55, 57–61
Object permanence 34
Physical contact 38, 41, 93, 96–97, 117
Play 93, 94–95, 117
Preferences for either parent 33, 36, 42, 88–92, 99–100
Pregnancy 9, 19, 55–56, 62
    Mother's attitudes 9, 55–56, 62
    Support systems 19
Reciprocal interactions 12–14, 57, 61, 230
Sensorimotor development 35
Sex differences in parental styles 59, 88–89, 93–98, 100–101, 117
Similarities in parental styles 13, 122–123, 126–127
Social class differences 35–36, 54–55, 231
Social development 34
Time with child 113–118
Verbal interaction 12–13, 16, 34, 230–231
Mother's attitudes 9, 51–62, 157–159, 170, 206–207, 211
    Birth 55–56, 211
    Child development 61
    Childrearing practices 52, 58
    Competency 52
    Early separation 60
    Employment 52–53
    Environmental variables 60
    Father absence 60
    Mother/child relationships 53, 54, 55, 57–61

Pregnancy 9, 55–56, 62, 206–207, 211
    Attachment 56
    Family style differences 206–207, 211
    Postpartum period 56
    Premature infants 60
    Role satisfaction 52–53, 170
    Self-concepts 52–53, 157–159
        Divorced families 157–159
    Social class differences 54, 60

Native American families 181–182
    See also *minority families*.
Negative behaviors of children 169–171
Nontraditional families. See *family style differences*.

Object permanence 31–32, 34, 35
    Attachment 31–32
    Contingent responsiveness 34, 35
Oppositional tendency in boys 78–79

Parent/child relationships 5–26, 33, 36, 39, 42, 52, 69–70, 72, 73–75, 88–92, 93–98, 99–100, 101–103, 104, 115–116, 117–118, 120–121, 135–136, 140, 162–173, 177–178, 207
    Attachment 5–26, 39, 89–92, 99–100
    Attitudes and infant behavior 103
    Aspirations for children 69–70, 207
        Family style differences 207
    Child control 73–75, 117–118, 163–172
    Child development 135–136
    Divorced families 162–173
    Indirect effects 101–103
    Influences 7, 9–10
    Minority families 177–178
    Preferences for either parent 33, 36, 42, 88–92, 99–100
    Prosocial behaviors of children 72, 73
    Sex-role development 92, 104
    Social trends 140
    See also *father/child relationships, mother/child relationships, sex differences in parental styles, similarities in parental styles*.
Parent education 45, 61–62
Paternal role. See *father/child relationships*.
Peer influence and prosocial behaviors of children 79–80
Permissiveness, sex differences in parental styles 117–118
    See also *child control*.
Physical care. See *caregiving*.
Physical contact 34, 38, 41, 93, 96–97, 117

Subject Index

Sex differences in parental styles 41, 93, 96–97, 117
Physical punishment 73, 138
  Aggression by children 73
  Sex differences in parental styles 138
Play 36, 93, 94–95, 116–118, 218–219
  Sex differences in parental styles 36, 93, 94–95, 116–118
Polymatric caregiving 44
Postpartum period 14–18, 55, 56
  Mother's attitudes and depression 56
Preferences for either parent 33, 36, 42, 88–92, 99–100
  Attachment 33, 89–92, 99–100
  Stress situations 90, 99–100
Pregnancy 9, 19–20, 55–56, 62, 205–207, 211
  Family style differences 205–207, 211
    Diet 205
    Drug use 205
    Mother's attitudes 206–207, 211
    Prenatal care 206
  Mother's attitudes 9, 55–56, 62
    Attachment 56
    Postpartum period 56
  Support systems 19
Premature infants 6, 7, 11, 12, 15, 21–23, 60
  Battering and failure-to-thrive 6
  Father's role 21, 22
  Initial contact with parents 21, 22
  Maximizing parents' attachment 21–23
  Mother's attitudes 60
Prenatal care, family style differences 206
Prosocial behaviors of children 69–80
  Adult behaviors 72–73
  Child control 73–74
  Cultural differences 77
  Effects of participation 77–79
  Helping behaviors 70–71
  Modeling 75–76
  Oppositional tendency in boys 78–79
  Parent/child relationships 72, 73
  Peer influence 79–80
  Reasoning and induction 74–75
  Responsibility 77
  Role playing 75–76
  Sex differences 78–79
  Socialization practices 72–73
  Television 76
  See also *social development*.
Proximal attachment behaviors 40–41, 59

Racism 237, 238, 239
Reasoning and induction, 74–75, 165–167

Compliance 165–167
Prosocial behaviors 74–75
Reciprocal interactions 12–14, 18, 37–39, 57, 61, 230
  Mother/child 12–14, 57, 61, 230
Reinforcement and child control 167–169
Relationships between parents, effects on children 126–127
Remarriage, attitudes of divorced parents 162
Research problems 225–240
  Adult-centered bias 227–229, 232
  Cultural bias 226–227, 232, 236–239
  Social class bias 227, 229–232
Responsibility and prosocial behaviors 77
Responsiveness. See *contingent responsiveness*.
Role playing and prosocial behaviors 75–76
Role satisfaction of mother 52–53, 170
Rooming-in 18

Security and infant's attachment 32
Segregation 238–239
Self-concepts 52–53, 125, 157–159
  Fathers in divorced families 157–159
  Importance of two parents 125
  Mothers 52–53, 157–159
    Divorced families 157–159
Sensorimotor development 34–35, 217–218
  Contingent responsiveness 34–35
  Mother's role 35
  Physical contact 34
Separation behavior and attachment 34, 36, 40, 42, 43, 89–90, 100–101, 218–219
Sex differences in children 33, 41, 43, 59, 78–79, 91–92, 110–113, 164–165, 166–167, 169, 217
  Attachment 33, 41, 59, 91–92
  Child development 217
  Compliance 164–165, 166–167, 169
  Day care effects 43
  Prosocial behaviors 78–79
Sex differences in parental styles 12–13, 16, 34, 37, 41, 88–89, 93–98, 100–101, 104, 113–123, 138, 167–168, 210–211, 230–231
  Biological basis 119–120
  Caregiving 88–89, 100–101, 115
  Child control 117–118, 167–168
  Domestic work roles 114, 138, 210–211
    Family style differences 210–211
  Physical contact 41, 93, 96–97, 117
  Physical punishment 138

Play 93, 94–95, 116–118
  Time with child 113–118
  Verbal interaction 12–13, 16, 34, 37, 230–231
Sex-role development 33, 91–92, 104, 110–113, 116, 126, 127, 138–139, 141
  Father's role 33, 92, 104, 110–113, 127, 138–139, 141
  Parental salience 91–92, 104
  Two parents, importance of 126
Sick infants 21–23
  Father's role 21, 22
  Initial contact with parents 21, 22
  Maximizing parents' attachment 21–23
Similarities in parental styles 13, 122–123, 126–127
Single mothers 202–203
  See also *family style differences*.
Sleeping patterns, family style differences 212
Smiling by infants 34, 35, 39–40
Social class differences 35–36, 44, 54–55, 60, 227, 229–232, 239
  Child control 239
  Cognitive development 44, 231
  Mother/child relationships 35–36, 54–55, 231
  Mother's attitudes 54, 60
  Television viewing by children 231
  Verbal interaction 230–231
Social-contract families 201–202
  See also *family style differences*.
Social development 31, 34, 35, 125
  Attachment 31
  Contingent responsiveness 34, 35
  Eye contact 34
  Mother's role 34
  Two parents, importance of 125
  See also *prosocial behaviors of children*.
Social trends and parenting 52, 140, 189–190, 225
Spanish-speaking American families. 185–186
  See also *minority families*.

Species-specific behavior at birth 11, 12
Stranger, response to 33, 40, 43, 44, 218–219
Support systems 14, 19, 62, 173, 178, 180, 189, 190–193, 209–211, 237
  Birth 19
  Cultural differences 14, 19
  Divorced families 173
  Kin-help systems 178, 180, 189, 190–192, 237
  Family style differences 209–211
  Pregnancy 19

Television 76, 231
  Prosocial behaviors 76
  Social class differences in viewing 231
Tension introduction 125
Time with child 33–34, 45, 100–101, 113–118
  Attachment 33–34, 45, 100–101
  Sex differences in parental styles 34, 113–118
Traditional families 204
  See also *family style differences*.
Two parents, importance of 123–127, 128, 140
  Children's self-concepts 125
  Contrast effects 125–126
  Indirect effects 126–127
  Meeting children's needs 124–125
  Normalcy 126
  Sex-role development 126
  Social development 125

Verbal interaction 12–13, 16, 34, 37, 230–231
  Father/child 34, 37
  Mother/child 12–13, 16, 34, 230–231

Working mothers 52–53, 113, 140, 150, 225, 226, 234–236
  Childrearing practices 53
  Day care 235
  Role satisfaction 52–53

Selected NAEYC Publications

Code#	Title	Price
132	**The Block Book,** edited by Elisabeth S. Hirsch	$3.50
213	**Caring: Supporting Children's Growth,** by Rita M. Warren	$2.00
104	**Current Issues in Child Development,** edited by Myrtle Scott and Sadie A. Grimmett	$3.50
125	**Demythologizing the Inner-City Child,** edited by Robert C. Granger and James C. Young	$4.00
133	**Developing Open Education in America,** by Kathleen Devaney	$3.75
110	**Early Childhood Education: It's an Art? It's a Science?** edited by J. D. Andrews	$4.00
108	**Education for Parenting,** by Mary B. Lane	$3.00
212	**A Good Beginning for Babies: Guidelines for Group Care,** by Anne Willis and Henry Ricciuti	$4.50
124	**"The Good Life" for Infants and Toddlers,** by Mary Elizabeth Keister	$1.75
211	**The Infants We Care For,** edited by Laura L. Dittmann	$2.00
109	**One Child Indivisible,** edited by J. D. Andrews	$5.25
135	**Parent Involvement in Early Childhood Education,** by Alice S. Honig	$3.00
306	**Play as a Learning Medium,** edited by Doris Sponseller	$2.75
129	**Play: The Child Strives Toward Self-Realization,** edited by Georgianna Engstrom	$2.50
309	**Science with Young Children,** by Bess-Gene Holt	$3.25
310	**Talks with Teachers,** by Lilian G. Katz	$3.00
311	**Teaching Practices: Reexamining Assumptions,** edited by Bernard Spodek	$2.25
202	**The Young Child: Reviews of Research, Volume I,** edited by Willard W. Hartup and Nancy L. Smothergill	$3.75
207	**The Young Child: Reviews of Research, Volume II,** edited by Willard W. Hartup	$5.75

Order from NAEYC
    1834 Connecticut Avenue, N.W.
    Washington, DC 20009

For information about these and other NAEYC publications, write for a free publications brochure.

Please enclose full payment for orders under $10.00.